Leadership for Success

Leadership for Success

THE JAMAICAN SCHOOL EXPERIENCE

Edited by
DISRAELI M. HUTTON
and
BEVERLEY JOHNSON

THE UNIVERSITY OF THE WEST INDIES PRESS
Jamaica • Barbados • Trinidad and Tobago

The University of the West Indies Press
7A Gibraltar Hall Road, Mona
Kingston 7, Jamaica
www.uwipress.com

© 2017 Disraeli M. Hutton and Beverley Johnson

All rights reserved. Published 2017

A catalogue record of this book is available from the National Library of Jamaica.

ISBN: 978-976-640-615-8 (print)
978-976-640-616-5 (Kindle)
978-976-640-617-2 (ePub)

Book and cover design by Robert Harris
Set in Scala 10.25/15 x 27

The University of the West Indies Press has no responsibility for the persistence or accuracy of URLs for external or third-party Internet websites referred to in this publication and does not guarantee that any content on such websites is, or will remain accurate or appropriate.

Printed in the United States of America

To those courageous principals of the
Jamaican school system who dare to make a difference

CONTENTS

Foreword *Stafford A. Griffith* ix
Preface xi
Acknowledgements xiii
List of Abbreviations xv
Introduction 1

1   The Leadership Role in Educational Transformation 9
DISRAELI M. HUTTON

PART 1. PRIMARY SCHOOLS

2   Towards School Effectiveness: The Jericho Story 25
BEVERLEY JOHNSON

3   The Challenges and Rewards of the Principalship 36
ESTHER McGOWAN

4   "If You Can Dream It, You Can Achieve It" 47
CARLENE McCALLA-FRANCIS

5   Strengthening Leadership Capacity: The Journey Continues 55
GARTH GAYLE

PART 2. TRANSITION: PRIMARY TO UPGRADED SECONDARY SCHOOLS

6   Effective Principalship: Innovative Leadership Skills 65
O'NEIL B. ANKLE

7   Transforming Lives through Education 80
BRADLEY ROBINSON

PART 3. UPGRADED SECONDARY SCHOOLS

8   Being Principal: The Experience of a Lifetime 91
EVERTON WALTERS

9	The Impact of Transformational Leadership 102	
	CYNTHIA PEART	
10	Challenges of a School Administrator 115	
	MONICA McINTYRE	
11	Dealing with Challenges, Successes and Setbacks 129	
	JOAN WINT	
12	Setting Challenging Goals: Achieving Inspiring Performance 140	
	PAULEEN PAMELA REID	

PART 4. TRADITIONAL HIGH SCHOOLS

13	Lessons Learned about the Jamaican Culture and Its Effects on Education 153	
	ERROL V. JOHNSON	
14	My Experience as a Principal 164	
	ESTHER TYSON	
15	Strong Leadership Makes a Difference 182	
	DENNIS M. CLARKE	
16	Improving Performance through Relationship and Culture 194	
	MARGARET CAMPBELL	
17	Student Success: A Primary Concern 206	
	FAITH CLEMMINGS	
18	The Campion Experience: Cutting Diamonds 215	
	GRACE BASTON	
19	Issues of Importance: Analysis, Reflection and Action 228	
	DISRAELI M. HUTTON AND BEVERLY JOHNSON	
20	Strengthening Structures and Systems for Successful School Leadership 246	
	DISRAELI M. HUTTON	

Index 263

Contributors 269

FOREWORD

LEADERSHIP FOR SUCCESS: THE JAMAICAN SCHOOL EXPERIENCE is written for all educators who are interested in learning from the experiences of principals who have been successful leaders. Very often, educators who have no experience or examples to guide their actions are appointed to lead schools. Far too often, those who acquire the needed skills as part of their formal training do not have the accompanying classroom experience to bolster their practice. Even if the theoretical foundation has been provided in their academic programmes, it often takes time and practice to measure up to the demands of school leadership. However, those who become principals are expected to demonstrate effective performance from the first day of work. This book has accumulated the practical experience of principals who have been very successful in getting schools to perform consistently. This information is presented using their voices. Additionally, the book provides guidance, based on the wide experience shared by the principals, which can serve as a starting point for entry into school leadership.

This book is intended for a wide cross-section of educators, policymakers, educational planners, parents and the ordinary citizens who care to know and have a better knowledge of how high-performing principals run schools effectively. The stories will serve as an inspiration to, and a positive influence on, current and aspiring principals. Educational institutions can use this book as a central source of instructional material from which to prepare educators for the role of school leadership. The book will also serve as good reading material for those in the general public who have an interest in the development and achievements of the school system. Specifically, this book is ideal for those who will use it in the preparation of the new principal for school leadership by making a connection between theory and practice.

For colleges and universities which are involved in training school leaders, including principals, the edited text has numerous examples which will assist in making relevant connections with the actual workplace. Additionally, while the need to invite school leaders to share their experience with those in training will continue, the availability of the documented stories of workplace experiences will go a far way in helping them to benefit from the shared experience of successful principals.

The book provides insights to non-educators who are interested in the field of education to help them in grappling with some of the main concerns faced by educators and policymakers alike. Perhaps more importantly, the strategies and approaches principals, teachers and other stakeholders employ, which are documented in this book, will help those in the field of educational leadership to make similar gains. This book represents a new stage in our quest to improve student performance at all levels of the school system. *Leadership for Success: The Jamaican School Experience* is written with the conviction that leadership is one of the most important factors in improving student outcomes and overall school success and effectiveness.

STAFFORD A. GRIFFITH
Director of the School of Education and Deputy Dean
Faculty of Humanities and Education
The University of the West Indies, Mona

PREFACE

SCHOOL PRINCIPALSHIP CONTINUES TO be the focus of much debate in Jamaica and globally as researchers and practitioners alike seek to ascertain what it is that makes some principals more effective than others. Research has consistently placed instructional leadership as the hallmark of effective leadership. Similarly, for the Jamaican principal, the business of instructional leadership is especially critical. This is so because, unlike many principals from developed countries, our principals do not always have an adequate support system; they sometimes have to single-handedly manage many responsibilities. Drake and Roe (1999) pose the million-dollar question: Should the principal be held accountable for the accomplishment of management tasks if he or she is primarily expected to exert educational leadership? If the answer is no, then careful consideration must be given to the roles of the principal. Despite the challenges faced by principals in Jamaica, some have been deemed effective and are making a significant difference in the academic performance of students. The question is, as posed by Johnson (2012): What are they doing that others are not doing? This book also seeks to shed some light on this question as it presents a discourse on leadership role in educational transformation and unfolds the journey of seventeen principals who have made a significant difference in the education landscape of Jamaica.

The stories told by these educators focus on their early years as principals; the difference they made to student and teacher performance; how they made teaching and learning a priority; the challenges they faced and how the challenges were overcome; how they dealt with issues such as student discipline, gender diversity, staff development, and mobilizing and motivating teachers; using data to make a difference; building an effective school culture; improving infrastructure; the role of personal traits; and fostering relationships with key stakeholders. Their stories are punctuated with relevant literature, thus adding to the intellectual integrity of the discourse. The language of the chapters is conversational and encourages reader participation and involvement.

The work is divided based on the school types existing in the Jamaican school system: (1) primary schools, (2) schools transitioning to upgraded high schools, (3) upgraded high schools and (4) traditional high schools. This approach was adopted because research has shown that the leadership behaviour of principals differs based on the type of schools they lead; it is expected that different strategies and approaches would be applied in meeting performance standards. Part 1 charts the journey of four primary school principals. Part 2 represents the experiences of two principals who transitioned from primary to upgraded high schools. Part 3 focuses on five principals who served in schools which are considered upgraded high schools. (These principals have lately made the transition from primary to secondary schools.) Part 4 highlights the journey of six traditional high school principals. The opening and the concluding chapters provide a framework for effective and successful leadership performance in school systems and highlight changes being pursued by the central ministry and the government at this time.

References

Drake, T.L., and W.H. Roe. 1999. *The Principalship*. 5th ed. Upper Saddle River, NJ: Prentice Hall.

Johnson, B. 2012. "The Relationships between the Principals' Roles in Instructional Supervision and School Effectiveness in Selected Primary Schools". PhD diss., University of the West Indies, Mona, Jamaica.

ACKNOWLEDGEMENTS

WE PAY TRIBUTE TO THE PRINCIPALS who took the time to document their experiences as school leaders. Their contribution to this edited book will certainly make a difference in improving the performance of schools and students in the Jamaican education system. For most, this was their first experience at attempting to write for publication. However, with encouragement they were able to complete their book chapters. Although only seventeen of the more than thirty-five principals contacted could appear in this volume, the effort of all is commendable. For the others, even though their narratives are not included here, their contributions to the Jamaican education system continue to be recognized by many of those who understand the role education plays in the development and advancement of the country. Perhaps this publication will be an inspiration for future action.

The completion of the manuscript would not have been achieved without the commitment and dedicated work done over a period of eight months by Desmarie Brooks, a graduate in economics from the University of the West Indies, Mona. She took on the task as if it were her own. It was even more encouraging when she took on the job of recontacting some authors to clarify aspects of the work they had submitted. We know that Desmarie has gained much knowledge about school leadership as a result of her experience with this book project. We also express sincere gratitude to the Human Resource Development Unit, Department of Sociology, Psychology and Social Work, which provided the funding for Desmarie's assignment as the in-house editor of this book. In addition, the unit was gracious in providing funding support for the publication of the text. This is the real reward for my (Disraeli M.

Hutton) twenty years as a lecturer and more recently as programme coordinator.

Some of our colleagues who took time to review a number of the book chapters were Carmel G. Roofe-Bowen, University of Technology, Jamaica; Grace-Camille Munroe, University of the West Indies; Esther McGowan, Morant Bay Primary; Cynthia C. Onyefulu, University of Technology, Jamaica; Charmaine Bissessar, Hugh Wooding Law School; Glenda Prescod, Mico University College; and Canute Thompson, University of the West Indies. These persons were the first to provide critical feedback on book chapters, and they offered useful ideas of how to address limitations resulting from the inexperience of writers who were mainly engaged on a day-to-day basis attending to the challenges of running schools.

It would have been remiss not to recognize a number of the students from both the masters in educational administration and PhD in education programmes of the School of Education, University of the West Indies, who took time out to review a number of the manuscripts and to offer valuable feedback which improved the overall quality of the book. These persons included Kadian Henry, Roselee Howell, Shermaine Hassock, Carol Hibbert, Joan Gordon-Shaw, Wilbert Nunes, Abdul Antoine and Courtney Palmer. The checking of references by these students and, in some cases, locating appropriate references was a task that meant extra time needed for this assignment. We acknowledge the contribution of Professor Carol Clarke, who edited the manuscript; this was done with a high degree of thoroughness. With her input and commitment to the project, the quality of the book has been significantly enhanced. We hope that this text represents one of many attempts made to document and share the wealth of knowledge regarding high-performing and effective principals in the Jamaican school system.

ABBREVIATIONS

CAPE Caribbean Advanced Proficiency Examination
CSEC Caribbean Secondary Education Certificate
CXC   Caribbean Examinations Council

INTRODUCTION

DISRAELI M. HUTTON

THE JAMAICAN SCHOOL SYSTEM HAS BENEFITED from concerted efforts by successive governments, especially since Jamaica gained independence in 1962, to improve school performance and, in particular, student outcomes. Undoubtedly, we still have a far way to go before we can express satisfaction that our students and school system are performing at a standard of international acclaim. All of this effort and, in particular, the innovative interventions, will make a difference, but I am still not convinced that schools will make a radical improvement without a persistent and truly national effort that involves the wide participation of stakeholders.

Jamaica has demonstrated its capacity to operate at a world-class level for decades with achievements in areas such as athletics, music and tourism. The opportunity now presents itself for the transformation of the country's economy with the preparation of a more effective workforce. And there is growing excitement to focus on a curriculum that is driven by science, technology, engineering and mathematics (STEM), which will be the platform for preparing our students to be the agents of change (Hutton 2015a). This is important because it seems that the stimulation for excellent and successful performance must come from an education system that provides the skill sets to make a difference in the quality of the workforce and the building of a nation on a whole. We have learned from the success of the three areas identified (athletics, music and tourism) that the Jamaican ethos, culture and personality are reflected in and indeed underpin these areas of national achievement. These three areas of achievement have demonstrated our ability to make a difference when will and determination are consistently applied.

As we seek to broaden the areas of success, it is necessary to become much more reflective of past gains and to start paying closer attention to the values which are reflected in performance that brings success to the country and people. The success and effectiveness of Jamaican high-performing principals lie in the fact that they implement goals and objectives which reflect the needs and concerns of the school for which they were the responsible officer (Hutton 2011). These principals exemplify authentic leaders who exhibit values that inform insights, experience and personal conviction. In many ways, this study of high-performing principals in the Jamaican public school system reveals qualities which are consistent with authentic leadership. Kernis (2003, 93) defines authentic leadership as follows: "When individuals come to know and accept themselves, including their strengths and weaknesses, they display high levels of stable, as opposed to fragile, self-esteem. Such individuals are also relatively free of the defensive biases displayed by less mature persons and consequently more comfortable forming transparent, open and close relationships with others. Furthermore, they display authentic behaviour that reflects consistency between their values, beliefs, and actions." As Walumbwa et al. (2008) further confirm, being an authentic leader is a model of leadership which principals who want to make a difference in leadership must adopt. In the Jamaican context, characterizing high-performing principals as authentic in their leadership behaviour is reinforced by the fact that they articulate a philosophy which is personal and at the same time reflects their own concerns, desires and ambition. One philosophical position embraced by high-performing principals, as reported by Hutton (2011), is that each child has the ability and capacity to learn, so it is the responsibility of the school, with the appropriate support system in place, to assist the learner to become educated.

Additionally, such principals posit the view that formal schools enable the majority of learners to acquire an education which would make them well-rounded citizens who contribute to self and society. Miller and Hutton (2014, 83), in a comparative study of principals in England and Jamaica, show that in both countries effective principals embraced the ideas of "wanting to give back to society, love for children and for their learning, [and] equity and inclusion for all children". Hence, the principal who desires to make a difference in the performance of schools in Jamaica must be capable of displaying leadership which is guided by a philosophy that reflects an understanding of the needs of Jamaica's school system but, even more importantly, from his or her perspective.

Related to the notion that the effective school leader has to be an authentic leader is the role that personal abilities or traits play in the leadership process. Despite studies which were done to show the limitations of personal qualities, time has shown that these qualities do matter and make a difference in leadership behaviour. Bass and Bass (2008, 103), addressing leadership from the standpoint of traits or personal qualities, note that "traits and their expressions may be captured as a snapshot, but they are more enduring unlike momentary moods or state of being as feeling angry or feeling happy". The enduring nature of traits suggests that these are dispositions which are associated with leaders and, specifically, effective and successful leaders.

The obvious question to follow from this assertion is, Are leaders born or are they a product of their environment? While the debate on this issue has continued for decades, there is enough evidence to suggest that both hereditary and environmental factors play an important role in leadership effectiveness. Avolio (2010, 731) provides credence to the role of traits in leadership performance when he outlines that "over a series of studies, we have found, for both men and women, that approximately 30 percent of leadership emergence was heritable, whereas 70 percent was due to environmental events". While recognizing the limited number of studies done in this area of leadership, Arvey, Rotundo, Johnson, Zhang and McGue(2006, 3) report on one study which shows that "48% and 59% of the variance in the transactional and transformational leadership dimensions respectively were associated with genetic factors". Further, the results of a similar study done by Arvey, Zhang, Avolio and Krueger (2007, 694) show that "30% of the variance in leadership role occupancy could be accounted for by genetic factors". Increasingly, evidence is being provided which supports the role of personal qualities in leadership effectiveness. Notable is the comment of a high-performing principal who was convinced that she was able to transmit enthusiasm and passion to those with whom she works (Hutton 2013, 87). The observation by this principal suggests that personal qualities can also be learned. The question is, is there a difference between those who seem to naturally exhibit personal qualities and those who acquire these skills through training or modelling?

Dinham (2008, 346) also conveys the importance of personal qualities in a study of school leaders who achieved outstanding educational outcomes when he points to fact that they "possess and utilize high-level interpersonal skills, . . . demonstrate empathy and compassion and are available at short notice when needed". The study of high-performing principals by Hutton (2013) identifies these personal qualities or traits to include working "enthusiastically in performing his/her role as principal", demonstrating "personal commitment to the school and the education of the students" and exhibiting "a high level of self-confidence in his/her ideas and the possibility of successfully pursuing them". Hutton (2011, 6) summarizes the personal qualities of high-performing principals as "individual fortitude, qualities and abilities, which are the central personal elements responsible for their success as principals in the school system".

Bass and Bass (2008) identify leader traits which can be placed in five categories, as follows: cognitive traits which include resourcefulness, judgement, imagination, creativity; social competency traits which include assertiveness, cooperativeness, interpersonal skills; emotional competency traits which include self-confidence, self-efficacy, hardiness; character traits which include integrity, honesty, resilience; and biophysical traits which include physical fitness and stature. Hoy and Miskel (2005) citing Yukl (2002) also place traits, or personal qualities, into three categories: personality, motivation and skills. *Personality traits* include self-confidence, stress tolerance, integrity; *motivation traits* include task and include interpersonal needs, achievement orientation and power needs; and *skills traits* include technical, interpersonal and conceptual aspects.

Hutton (2015b), in his proposed model for effective school leadership, places traits into three categories: personal-character qualities, work-performance qualities and relationship-maintenance qualities. Examples of *personal-character qualities* include being enthusiastic, assertive, determined, passionate, ambitious, insightful, self-motivated, engaging, confident, forthright, committed; examples of *work-performance qualities* entail being reliable, disciplined, hard working, professional, inclusive, participative, facilitative, visionary; and examples of *relationship-maintenance qualities* involve being trustworthy, honest, fair-minded, empathetic, compassionate, loving, supportive. In all three categories, traits are presented as qualities which are innate and highly person-centred, and how these qualities are combined and applied make the significant difference in leadership. It is therefore possible that one may demonstrate these qualities but remains outside of a formal leadership setting, and it is only when the practice of leadership is ignited that personal qualities will make a difference in human performance.

One of the promising strategies being employed by educators across the world is the use of student data to determine performance deficiencies and plan appropriate intervention to improve outcomes. McMillan (2000) indicates that not enough is being done to prepare teachers and administrators to incorporate this strategy as part of their professional development. In Jamaica, since the publication of the final report of the Task Force on Educational Reform (2005), much effort has been made to improve student outcomes. The report establishes some key performance indicators which signal a level of success. For example, the report sets a target for the national mean score for the Grade Six Achievement Test (GSAT) to be 85 per cent of students achieving mastery in each subject area. Similarly, for the Grade Four Literacy Test (GFLT) to be 85 per cent of the targeted cohort to demonstrate mastery, and 60 per cent of the cohort attaining grades 1–3 in five Caribbean Secondary Education Certificate (CSEC) subjects, including English and mathematics. This level of achievement was set to meet the United Nations' Education for All 2015 target. After nine years some progress has been made, but there is still some way to go in terms of improving student outcomes (see table 1.1).

One of the initiatives that has been implemented by schools to improve performance is the use of student and, to a lesser extent, teacher data to determine instructional strategies to address specific learning problems. However, it would appear that principals and teachers alike need much more in-depth training in generating, analysing and applying data to improve instruction. The training of aspiring principals will help as they are absorbed into the education system with a firm understanding of how to apply data.

Currently, there is a need for schools to take a more comprehensive approach to the use of data to assess students' outcome. Huba and Freed (2001, 8) define assessment as "the process of gathering and discussing information from multiple and diverse sources in order to develop a deep understanding of what students know, understand, and can do with their knowledge as a result of their educational experiences; the process

Table 1.1 Comparison of Students' Performance in Selected Assessments

Selected Assessments	2005	Target	2014
GFLT (achieving mastery)	63.5%	85%	77%
GSAT (mean national score)	52%	85%	66%
CSEC (passing 5 or more)	20.2%	60%	34.5%

Data from selected sources: Planning and Development Division, Ministry of Education (2015); PIOJ (2005)

culminates when assessment results are used to improve subsequent learning". Central to the definition given here is the need to use a number of sources to determine learning outcomes of students. But in order to improve student outcomes, the quality of assessment must also be improved. Western and Northern Canadian Protocol (2006, 8) identify "four basic principles or quality issues that are important in classroom assessment: reliability, reference points, validity, and record-keeping". Reliability, for example, seeks to ensure that learning is tested by using various means recognizing the shortcomings of any one or two assessment formats. Additionally, assessment was focused mainly on learning which occurs after teaching takes place, and it is used to determine what the learner knows and is able to do. But there is also assessment of learning which tests for previous knowledge and other forms of prerequisite knowledge. The output from this approach to assessment is used to enhance and align teaching and learning activities to suit the needs of learners. Assessment as learning is focused on the learner, who becomes a legitimate participant in the assessment process. This approach is usually not emphasized, but it is an alternative that will encourage motivation and interest in the teaching-learning process.

So, consistent with emphasizing reliability by using a variety of assessment approaches, assessment types also broaden the means for determining student outcomes (Western and Northern Canadian Protocol 2006). The other area of assessment which can impact students' performance and teacher effectiveness concerns the nature and type of data used. Western and Northern Canadian Protocol (2006) mentions four types of data which can be used in the students' assessment process: achievement data, demographic data, programme data and perception data. The need to take a more comprehensive approach to the evaluation of student performance will also enhance the reliability of the process. More importantly, going beyond the use of achievement data will give a more comprehensive profile of the learner.

There is an urgency to improve the performance of the education system and improve student outcomes in all areas of learning. More concerted attention is being paid to improve learning for all students than at any other time in the history of Jamaica. When a concerted national approach is taken, the results are in the main successful. In 1974, literacy in Jamaica was below 47 per cent, but a national approach whereby persons from "all walks of life" were mobilized, resulted in the literacy rate increasing to 75 per cent by 1994 (Hutton 2012). Similarly, an effort to manage the birth rate in Jamaica has had success. The campaign "Two Is Better Than Too Many" has been declared a success by both local and international experts. In fact, there is a clear danger that the Jamaican economy will suffer in the long run because, with a birth rate of 2.5 per family, Jamaica will not be able to sustain the hearty workforce needed to bolster the country's economic activities when robust economic growth is realized.

References

Arvey, R.D., M. Rotundo, W. Johnson, Z. Zhang and M. McGue. 2006. "The Determinants of Leadership Role Occupancy: Genetic and Personality Factors". *Leadership Quarterly* 17 (1): 1–20.

Arvey, R.D., M. Zhang, B. Avolio and R. Krueger. 2007. "Developmental and Genetic Determinants of Leadership Role Occupancy Among Women". *Journal of Applied Psychology* 92 (3): 693–706.

Avolio, B.J. 2010. "Pursuing Authentic Leadership Development". In *The Handbook of Leadership Theory and Practice: A Harvard Business School Centennial Colloquium on Advancing Leadership*, edited by N. Nohria and R. Khurana, 739–68. Boston: Harvard Business School Press.

Bass, B.M., and R. Bass. 2008. *The Bass Handbook of Leadership: Theory, Research, and Managerial Applications*. New York: Simon and Schuster.

Dinham, S. 2008. *How to Get Your School Moving and Improving: An Evidence-Based Approach*. Victoria, Australia: Australian Council for Educational Research.

Hoy, W.K., and C.G. Miskel. 2005. *Educational Leadership and Reform*. IAP.

Huba, M.E., and J.E. Freed. 2001. *Learner-Centered Assessment on College Campuses:*

Shifting the Focus from Teaching to Learning. Needham Heights, MA: Allyn and Bacon.

Hutton, D.M. 2011. "Revealing the Essential Characteristics, Qualities and Behaviours of the High-Performing Principal: Experiences of the Jamaican School System". *International Journal of Educational Leadership Preparation* 5 (3): 1–15.

———. 2012. "Implementing the Career Advancement Programme: Learning from the Experiences of Previous Policy Initiatives". *Caribbean Journal of Education* 34 (1–2): 96–125.

———. 2013. "High-Performing Jamaican Principal: Understanding Their Passion, Commitment and Abilities". In *School Leadership in the Caribbean: Perspectives, Practices, Paradigms*, edited by P. Miller, 6–79. Oxford, UK: Symposium Books.

———. 2015a. "STEM Philosophy and Framework for the Jamaican Education System". Position paper for STEM initiative. School of Education, University of the West Indies, Mona, Jamaica.

———. 2015b. "Leadership Performance Model for Effective School Leadership". Manuscript.

McMillan, J.H. 2000. "Fundamental Assessment Principles for Teachers and School Administrators". *Practical Assessment, Research and Evaluation* 7 (8). http://pareonline.net/getvn.asp?v=7&n=8

Miller, P., and D.M. Hutton. 2014. "Leading from 'Within': Towards a Comparative View of How School Leaders' Personal Values and Beliefs Influence How They Lead in England and Jamaica". In *Building Cultural Community through Global Educational Leadership*, edited by S. Harris and J. Mixon, 70–90. Beaumont, TX: NCPEA.

PIOJ (Planning Institute of Jamaica). 2015. *Economic and Social Survey Jamaica 2014*. Kingston: Planning Institute of Jamaica.

Planning and Development Division. 2015. *Student Performance in Selected Assessments*. Kingston: Ministry of Education.

Task Force on Educational Reform. 2005. *A Transformed Education System: Report*. Rev. ed. Kingston: Jamaica Information Service.

Walumbwa, F., B. Avolio, W. Gardner, T. Wernsing and S. Peterson. 2008. "Authentic Leadership: Development and Validation of a Theory-Based Measure". *Journal of Management* 34 (1): 89–126.

Western and Northern Canadian Protocol. 2006. *Rethinking Classroom Assessment with Purpose in Mind: Assessment for Learning, Assessment as Learning, Assessment of Learning*. Manitoba: Western and Northern Canadian Protocol for Collaboration in Education. https://www.wncp.ca/media/40539/rethink.pdf.

Yukl, G.A. 2002. *Leadership in Organizations*. 5th ed. Upper Saddle River, NJ: Prentice Hall.

CHAPTER 1

THE LEADERSHIP ROLE IN EDUCATIONAL TRANSFORMATION

DISRAELI M. HUTTON

THE JAMAICAN SCHOOL SYSTEM HAS RECEIVED a greater level of attention since the publication of the final report of the Task Force on Educational Reform in 2005. The performance of the education system then was considered far below what was required to support the economic development of the country and the creation of an educated society. This report outlined the performance targets for education to be achieved by 2015. The significance of this date is that it coincides with the United Nations' target for achieving education for all by all countries. The national shared goals for the Jamaican education system were developed out of a national consultation effort. More importantly, the report identified the key issues affecting the education system, which include governance and management of the education system, curriculum, teaching and learning support, stakeholder participation, finance and discipline (Task Force on Educational Reform 2005). Addressing these issues is challenging, but it is necessary to get the education system to work well because the quality of life of the Jamaican people is dependent on the preparedness of a workforce; one which is world class and has the ability to produce quality goods and services to meet the needs of its people. Education is also essential in assisting persons to realize their own potential and to develop social, emotional and moral skills which are necessary to demonstrate qualities such as tolerance, love and care.

Concerns for Leadership

The role of leadership in improving the performance of a school has been affirmed at the national and international levels by both practitioners and academicians. There is general acceptance that leadership is the second most important factor, outside of the teacher and teaching, that affects the quality of student performance (Louis, Leithwood, Wahlstrom and Anderson 2010). New Leaders for New Schools (2009), using what it refers to as the Urban Excellence Framework in the United States of America, indicates that of the school-related factors which impact students' achievement, nearly 60 per cent are associated with principal and teacher effectiveness, with principals responsible for 25 per cent and teachers, 33 per cent. It points out that in order to improve performance, we must address both teacher quality and leadership.

Consistent with the traditional view of the leader, she or he is the significant person with the responsibility to influence the running of the organization and ultimately impacting the performance of the organization. The operative word is *influence*, which means working towards achieving organizational goals that are realized through the efforts of colleagues and other employees in the organization. The other view of leadership is one that is defused and experienced throughout the organization.

For the education system, other leaders include vice principals, senior teachers, classroom teachers and student leaders. All these categories of persons are assigned specific areas of responsibility. Beepat (2013) argues that a more systemic approach should be taken to leadership wherein there is less reliance on the individual leader. The distributed approach to leadership is receiving more attention because it is recognized that the individual leader, no matter the significance of his or her performance, will have to vacate the position at some time in the future. There is no guarantee that a replacement from within or without will provide the same level of impact as the outgoing principal. Regardless of the strength of the leadership at other levels of the organization, there is need for coordination at the top of the organization. This suggests that for organizations to function efficiently and to realize the outcomes and overall pursuit of goals, the effective and successful leader is a necessary requirement.

What Effective Leaders Do

Over the past twenty years, the role of school leaders has changed and has become more challenging. Numerous research studies have sought to determine which factors are emphasized by effective leaders in the education system. In the late 1970s and early 1980s, a group of persons including educators, policymakers and ordinary citizens tried to address the task of reforming public schools in the United States. Findings that arose from research conducted by this group and led by Ronald Edmonds was shared with schools and school districts. These efforts became known as the effective schools movement. Lezotte (2007) outlined the original five characteristics or correlates of effective schools which were first presented in an Edmonds publication in 1982. The correlates as listed by Lezotte (2007, 4) were as follows: the leadership of the principal notable for substantial attention to the quality of instruction; a pervasive and broadly understood instructional focus; an orderly, safe climate conducive to teaching and learning; teacher behaviours that conveyed the expectation that all students obtain at least minimum mastery; and the use of measures of pupil achievement as the basis for programme evaluation. Three of the correlates presented by Lezotte are related to leadership, the teacher and the students. And the remaining two correlates, learning and instruction, are the connecting thread which brings the three into meaningful action to improve school performance. It should be pointed out that the origin of effective schools was based on strategies emanating from systematic research and practice. With a basic understanding of the requirements for effective schools based on what was learned from research and practice, Lezotte (2007) reported that the correlates have undergone a number of refinements; they are now represented as (1) instructional leadership, (2) a clear and focused mission, (3) a safe and orderly environment, (4) a climate of high expectations, (5) frequent monitoring of student progress, and (6) positive home-school relations. Much more research has been done to understand effective schools and effective principals, but it is evident that the original constructs which effective schools revealed through the work of Ronald Edmonds and his colleagues continue to figure significantly in the dimensions and categories related to effective schools. An examination of the characteristics of effective schools by Sammons, Hillman and Mortimore (1995) lists eleven factors related to effective schools. These represent three broad categories: leadership input, student emphasis and organization support.

Organizational support includes factors such as learning organization and learning environment. These factors underpin both leadership input and student emphasis. The learning organization benefits from experiences gained from others as well as their own experiences. The learning environment involves the support system put in place to assist students. Having a strong and responsive support system is identified as one of the factors related to high-performing principals (Hutton 2011).

Student emphasis factors include (1) a home-school partnership, (2) concentration on teaching and learning, (3) purposeful teaching, (4) progress monitoring, (5) positive reinforcement, and (6) pupils' rights and responsibilities. All of these factors are related to learning issues, and these issues continue to be the focus of effective teaching nineteen years after Sammons et al. (1995) identified these elements. What is also of importance is the emphasis on students' rights and responsibilities. This includes recognition of the role students play in the process of teaching and learning, which may be taken for granted by some school leaders. In fact, "The Convention on the Rights of the Child" as outlined by the United Nations Economic, Social and Cultural Organization (UNESCO 1995, 3) guarantees their "right to participate and give opinions, to exercise freedom of conscience, and to actively participate in community life through freedom of expression and association" which are expected to be facilitated both at school and home.

The category dealing with organizational support includes (1) professional leadership, (2) shared vision and goals, and (3) high expectations. To be a professional leader means that you have to engage in a process of systematic training to acquire the requisite skill for effective leadership. Learning must be continuous in order to maintain and improve on the competencies which are essential for effective performance.

Further elaboration of select characteristics based on the results of the review by Sammons et al. (1995) provides a general picture of the nature of these characteristics. For example, a school that is characterized by *professional leadership* is one whose leader (a principal) leads through action taken deliberately and purposefully. Leadership is participatory in nature, with senior teachers involved in critical decisions related to policy. The teachers are involved in those areas which are directly related to their roles and responsibilities including the planning of the curriculum. Being the leading professional, the principal stays abreast of matters related to the implementation of the curriculum.

As for *students' rights and responsibilities*, student performance in school is enhanced when there are systems in place to support the development of self-esteem, the role students play based on the responsibilities and duties that are assigned to them, and self-determination – the extent students help to determine what they do and learn at school. Teachers have an important role to play in the confidence students display at school. Confidence is usually an indication of self-esteem. Specifically, confidence is demonstrated when teachers treat students with respect and dignity. So despite their circumstances, students have a right to feel wanted and to be a part of the life of the school. Failure in this area may lead to disruptive behaviour, the first sign of problems to come. Students respond positively when they are given tasks and responsibilities that are engaging, worthwhile and important. This is a way of practically demonstrating that students are valuable members of the school community and that they are making a difference. Allowing students control over what they learn is also a way of enhancing their performance. Further, giving them responsibility for decisions about what they learn will generally result in what coincides with their interests and preferences.

Another characteristic, *home-school partnership*, refers to the quality of the relationship between home and school, which has been shown to make a difference in learning. The extent of parental involvement will vary based on school types – primary versus secondary. In addition, parental involvement spans school and home. At school, parental involvement could include working directly with students in the classroom or working with the schools to support the staff – for example, taking children on school trips. At home, parental involvement could include providing personal support for homework assignments. Ultimately, the support will vary depending on the type of assistance the schools need and the capabilities of communities and parents. For example, the parents could play a more supportive role in areas such as school self-evaluation and school development-planning activities, which require more administrative and technical skills (Sammons et al. 1995).

Management Responsibilities of the Principal

Much has been said about the need for principals to be effective leaders, but the management responsibilities of the job must be performed if the school is going to operate effectively. Bass and Bass (2008) indicate that studies have shown that for schools to perform effectively principals must demonstrate both leadership and management skills. The concern for leadership is also expressed in the distinction that some persons make between leadership and management. Generally, it is expected that those who lead must also have the required skills to manage effectively. An Ohio study on leadership emphasized the importance of both leadership and management which are expressed in the constructs of "concern for people" and "concern for tasks" (Bass and Bass 2008). Yukl (2013, 22), commenting on those theorists who view managers as fundamentally different from leaders, said that "managers value stability, order and efficiency, and they are impersonal, risk-aware, and focus on short-term results. . . . Leaders are concerned about what things mean to people, and they get people to agree about the most important thing to be done." Indeed, some educators suggest that the difference between the two skills is so wide that the same person cannot perform both effectively. In identifying the difference between management and leadership, Northouse (2013, 13) observes that the "overriding function of management is to provide order and consistency to organizations; whereas the primary function of leadership is to produce change and movement. Management is about seeking order and stability; leadership is about seeking adaptive and constructive change." Yukl (2013, 22) expands on the differences between management and leadership thus: "Managers value stability, order, and efficiency, and they are impersonal, risk-averse, and focused on short-term results. Leaders value flexibility, innovation, and adaptation; they care about people as well as economic outcomes, and they have a long-term perspective with regard to objectives and strategies." Gorton, Alson and Snowden (2007, 6) see the difference between leadership and management in terms of the nature of the actions taken in the organization. From this perspective, the administrator would be rightfully seen as a leader if he or she is the one who initiates change in the organization. We must take into account the contending position expressed by Yukl (2013, 22), who maintains that "the most extreme distinction assumes that management and leadership cannot occur in the same person". Can we separate the leader from the manager, and how could we successfully do so? The fact that leaders have caused organizations to consistently realize goals and objectives in an effective and efficient manner suggests that directly or indirectly, the effective leader can also be an effective manager. Even though there is debate about whether effective leaders can also display the skills required for effective management, what is certain is that we can define the skills for both managers and leaders.

In practice, this may mean that those who are recruited to fill the top job must have the requisite competencies to address the deficiency existing in the organization. If leadership is determined to be central to the performance of the organization, then the right person for the job must be able to influence and motivate subordinates. On the other hand, if the challenge facing the organization is about improving the functions of the organization, such as planning, organizing and evaluating, an effective manager should be recruited. In the real world, while this distinction may be recognized, a school, for example, will seek to recruit principals who are capable of being both a good leader and a good manager.

There is a direct relationship between leadership and management (Bass and Bass 2008); that is, as a leader moves from a low-level leadership position, such as a shop-floor supervisor to a middle manager and from a middle manager to a senior manager, more emphasis should be placed on leadership than management. From a theoretical standpoint this seems logical, but in practice (as in the case of the Jamaican school system) the emphasis may be determined by the context or given situation the principal is facing at a particular time or period.

Is Management Important for Effective Leadership?

The Centre for Educational Effectiveness (2014, 2) outlines two dimensions associated with effective leadership. First is the allocation of resources, which includes the use of financial resources, time, facilities and technology. The second is management of people and processes including the recruitment, hiring, induction and development of qualified staff and the employment of "critical processes which include planning, implementing, advocating, supporting, communication and monitoring". Among the five areas of performance identified by Seremet, Ward, Williamson and Lani (2014) are the implementing and monitoring of the school improvement plan. We can assume, therefore, that the leader plays an integral role at all stages of the development and implementation of the improvement plan, with implementation and monitoring being the critical performance component.

Lunenburg (2010) mentions seven tasks and related skills necessary to perform the managerial functions of principals. These include building sound relations with the central office, monitoring organizational information, maintaining the school building, coordinating school activities, managing financial resources, directing school support services and staffing. These functions are consistent with those carried out by principals generally. Hutton (2011, 6–7) elaborates further on these high-performing principals as those who "spend time on the ground monitoring, observing and intervening in order to manage and maintain a balance between and among all facets of the school. Both interpersonal and communication skills are assets which are exhibited by . . . these principals." Evidently, management is an integral part of the job of high-performing principals.

Perhaps the real question is, How do school leaders perform both the management and leadership roles especially when school leadership is becoming more demanding and expectations of stakeholders are high and uncompromising? This can be addressed through teamwork, sharing responsibilities at the leadership level or strengthening the leadership team in a number of school settings. The real solution is distributed leadership, as it is impossible and unreasonable to expect principals to take sole responsibility for the running of schools, especially the large ones whose population is over fifteen hundred students, as in some cases in Jamaica.

Examining Critical Management Roles

By examining the jobs they do from different perspectives, Lunenburg (2010) provides a framework we can use to discuss the role of management. These roles include leadership functions, administrative roles, management skills, task dimensions, human resource activities and behavioural profiles of effective versus successful administrators. The leader functions are similar to the essential functions of management. These include the four functions of planning, organizing, leading and monitoring. According to Lunenburg's model (2010, 5), all four management functions are tied together, with leadership playing the driving role. Administrative roles describe what the principals do on a day-to-day basis. These include "heavy workload at a fast pace", "variety, fragmentation, and brevity", and "oral communication". Studies done in non-educational settings provide similar patterns of management. Among the actions which signal what managers usually do, Yukl (2013) identifies four activity patterns. These are (1) the hectic and unrelenting pace of work which is revealed in the long hours at the workplace and the fact that work is also done at home; (2) the wide variety of work tasks, some of which are completed in a short period of time; (3) activities which are usually reactive and fragmented, and lacking the systematic approach of an organized manager; and (4) time not spent with superiors and subordinates as expected but with others above their bosses or those below their subordinates.

According to Lunenburg (2010), the management functions – planning, organizing, leading and monitoring – are placed in three categories called leadership skills. He makes reference to the technical, human and conceptual skills advanced by Katz and Kahn (1966). For Lunenburg, these skills are directly related to what leaders can achieve in the organization, and when they are performed at different levels of leadership the emphasis changes accordingly. The technical skills are usually exhibited by department heads and team leaders in organizations related to a specific field of discipline. Northouse (2013, 44) indicates that "technical skills involve a hands-on activity with a basic product or process within the organization". Lunenburg (2010, 7) describes technical skill as "the ability to use the knowledge, methods, and techniques of a specific discipline or field". Hoy and Miskel (2005) identify some of the specific technical skills as managing budgets, interpreting test results and evaluating personnel. While the technical skills are important for managers at all levels of the organization, those in a supervisory role are best positioned to apply these skills.

Since principals spend so much time interacting with persons inside and outside of the organization, human skills are necessary for building and maintaining good working relationships. Northouse (2013, 45) describes these skills as "the abilities that help a leader to work effectively with subordinates, peers, and subordinates to accomplish the organization's goals". Hoy and Miskel (2005, 382) give examples of human or interpersonal skills that include "communicating . . . through written and oral media, establishing and maintaining cooperative and collaborative relationships, being sociable, and showing sensitivity, empathy, consideration and tact". In describing the importance of human skills, Lunenburg (2010, 7) advances the idea that "excellent schools and excellent leaders provide warm, nurturing, caring, trusting, and challenging environments. In this view, effective principals are cheerleaders, facilitators, coaches, and nurturers of champions." These skills are necessary at all levels of management because managers' interaction spans the supervisory level to the top management level.

The conceptual skills call for the leader to take a holistic view of the organization in the roles of problem solving and decision making. Northouse (2013, 46) opines that "conceptual skills involve the ability to work with ideas. . . . Conceptual skills are central to creating a vision and strategic plan for an organization." Hoy and Miskel (2005, 382) describe such skills as "the abilities to form and work with concepts, to think logically, and to reason analytically, deductively, and inductively". Lunenburg (2010, 9) adds to the importance of the conceptual skills by saying, "Because top-level administrators devote a large portion of their time to planning, they draw on conceptual skills to think in terms of relative tendencies, probabilities, patterns, and associations."

Regarding human resource activities, Lunenburg reports on a study done by Kreitner and Kinicki (2010) which identified the ability of effective and ineffective leaders to work with others in the organization. The findings show that the ineffective leader showed a number of shortcomings which include (1) insensitivity towards others; abrasive, intimidating, bullying style; (2) cold, aloof and arrogant; (3) betrayal of trust (failure to accomplish stated intentions); (4) overambitiousness, thinking of the next job, playing politics; (5) overmanaging; inability to delegate or build a team; (6) inability to plan and organize work; and (7) inability to adjust to new and changing conditions.

Retaining the Focus on Effective Leadership

With the recognition that effective leadership will make a difference in the performance of school and students, we should endeavour to strengthen leadership. Commenting on the challenges facing school leadership in the Caribbean, Borden (2002) indicates that the role of principals continues to focus more on management and less on leadership. Beepat (2013, 71), making reference to the issue of leadership in schools, mentions that "one observes that school management is still the dominant model adopted by school principals who function more as managers rather than educational leaders". So the focus on management concerns continues to persist even in light of successes stemming from an emphasis on effective leadership in schools in Caribbean countries such as Jamaica. In fact, a review of the strategic plans for the education sector in the countries of the region show that these plans all call for the provision of training in leadership and management (Beepat 2013; OECS 2013; Task Force on Educational Reform 2005). But while recognizing the need to improve the effectiveness of leadership, there are real systems problems which may be hindering or retarding the drive to improve leadership performance. One such limitation is the continued dominance of bureaucratic structure in many countries, such as Jamaica and the rest of the Caribbean region, even though Jamaica has made strides to address this situation in a number of respects.

Leadership effectiveness is more likely to be enhanced when greater responsibility and authority are assigned to principals and the schools they operate. The decentralization of the education system to give more responsibility to the regional entities in Jamaica is a step in the right direction. But the effectiveness of schools essentially lies in the hands of those who are responsible for leading them. These are the principals who work with the school board. The decentralization and democratization process empowers schools; so, while the strengthening of regional entities represents progress, the extension of this level of autonomy to the school will strengthen the systems and the structure for greater creativity and innovation from the leadership of schools.

Conclusion

We can learn from our knowledge and experience of effective leadership and management to improve on the performance of schools in Jamaica and the wider Caribbean region. The examination of what effective leaders do should give aspiring, neophyte and experienced principals enough insights into what to do to improve school performance and student outcomes. The studies on high-performing principals were done within a context that may be different from the more developed countries. For example, improvement of the physical plant was identified by high-performing principals as an important factor which had a positive psychological impact on the school community. In addition, these two studies show that the Jamaican schools are now embracing more fully the concepts of effective leadership and also instructional leadership. There is need for this trend to be accelerated so many more leaders can be trained to improve their effectiveness in the classroom.

The area of management, which is being treated as less important than leadership, should be re-examined by those educators who want to minimize the role of management. What is clear, for most of the factors identified for effective leadership, is that the management role and responsibilities are important. In fact, it would seem that principals cannot be effective if management functions are not implemented effectively and efficiently. Therefore, the conclusion could be reached that for the education system, at least, the effective principal must also demonstrate effective management competencies. The distinction made between the successful and the effective principal cannot be dismissed. It would seem that the successful leader has to wrestle with the systems and structural deficiencies of the organization, which in many cases are related to the management and organizational functions. Questions could be raised regarding the fact that a successful leader may not have the skills to be an effective leader or vice versa. This is more likely in a scenario in which a successful leader seeks to take advantage of networking and achieve rapid promotion in an organization. What is emerging from the schools with principals who have high visibility is that students' success and academic performance cannot be facilitated by strengthening structures and systems alone. In other words, improving the physical conditions of the schools, managing teacher performance to ensure greater productivity and building external networking are not enough. Most vital input is the quality of relationships established with the staff, especially the academic staff. The effective leader must be in a position to ensure that both the goals of the organization and the goals of the staff are being realized. Any attempt to minimize the goals of the staff will in fact diminish their commitment to the organization, leading to a reduction in organizational performance and student outcomes.

References

Bass, B.M., and R. Bass. 2008. *The Bass Handbook of Leadership: Theory, Research, and Managerial Applications*. New York: Simon and Schuster.

Beepat, R. 2013. "From Management to Leadership: The Case for Reforming the Practice of Secondary Education in Guyana". In *School Leadership in the Caribbean: Perceptions, Practices and Paradigms*, edited by P. Miller and A. Minott, 63–78. Oxford: Symposium Books.

Borden M. 2002. "School Principals in Latin America and the Caribbean: Leaders for Change or Subjects of Change?" http://www.iadb.org/wmsfiles/products/publications/documents/646204.pdf.

Center for Educational Leadership. 2014. "Four Dimensions of Instructional Leadership". University of Washington. http://info.k-12leadership.org/hs-fs/hub/381270/file-782283039-pdf/documents/4dimensions_instructional_leadership_framework_v1.0.pdf?&__hssc=184520185.1.1417205131444&__hstc=184520185.abec99d3dbced288ae07d7611f7ecdc1.1399217295273.1417195490741.1417205131444.3&hsCtaTracking=1af5be0b-c921-4012-aa7d-0a2210397436%7C97e7a42b-2d99-4ce0-9a96-d1c95c62fc05.

Gorton, R., J.A. Alson and P. Snowden. 2007. *School Leadership and Administration: Important Concepts, Case Studies and Simulations*. New York: McGraw-Hill.

Hoy, W.K., and C.G. Miskel. 2005. *Educational Administration: Theories, Research and Practice*. New York: McGraw-Hill.

Hutton, D.M. 2011. "Revealing the Essential Characteristics, Qualities and Behaviours of the High-Performing Principal: Experiences of the Jamaican School System". http://cnx.org/exports/e191eab3-6d7d-471e-a836-5223c4c18f49@4.pdf/revealing-the-essential-characteristics-qualities-and-behaviours-of-the-high-performing-principal-experiences-of-the-jamaican-school-system-4.pdf.

Kreitner, R., and A. Kinicki. 2010. *Organizational Behavior.* 9th ed. New York: McGraw-Hill.

Lezotte, L.W. 2007. "Effective Schools: Past, Present, and Future". http://www.effectiveschools.com/images/stories/brockpaper.pdf.

Louis, K., K. Leithwood, K. Wahlstrom and S. Anderson. 2010. *Learning from Leadership: Investigating the Links to Improved Student Learning.* Seattle: Centre for Applied Research and Educational Improvement.

Lunenburg, F.C. 2010. "The Principal and the School: What Do Principals Do?" *National Forum of Educational Administration and Supervision Journal* 27 (4): 1–13.

New Leaders for New Schools. 2009. "Principal Effectiveness: A New Principalship to Drive Student Achievement, Teacher Effectiveness and School Turnarounds". http://files.eric.ed.gov/fulltext/ED532065.pdf.

Northouse, P.G. 2013. *Leadership: Theory and Practice.* 6th ed. New Delhi, India: Sage.

Sammons, P., J. Hillman and P. Mortimore. 1995. "Key Characteristics of Effective School: A Review of School Effectiveness Literature". International School Effectiveness and Improvement Centre, Institute of Education, University of London. http://www.highreliabilityschools.co.uk/_resources/files/downloads/school-effectiveness/psjhpm1995.pdf.

Seremet, C., B. Ward, C. Williamson and H.S. Lani. 2014. "School Improvement Maryland Indicators for Effective Principals Leadership in Improving Student Achievement". http://mdk12.org/process/leading/p_indicators.html.

Task Force on Educational Reform. 2005. *A Transformed Education System: Report.* Rev. ed. Kingston: Jamaica Information Service.

UNESCO. 1995. *The Convention on the Rights of the Child.* Paris: UNESCO. http://www.unesco.org/education/pdf/34_72.pdf.

Yukl, G. 2013. *Leadership in Organizations.* 8th ed. New York: Pearson.

PART 1
PRIMARY SCHOOLS

CHAPTER 2

TOWARDS SCHOOL EFFECTIVENESS
The Jericho Story

BEVERLEY JOHNSON

I STARTED AS PRINCIPAL AT JERICHO PRIMARY SCHOOL on May 1996. I rang the bell that fateful morning amidst the chaos and confusion. I conducted devotion and started with the prayer chorus "They that wait upon the Lord shall renew their strength". I prophetically declared that morning that Jericho would mount up with wings and like the phoenix rise from the ashes. It did. The school was underperforming. The piloted Grade Six Achievement Test results showed that 50 per cent of the girls and 70 per cent of the boys were failing. The infrastructure was very poor. The school which housed four hundred students was one big room, 72 feet by 48 feet, donated by the Canadian government. It housed twelve classes – separated by blackboards, the principal's office and a kitchen. The building was badly deteriorated and termite infested.

Vandalism was normal. As a matter of fact, the school was vandalized the night before I assumed leadership. On my arrival, the then Jamaica Broadcasting Corporation, one of the major media houses, was there to investigate and report on the matter. This national media attention brought an unwelcome spotlight, which was most unsettling for the school community. Staff and students were demoralized, demotivated and desperate. Many people in the community did not send their children to the school for an extended period of time, and only those who had little or no other choice would allow their children to attend. We had to wait until December 1996 to get our quota of children for grade 1. My task was to transform this institution to an effective school where meaningful learning could take place.

When I assumed leadership, the school had so many challenges – very poor infrastructure, overcrowding, limited material resources and poor student performance, to name a few. At the time, although I knew that the students' performance was paramount, I also recognized that their performance could not improve at the rate it should, given the many limitations. Consequently, most of my time was spent on procuring the needed materials and improving the infrastructure of the school. How did I manage to accomplish that? I quickly sought the support of the parents, business community, other stakeholders and even overseas donors in providing material and financial support. I had to convince the parents that they had a critical role to play in assisting in transforming the institution. This is in keeping with school effectiveness research which suggests that parent/community involvement is one of the correlates of school effectiveness.

At the first parent-teacher association meeting, while we were discussing the poor infrastructure of the school, parents were blaming the government and, in particular, one lawmaker. The statement I made which got them thinking seriously about their role was, "Show me Mr Patterson's [then prime minister] or Mr Pickersgill's [a member of parliament] children in the school." The statement was made to provoke their thoughts and invite them into the leadership of the school. After enlisting the parents' support, I began to engage other stakeholders to assist with the school. The engagement with the member of parliament allowed the school to be assigned a company (AEROTEL) which acted as a sponsor. The sponsorship led to the rehabilitation of the school to create self-contained classrooms and peripheral fencing through the Jamaica Social Investment Fund. The school yard was paved via funding from Petrojam, the local petroleum company. The New Horizon Project (which targeted primary schools to improve performance in literacy and numeracy), overseas donors and past students assisted with acquiring books, computers and other equipment. However, it did not happen overnight; it took commitment, consistency and resilience on my part. Promises were made which were not forthcoming and I kept on "asking, seeking and knocking".

The Role of Personal Qualities and Competence in Effective Performance

Passion

Anything we undertake successfully must begin with a passion. The passion is what drives any relationship and keeps the fire burning. To be a successful leader, we must first have a passion for learning, a passion for teaching, a passion for people and a passion for work. I am very passionate in whatever I am doing and believe I should give one hundred per cent to all I undertake. It is no coincidence, therefore, that I chose to attend the then Mico College, whose motto states: "Do it with thy might". It was not hard to advance into the role of principal as I had already possessed the necessary personal ingredients to do the best job – passion, faith in God and a positive attitude.

It was my passion for the job coupled with my faith in God and my positive attitude that allowed me to go on. As a principal, I shared the school leadership with all the stakeholders. I allowed them to realize that they were a part of the leadership structure. One of the first things I did was to have a meeting with the board members and go through the code of regulations with them so that they could be aware of the leadership role they had to play. The teachers too were invited to share in the leadership as they were integral in a lot of the decisions that were made. The parents were invited into partnership and leadership. Even the students were made to realize that they were a part of the leadership chain. This is what Lambert (2003) calls "building leadership capacity". Despite this critical role of the principal in building this leadership capacity, it is a principal's personal qualities and competence that are critical to his or her effectiveness.

Commitment

According to Gills (1997, 29), without commitment, leaders "cannot make the transition from mountaintop of academic knowledge to the trenches of dedicated service". During my tenure at Jericho, I was met with many challenges that threatened my resilience and even safety as an educator. I was held up at gunpoint and my car was stolen, only because I tried to do an effective job in bringing some semblance of order and discipline to the school. I had to make changes to the break-time routine, as vendors who came from the morning period were a threat to the school's discipline. The school had no peripheral fence and so it was difficult to contain the students during the break period. Despite my attempts to solicit the vendors' support, they continued to undermine the discipline and effective operation of the school. I then had to take the decision to suspend a full-scale break and allowed students to have a "working break". This was met with much resistance from the vendors, who had to cease their morning visits. The theft of my car and the threat to my life were allegedly carried out to get me to leave. However, I was committed to the task of transforming that school and made it clear at parent-teacher association meetings that I was not daunted and would not relent. Eventually, when everyone saw the level of commitment and resilience, and with certain measures in place, the vandalism and resistance ceased and the school was allowed to flourish and grow.

Knowledge

Knowledge is seen as power, profit and pedagogy. When leaders have knowledge, it provides them with expert power which makes them more credible. Moreover, knowledge is seen as profit. According to Senter (2011, para 3), "Knowledge generates new opportunities, provides new solutions, and creates new resources ... every opportunity to gain knowledge is an opportunity for success." As a leader, the principal, being the "principal teacher", has to have teaching knowledge in addition to knowledge of educational administration and leadership.

Education, training and the experience of educators should put principals in a very strong position as effective educators. Davis (1998) states that education and training by their very nature, contribute to human performance. However, education and training alone cannot suffice. The education system needs educators who are dedicated, hardworking and committed to the tasks at hand.

As a beginning principal, I did not have any formal training in educational administration and therefore went into the job poorly prepared for some of the challenges. However, what I lacked in knowledge I quickly made up for in my enthusiasm to research and learn from those who were experienced in leadership. Principals should and must have the right attitude to learn, to seek advice and to be receptive to suggestions from others. I can recall just after assuming the post of principal in 1996 that my then territorial education officer introduced me to the idea of writing a school development plan. The idea was quite new to me but I ran with the idea and quickly developed a plan for my school with the help of other stakeholders. This gave the school an advantage over many other schools when we got involved in the New Horizon Project for primary schools. When my school started on the project, I was introduced to the concept of "instructional leadership". I recognized then that I was limited in my knowledge of school leadership. However, I was motivated to learn more and quickly enrolled at the University of the West Indies and undertook a master's in educational administration. My thesis focused on "the perceptions of teachers and principals about the principals' roles in instructional supervision". I gained the degree with distinction. Moreover, I gained a lot of knowledge which better prepared me for my role as an instructional leader.

Drake and Roe (1999) see the principal as a professional person being torn apart, on the one hand, by intense interest and desire to lead in instruction and learning and, on the other hand, by the responsibility to "keep school" through proper administration and management of people and things. I was torn between my role to ensure a safe and conducive physical environment for the students and trying to ensure that the teachers were doing an effective job in facilitating the students' learning. It was no easy task.

Integrity and Honesty

Integrity and honesty are two other personal characteristics that are necessary for effective leadership. You must say what you mean and mean what you say. As a principal, I tried to maintain a certain level of integrity and honesty in the daily operations of the school. I made it my duty to treat all teachers fairly and professionally and tried not to allow my personal feelings to dictate how I treated my staff. I can recall a personal problem I had with my son's teacher. She discriminated against my son and displayed a very poor attitude when she was accosted. Moreover, she was in an acting position and was someone I tried to assist, so I could have easily allowed my personal feelings to get the better of me. Despite her attitude, however, she was a good teacher; and hence I had to make a professional decision whether to continue her service, because I recognized that it was not about me and my personal likes or dislikes but what was best for the students and the school as a whole.

Interpersonal Relationships

Principals must recognize that they cannot do the job by themselves no matter how good they think they are; hence it is critical to foster and maintain a good relationship with staff. At Jericho, I tried to do this. I was careful in how I spoke to my staff no matter how upset I was. I tried never to embarrass or to be condescending to any member of the staff, ancillary or otherwise. I treated everyone with utmost respect even when this respect was not reciprocated. I can recall an incident wherein I asked a teacher a question in the staff room and the way she responded was disrespectful. I could see the disbelief on the other teachers' faces. However, instead of responding according to a natural instinct to put her in her place there and then, I quietly said to her, in front of the staff, "Miss, could I have a word with you in my office?" I had to let the staff know that I was going to deal with the matter but I was not prepared to have an open "showdown". We do not have to respond negatively to unpleasant situations; as the popular adage states, "He who angers you, conquers you."

Teacher Professional Development: Mobilizing and Motivating Teachers

Very soon after assuming the role of principal at the Jericho Primary School, I recognized that I needed to lift the very low morale of the staff. I instituted a Teacher of the Term competition to encourage teachers to raise the level of their performance. I challenged them to set very high expectations, commended them for their hard work and tried to improve their working conditions. In addition, we planned focused staff-development workshops for the staff. We catered to teachers' personal welfare as the many visits to hotels for a day or a weekend proved beneficial in lifting teachers' morale and providing them with time to refresh. There were other events and benefits, such as birthday clubs and a welfare fund to provide grants and loans to teachers. Each teacher was also provided with a free lunch each day. Moreover, teachers were encouraged to, and supported in, study. What were the results? Motivated teachers who rose to the occasion and delivered well. In fact, teachers did not leave the school unless they retired or migrated.

Staff Appraisal/Teacher Evaluation

Teacher evaluation is critical to the teaching and learning process as it facilitates instructional improvement. While I was principal at Jericho, staff evaluation was critical for me. I made regular visits to the classrooms to ensure that teachers were delivering the curriculum effectively. This was done not to expose teachers doing the wrong things but to help to monitor and sometimes even model lesson delivery so that teachers could improve their craft. This process also facilitated the selection of the Teacher of the Term/Year. I was very visible and "managed by wandering around" (MBWA). My visibility encouraged teachers and students to be at their best at all times, thus engendering a culture of accountability and excellence. Because some teachers did not understand the role of the principal in instructional supervision they resented the "intrusion" and felt I was treating them as if they were on teaching practice. I had to educate them as to my role and it became a normal part of the routine of the school. It was therefore very easy for us when the Ministry of Education introduced the system of staff appraisal. It was during my regular classroom visits that teachers' weaknesses were detected, and this facilitated focused staff development.

The Need for Continuity

As a school embarks on its journey to improve effectiveness, continuity and sustainability become critical. As a principal, I always encouraged my teachers to study so that they could be prepared to assume the role of principal when I was ready to leave. I even invited them to be principal for a day while I taught their classes. Of course, no one was brave enough to take it on. In addition, I did a succession plan which served as a guide for selecting my successor from the staff. There were teachers on staff who I believed possessed the ability and the right attitude to be effective leaders, so I encouraged, mentored and supported them. It was therefore an easy transition for one of them to assume the role of principal when I retired.

Making a Difference in Student Performance

When I started at Jericho Primary, the students were performing poorly, as the school's mean score both for internal and external examinations was about 40 per cent. I had to take a multifaceted approach to improve the students' performance. At the beginning of the first term, all classes took a diagnostic test to help the school in general and the teachers specifically to plan for the students. I spent a lot of time analysing each child's achievement and prepared graphs and tables to show the results to the entire staff. I believe that all the teachers should be aware of the performance of the entire school and see how this relates to their own context. In addition, decisions must be data driven. At the end of the first term, the same tests were administered to track the students' growth and development. The results were compared to the diagnostic tests and shared with teachers. At that point, students' individual scores were compared to see the value added. It was not just a matter of students getting A or B; the level of improvement was addressed. In addition to sharing the results with teachers and holding them accountable for the students' progress, students were held accountable for their own performance. I would meet with individual classes to share results and with individual students to discuss their performance, especially in cases in which no improvement was detected. Students had to account for their non-performance and, based on what they said and what the teachers reported, individual parents were summoned.

Parents have to recognize that they have a critical role to play in their children's education and must be encouraged and invited to play that role well. They must be encouraged. Cotton and Wikelund (1989) suggest, for example, that teachers and administrators need to assess their own readiness for involving parents and determine how they wish to engage and partner with them.

Gender Focus

The issue of gender of students cannot be overlooked. Research on standardized tests worldwide reveal that on average girls outperform boys. King and Gurian (2006, 56, cited Gurian and Stevens 2005) said that "all over the world boys are struggling in school, with lower grades, more disciplinary problems, more learning disabilities, and more behaviour disorders than girls". This gender gap has serious implications for the school as well as the students. I pose the question, Is something wrong with how we are teaching our boys?

At Jericho, the majority of the students who were failing were males; hence we embarked on an action research and experimented with single-sex classrooms. What was happening that caught my attention? The boys were performing poorly, there were more behavioural problems among boys and these boys generally had poor attitudes towards learning.

Attending the International Reading Association Conference in New Orleans in 2001 (compliments of New Horizon Project) heightened my interest in gender studies. I attended a session entitled "Boys Will Be Boys: You Cannot Teach Boys the Same Way You Teach Girls". I thought then and still think that perhaps our boys were failing because of how we teach them. I came back very excited and shared the information with my staff and tried to get their support in undertaking this research. We started a more sustained focus on the boys. Among some of the programmes we experimented with were: single-sex classes for all grades each Wednesday (2002–2006), single-sex classes for all grade 3 and grade 6 students (grade 3 with a male teacher, grade 6, female) (2006–2007), male teachers for both grades (2007–2009). Further, we initiated fathers' parent-teacher association once per term, boys' choir and staff-development workshops on teaching to the minds of boys. With the recruitment of more male teachers, "father and son day"/"mother and daughter day" and "father and daughter day"/"mother and son day" were also included.

The observation and analyses of data revealed that boys' performance, attendance, general attitude and behaviour improved tremendously. Even though the girls were also making improvements, generally, the boys showed greater gains. Additionally, most female teachers found it difficult to teach boys' classes and relate to boys, and boys reacted differently to male teachers.

Teachers who teach boys' classes say boys talk more freely in all-boys' classes. At first, some grade 6 boys did not like all-boys' classes but after a while they felt more comfortable, even though they missed interactions with girls. It was also found that boys began showing more interest in the Jamaica Cultural Development Commission Festival of Arts since a male teacher began teaching dance classes. While there may be other variables, the action research has had a positive impact on boys' achievement. There is nothing to lose in doing action research, hence, it is worth exploring. We have a moral obligation to act in the best interests of all students.

Conclusion

A school's journey towards school effectiveness can be facilitated through the personal characteristics of the principal – a principal who has a passion for the job, who is committed to the task, who is knowledgeable and honest, and who engenders good personal relationships and maintains his or her integrity. Moreover, a principal must be able to motivate, mobilize, model and monitor the staff in working effectively so that students' overall welfare can be fostered. Most importantly, such a journey calls for a principal who recognizes his or her instructional role and takes it seriously in making the children's welfare paramount. This kind of principal makes decisions that are data driven and participates in action research. Principals must therefore open their minds to clarity and wisdom, open their eyes to insight and vision, open their ears and mouths to greater communication, offer their hands for greater service and open their hearts to greater loyalty and unity if they are to have effective schools.

References

Cotton, K., and K. Wikelund. 1989. "Parental Involvement in Education". http://educationnorthwest.org/sites/default/files/parent-involvement-in-education.pdf.

Davis, S.H. 1998. "Superintendents' Perspectives on Voluntary Departure of Public School Principals: The Most Frequent Reasons Why Principals Lose Their Jobs". *Educational Administration Quarterly* 34 (1): 58–90.

Drake, T.L., and W.H. Roe. 1999. *The Principalship*. 5th Ed. Upper Saddle River, NJ: Prentice Hall.

Gills, J.P. 1997. *The Dynamics of Worship*. Tarpon Springs, FL: Love Press.

Gurian, M., and K. Stevens. 2005. *The Minds of Boys: Saving our Sons from Falling Behind in School and Life*. San Francisco: Jossey-Bass.

King, K., and M. Gurian. 2006. "Teaching to the Minds of Boys". *Educational Leadership* 64 (1): 56–61.

Lambert, L. 2003. *Leadership Capacity for Lasting School Improvement*. Alexandria, VA: Association for Supervision and Curriculum Development.

Senter, M. 2011. "Knowledge Is Power". ABCO blog post, 11 February. http://abcohvacr.com/knowledge-is-profit/.

CHAPTER 3

THE CHALLENGES AND REWARDS OF THE PRINCIPALSHIP

ESTHER McGOWAN

THE FIRST QUESTION THE PANEL ASKED me at my interview for the post of principal was what did I have to offer to the institution that was new. My response was that I wanted to return the school to the community.

Challenges of School Administration

A number of challenges face me as the new administrator. First, there is a limitation on the resources available to meet the needs of the school and this significantly reduces the operating effectiveness of the institution. Another challenge is the inadequacy of time the job allows to work and interface with students. So the principal needs to be involved in the instructional aspect of the school, taking on the role of principal teacher, assisting teachers and students in the learning process. As part of my routine, I like to visit my teachers during the morning session. This is the time when teachers and students seem to be more alert and responsive and ready for any challenge. It would seem that principals are the ones who are responsible for all that takes place in the teaching-learning process. Moreso, they are seen as the backbone of what goes on in the classroom. Principals should therefore practise good time management in order to overcome the challenge of inadequate time.

As in any organization, in education, change is always met with some amount of resistance. There is usually a small pocket of individuals who resist the initiatives to improve performance. This occurs even though it is evident that the particular change is able to bring about improvement. Maltz (2011) offers some strategies that may be used to manage resistance to change. These include providing adequate information about change and being generally sensitive to fears about change, convincing others that a real reason exists for the change and committing sufficient resources to the change to ease the transition process and alleviate frustration.

Strategies for Survival

Since the partnership between school and community is so critical, the school then has to take an engaging approach to building and maintaining relationships with the community and alumni. The new thrust at my school was to move beyond the efforts of our teachers and principal and engage external stakeholders to partner with the institution in the education of our children. We held parent-teacher association meetings in various communities, but some parents did not attend. Another initiative was recognizing outstanding parents and community members. This was a way of encouraging them and giving them a sense of achievement. A few non-governmental organizations (NGOs) assisted in painting the buildings and tiling the bathrooms. Parental participation and getting assistance from NGOs still remain a challenge. Stakeholders, however, must come to realize that education is not just the responsibility of the principal and teachers but it is a partnership that is able to bring about better student outcomes (Callender and Hansen 2004).

Professional Development

The field of education is constantly evolving and changing. Various researches on learning and the development of children are emerging. It is therefore of paramount importance that educators learn and keep abreast of the advances and issues which are taking place in education, and the principal plays an essential role in ensuring that this is done. Since new strategies are constantly evolving, teachers need to be involved in professional development to be effective. At the time of succeeding my predecessor, only a mere 2 per cent of the staff were degree trained. I went on a campaign to encourage teachers to further qualify themselves so they would become better professionals and more effective school performers. They seized the opportunity to further develop their professional skills. At present, 75 per cent of the staff has at least a first degree.

We conducted regular staff-development sessions at school. In many cases, teachers were themselves presenters. This became a means of boosting the teachers' morale and confidence. These sessions encouraged them to become lifelong learners. The staff became more aware and abreast of various methods and strategies that they were able to utilize, and in turn, able to contribute to the effectiveness of the school. In an attempt to enhance the professional and personal growth of the teachers, staff members were encouraged to attend workshops and conferences even with the shortage of funds. Providing resources is also an integral way of enhancing professional development.

Staff development involves planning for student learning. Each Thursday afternoon, all grades engage in a planning session. Teachers meet with grade-level cohorts, review the week's work, discuss outcomes and make plans for the coming week. This is a very interactive session wherein best practices are shared, offering opportunities for shared learning. This is an opportunity to identify the best instructional strategies that will eventually lead to student achievement. Professional development has really become a way of life at the school. Teachers have bought into it and are always looking for opportunities to become involved. As Larson-Knight (2000) argues, a principal's behaviours that are associated with promoting professional growth and staff development are certain to yield positive effects for students.

Making Teaching and Learning Your Number One Priority

Principals must be prepared to learn and research if teaching and learning is to become their priority. Looking back on my own career, I realize that in addition to being a teacher, I have also taken on other roles – a teacher educator and an educational researcher. As a teacher educator, I was responsible for providing instruction and supervision for my teachers and also became engaged in research in order to advance my knowledge in the field of education. I had to equip myself with not only new knowledge and skills but also new ways of behaving. I associated with experienced and successful administrators and modelled their action. My teachers were engaged in differentiated instruction to cater to the needs of each individual student. Catering to the different intelligences therefore became my main focus. The moment you enter the institution, the vision of the Ministry of Education greets you: "Every Child Can Learn . . . Every Child Must Learn".

Instructional leadership clearly defines the role of the principal in fostering the development of staff and students. At the same time, efforts were made not to neglect other duties whiledealing with the general management of the school. Due to the fact that teaching and learning were now my priorities, classroom visits became routine, regular assessments were conducted and feedback given. At times I also became engaged in regular teaching sessions which were observed by teachers. Principal "walk-throughs" were done, which gave me a clear picture of how well the children were progressing.

Making a Difference in Student Performance

The principal's role has become increasingly complex and difficult as schools and organizations have changed and stakeholders are calling out for more accountability. Principals today cannot sit back in their offices and expect things to happen. The contemporary principal must become an educational leader. Waber (1971) studied four effective schools to identify what determines student achievement. The results of the study suggest that all four schools had strong leadership which focused on instruction, set high expectations for all students and monitored student progress frequently. Student achievement, therefore, is dependent to a large extent on the leadership of the institution and principals should identify a vision for the school with regard to student achievement.

It is this vision which will propel the leader to move forward. The vision pushes you to reflect on areas which need improvement and to develop programmes or activities to target these areas. Experience suggests that the more knowledgeable the principal is of the curriculum, the better students will perform. The principal must be an expert on teaching and learning. The principal must demonstrate the concept of being a teacher and a learner at the same time. Prater (2011) reports that principals who are perceived to be more competent influence student achievement irrespective of the school community context in which they operate. As principals, we need to show our students that we are interested in their well-being. During lunch periods, I try to have short talks with my students. I interact with them and encourage them to feel at ease with me. I also try to find out their dreams and aspirations and guide them towards achieving their goals. It is therefore my aspiration as a principal to help students meet their fullest potential by establishing an environment in which they are afforded opportunities to share their ideas, to explore options and to learn new coping strategies.

The Role of Personal and School Philosophy

Being a leader is more than simply holding a leadership position or having the ability to lead. I believe that everyone has the capacity to become a leader, but not everyone exercises his or her leadership abilities. In addition, individuals have different ideas about leadership. My idea of leadership has evolved over time, and being in leadership positions in other areas has assisted in shaping my personal philosophy and my philosophy of education.

Hong (2010) opines that your personal philosophy drives your actions, which in turn will create your results. Further, it allows you to be proactive instead of reactive. My philosophy is that, as a leader, you must be able to effect change through leading by example and taking the initiative. As a leader, you are always striving for excellence, always developing and improving.

The Role of the Board and Regional Office

It is the role of the school board to provide policy and strategic guidance for the school. The composition of our school board helped in contributing to the success of the institution. Members were visible on the school compound and were extremely supportive of the goals of the institution. There was also ongoing supervision, which really kept me on track. The board initiated a scholarship programme to allow past students to contribute. We worked as a team with a unified mission and vision. Decisions were made collectively and meetings were held frequently. The board was led and managed effectively.

The chairman acted as a facilitator of relationships with the other members. Healthy discussions and the different points of view were facilitated. No major activities took place in the school to which the board was not invited.

The regional office provided guidance and support. The education officer was extremely accommodating. It was through consistent workshops held by the regional office and conducted by the education officer that I came to have a full understanding of what a school improvement plan really is and, more so, of its importance. There was, however, some bureaucratic red tape which sometimes got me frustrated.

Ethics and Fair Play in Effective Leadership

Ciulla (2004) purports that a healthy, moral relationship between leaders and followers is central to effective leadership. Leaders who are ethical demonstrate the kind of behaviour which stimulates trust and that is very important to those who are led. An ethical leader empowers his or her staff and gives them a sense of competence and accomplishment (Ciulla 2004).

Being unethical in the institution can include arriving late while insisting that the staff arrives early or being disrespectful to the ancillary staff while expecting them to respect you. It cannot be that the principal is demonstrating a different set of values from the staff. This is certainly a recipe for disaster. I make clear my values and ethics and live by them through my leadership style and actions. In doing so, I have gained the respect and admiration of staff members. As principals, we must make clear what we want and expect to engender trust. For example, when I took up office, I made it clear that the position of senior teacher would be based not on years of service but on performance. I have held to this position since.

Moral Imperatives for Effective Principalship

Brush and Glover (2003) opine that moral leadership is usually based on the values and beliefs of the leader. The article suggests that this approach is similar to transformational leadership, but with a stronger value base which may be spiritual. Moral leadership provides the school with a clear sense of purpose. The authors argue for both moral and managerial leadership, pointing to the vital role of management and showing that moral leadership is required to develop a learning community. They maintain that one of the moral imperatives schools face is to transform themselves into learning communities.

Dealing with Student Discipline

Even though there might be a policy on discipline, many times it becomes a challenge when confronted with unacceptable behaviours from students. You might discipline a student and find that, shortly after, the same or even worse behaviour is displayed. It is at this point that you might discover there are some underlying issues (whether social, emotional or otherwise) responsible for their misbehaviour. At this point, the child is referred to the guidance counsellor. That is why it is so important for administrators to really know their students. I have discovered that in talking with students, especially during the lunch break, you learn a lot from and about them as well as their teachers. A little hug, a simple touch or even calling them by name can also make a difference.

Many disciplinary problems are a result of students' disengagement or failure to tap into their interests. You might find a child who constantly misbehaves for an entire school year. The moment the child is transferred to another class, however, he or she becomes a different child, settles down and begins to do well. What has really happened? The teacher's approach is quite different. That teacher has discovered the student's learning style and interests and has been zeroing in on them. So I have discovered that monitoring students and making the necessary adjustments according to their intellectual level and interests reduces unacceptable behaviours.

Working with Parents and Guardians

Working with parents can be very difficult at times. There are those parents who make an effort to cooperate with the school. They are always at the parent-teacher association meetings; they check with their child's teacher on a regular basis and are involved in a number of school activities. On the other hand, there are those parents who are very difficult to deal with. They never attend parent-teacher association meetings; they do not take part in any school activities; you see them at school only when something goes wrong between the child and the teacher; and they make unkind comments about the teacher in the child's presence. I have to ensure that enough information is given at the first parent-teacher association or grade meeting for the school for parents to understand their roles as partners in education and to forge good relationships. It is always important to develop and maintain good relationships with parents.

Dealing with Challenge, Success and Failure

Challenges stretch your thought; they steer you towards new directions. One of the greatest challenges when I came into office was managing criticisms. I was always concerned about what people would do or say when dealing with certain matters. It was frightening to think how others would respond to certain issues. I have learned, however, that people will always criticize, especially when you are in a leadership position. You learn from the critics and you also grow. It is best to not take criticisms personally. This can lead to animosity between staff and school principal. Always bear in mind your ethical and moral principles.

Another challenge I faced when I became principal was improving the literacy rate, which was at 44 per cent. And this was really a challenge. What made the situation even worse was that the school nearby was making strides in literacy. We identified the weak areas – comprehension and writing – and delved into rigorous staff-development exercises with these areas as our focus. The following year, the literacy rate increased to 53 per cent, then to 63 per cent. We are now at 80 per cent. As a matter of fact, we were at 82 per cent for one year. We also focused on getting it right in the lower grades. This certainly worked and is still working.

Teacher Supervision and Evaluation

Knight (2007) agrees that the goal of supervision and evaluation is to positively impact a teacher's proficiency in the use of research-based practices, which in turn improve student achievement. It cannot be that teachers are left on their own to determine what they feel like teaching, how they feel like teaching and when they feel like teaching. There must be some amount of cohesiveness. That is exactly why every Thursday afternoon, teachers meet in their respective grade-level teams and plan the best strategies (among other things) to use to impart their lessons. What I have also found to be effective is small-group staff-development exercises.

Middle management is also coached to undertake effective supervision and evaluation. The absence of evaluation is an absence of direction. Evaluation directs which way to go and why. Programmes cannot run for years without being evaluated. After observing a lesson, the teacher is usually the first party to ask about his or her performance. I try my best to avoid creating a hostile atmosphere. This is due largely to the fact that a collegial rather than a hierarchical atmosphere is created and maintained.

Improving the School Plant and the General Environment

All stakeholders like to be in an environment which is welcoming. It gives a feeling of security and satisfaction. We solicited assistance from the business community and painted the school. We even changed the colour to a more welcoming one. The entire school community was excited. Knowing that children are more susceptible to environmental diseases than adults and that children therefore need a healthy school environment, all the bathrooms but one were tiled, with the remaining one to be done shortly. The problem of security was a major issue. I continued to lobby the ministry for a perimeter fence and this was eventually installed. The need then arose for a security officer to guard the gate. At the time, two of the ancillary workers took turns to supervise the gate at various times. However, this posed a problem as those ancillary workers had other duties to perform. The issue was brought to the attention of the ministry, which after a time advised the board to employ a guard. Teachers and children feel much safer and parents are also more comfortable to know that their children are safe. Improving the general environment is a process which continues today.

Mobilizing and Motivating Teachers

I use my teachers to conduct staff-development sessions. It is amazing to see the ideas that these teachers present. They feel motivated to know that they are contributing. In the most recent school improvement plan, one of the objectives for the school year is to present certificates to teachers who are contributing significantly.

Principals must let teachers know that they are valued. It is important to congratulate them for tasks they perform (no matter how simple these might seem) and help them to buy into the goals and objectives of the institution. Compared to former years, at least 95 per cent of the staff is present at any school activity. This is a remarkable improvement over former years. This improvement could be linked to the fact that teachers are specially treated at that times of the year these activities are held – namely, at Christmas and on Teachers' Day. They are given certificates at some staff-development sessions and they appreciate these gestures. They are recognized publicly for their contributions to the various school activities.

Conclusion

Over the years, and more so in recent times, educational transformation has been the focus of stakeholders in Jamaica. This focus has placed the principal in a critical position; the principal is responsible for the failure or success of the school. Since the quality of leadership is rated as the second most important factor in improving the performance of schools, principals must be able to initiate and effect change which is able to move the institution forward. The days of sitting and waiting on the ministry to act are long gone. *Creativity, risk-taking, transforming* and *motivation* are just a few of the concepts which, when acted upon, add up to producing successful schools.

References

Brush, T., and D. Glover. 2003. *School Leadership: Concepts and Evidence*. Report of the National College of School Leadership. http://dera.ioe.ac.uk/4904/1/download%3Fid%3D17370%26filename%3Dschool-leadership-concepts-evidence-summary.pdf.

Callender, S., and A. Hansen. 2004. "Family-School Partnerships: Information and Approaches for Educators". *Helping Children at Home and School II: Handouts for Families and Educators* 28, S2–S25.

Ciulla, J.B. 2004. "Ethics and Leadership Effectiveness". In *The Nature of Leadership*, edited by J. Antonakis, A. Cianciolo and R. Sturnberg, 302–27. Thousand Oaks, CA: Sage. http://www.iei.liu.se/fek/tgtuo4/kursmaterial/1.519969/Ethicsandleadershipeffectiveness.pdf.

Hong, J. 2010. "Why You Absolutely Need a Personal Philosophy – and How to Create One". www.justinhong.com/2010/11/personal-philosophy.

Knight, J. 2007. *Instructional Coaching: A Partnership Approach to Improving Instruction*. Thousand Oaks, CA: Corwin Press.

Larson-Knight, B. 2000. "Leadership, Culture, and Organizational Learning". In *Understanding Schools as Intelligent Systems*, edited by K. Leithwood, 125–40. Stamford, CT: JAI Press

Maltz, M. 2011. "Managing Resistance to Change". http://static1.squarespace.com/static/5408e065e4b0d384103dad1a/t/54359c71e4b0827fe8f405a4/1412799601429/ManagingResistance.pdf.

Prater, M. 2011. "Student Achievement: Principals do Make a Difference". *Growth Through Learning* (blog). https://growththroughlearning.wordpress.com/2011/05/28/student-achievement-principals-do-make-a-difference/.

Waber, G. 1971. *Inner-City Children Can Be Taught to Read: Four Successful Schools*. Washington, DC: Council for Basic Education.

CHAPTER 4

"IF YOU CAN DREAM IT, YOU CAN ACHIEVE IT"

CARLENE McCALLA-FRANCIS

I STARTED AT KENSINGTON AS A classroom teacher in 1996. The school had an enrolment of 100 students. When I assumed the principalship in 1999, the school had an enrolment of 350 students. Today, the enrolment stands at 1,350 students, moving in rank from a grade 1 (under 300 students) to a grade 5 school (over 1,000 students). At the time I took the job, there were four other new schools in the Portmore community which were competing for students. Due to the fact that I was an inexperienced principal, many parents in the community opted to send their children to the other schools.

I resorted to taking students from the outskirts of Portmore, from such tough communities as Majestic Gardens, Lakes Pen and Central Village. Those were the students who did not want to remain in their communities due to the stigma attached to these "inner-city schools". Although my student intake was from volatile communities, I did not have any major disciplinary problems. There are misconceptions about inner-city schools. My students became immersed into the culture of the Kensington school and conformed to the standards. The parents were involved and enthused that they were a part of the school community.

One year a child from Central Village got her Grade Six Achievement Test for Wolmer's Girls School and the community held a dance to celebrate her achievement. This event encouraged community members to send their children to Kensington since the new environment facilitated their children's entry into traditional high schools. After those communities helped to make and give Kensington its name, the Portmore community began to own the school and wanted to send their children here. During registration, the community members were disappointed because they could not get their children registered. However, I was not going to refuse the children from Central Village and the other communities in the outskirts of Portmore which had supported and helped to build the school.

The school began with five veteran teachers who were responsible for mentoring the inexperienced teachers. One of the things I did was to ensure that I employed new teachers who did not come with any experience or expectations. We familiarized the new teachers with our expectations and they adapted easily and quickly conformed to the culture of the school. McCann, Johannessen and Ricca (2005) outline the provision of a comprehensive induction programme with a meaningful staff-development programme which is supportive of new teachers' professional growth and conveys the staff's seriousness about the craft of teaching. Furthermore, Johnson and Kardos (2005) prescribe a synergy of veteran teachers' knowledge and novice teachers' enthusiasm with the purpose of improving teaching and learning.

Making a Difference in Students' Performance

The school's motto, "If you can dream it, you can achieve it", is used as a mantra for motivating students to become high achievers. The students are constantly assessed and encouraged to perform at a high standard. Students are not streamed based on academic performance but placed in classes based on teachers' personalities. My first degree is in primary education and for my second degree I majored in psychology and took courses in educational administration. Due to my training in psychology, I provide each teacher with a book on psychology so that they know how to place students. Moreover, every year I sit with each teacher and ask her or him to tell me about the students and I help to place them with the teachers who best fit the students' personalities. I know my teachers and that helps in the placement. Additionally, no more than five students from each grouping would be placed together in the following year's grouping. This allows them to develop their interpersonal and social skills.

I do not test students before enrolling them. The school has students who are not performing at the optimum level and so the school employs a number of strategies to assist those students. I am involved in this through supervision and evaluation, coordinating the curriculum and monitoring students' progress. Bergesen (2007) describes this dimension as one wherein students are frequently assessed using different assessment tools in order to identify those who are in need of special or individualized help. Improvements are usually made to the instructional programme of the school based on students' assessment results. Those students who are in need of help will be provided with additional support during or after school. The focus here is on identifying students' strengths and weaknesses so that areas of weakness can be strengthened. Teaching methods and strategies are also adjusted based on students' progress and needs. We also run a "pull-out programme" where students with learning challenges, such as reading, can receive attention in the reading lab, in Saturday classes and in extra lessons.

Moreover, we have an extended day to facilitate preparation for the Grade Six Achievement Test. We focus on comprehension and reading, especially in preparation for the Grade Four Literacy Test. Teachers have to provide weekly reports for students who perform below the acceptable level. The ministry's minimum passing mark for comprehension is 14/30; however, we use a mark of 20/30 or lower as an indication that students need help. (Thirty is the standard score for the comprehension component.) We administer mock exams with the students using the same standard and under similar conditions prescribed by the Ministry of Education. Consequently, in any given year we can predict the performance level of the students sitting the national exam. In 2014, only two students failed the writing task for the Grade Four Literacy Test and they did so by one point. According to Sammons (1999), schools are effective if student performance exceeds expectations. This is determined by comparing the student's present level of achievement to the level at which he or she entered. It can therefore be said that an effective school, through its transformation process, adds extra value to its students when compared with other schools which take in students from a similar background and educational level.

Mobilizing and Motivating Staff

Teachers meet every Thursday and Friday afternoon to plan and to write lesson plans. I encourage and support team teaching and demonstration lessons. Within the school, teachers rotate among the classrooms so that the students can get the best teaching and learning experience. Teachers are supportive of each other. Those who are studying get assistance with assignments from other teachers. The result is that teachers are very dedicated to their jobs and will go the extra mile to ensure that the school programmes are embraced, encouraged and enhanced. I support my staff fully and provide incentives and opportunities for their social development. I do everything for my teachers. If they are in need of a house, I source the information regarding types of benefits available from National Housing Trust and provide support to assist with the process of buying a house. If a teacher has challenges accessing emoluments or documents from the Ministry of Education, I intervene for them to expedite the process. Support is also provided for teachers through baby and bridal showers and through contributions to funerals. Each year, every teacher gets a personalized Christmas card, and at Easter, everyone gets bun and cheese. Additionally, during the month of August, the staff is given a weekend on the North Coast. As Stipek (2006, 48) posits, "Teachers who feel respected, trusted and cared about as individuals are in much better position to offer the same support to students." Hence, it is incumbent upon the principal to foster and promote such a positive culture.

Staff appraisal is an integral part of our structure. Staff members are periodically appraised and these appraisals are viewed as an important matter. The board is allowed to participate in the appraisal of teachers, and the chairman of the school and the president of the parent-teacher association are invited to be a part of the panel selected to oversee the process. At the end of the appraisal process we discuss what will be the ranking. The teacher is allowed to say whether he or she agrees with the rank given and we discuss it and make any necessary changes. We also consult with the teacher about their strengths and weaknesses and how best to correct weaknesses. According to Checkley (2000), this feedback is needed to institutionalize a redefinition of teaching and learning as teachers are provided with the information they need to improve or adjust their teaching.

I have a good relationship with my ancillary staff who are not treated any differently from my academic staff. They are included in staff trips and other staff-development opportunities. In this way, a collaborative culture is developed within the school. I also get along well with the vendors, who are allowed to sell during the lunch period but are not allowed to set up permanent structures on the compound. They are also required to clean up the entire school premises after they have finished for the day as they have contributed to the students littering the school compound.

Student Welfare and Discipline

As educators, we are responsible for the nutrition of the students. I realized that many mornings the students' breakfast was just a bag of juice or some other snack, simply because their parents had given them only enough money to purchase a snack before class. Based on that, we started a cup-soup programme in the morning whereby students would receive something warm and filling instead of the unhealthy snacks. I see all the children at my school as "my kids". They belong to me and that is why I am very firm. Yes, I was a teacher and principal who used to utilize corporal punishment as a form of discipline. However, I have stopped and have been using other methods. These include interviews with parents, withholding privileges and instituting a token system for internal business transactions. We use a method whereby after "three strikes" (misbehaviours) we withhold privileges. Teachers use grouping systems for students in their classes and provide incentives for groups with the most merits. (Merits are given when students comply with class and school rules and complete assignments.) Other methods besides corporal punishment will work in curtailing indiscipline. No one method for managing students' behaviour is "law", and it is advisable to use a situational approach. If a teacher cannot control his or her class, more pressure is put on the principal and this affects his or her instructional role.

Relationship with Community

Parents are very supportive. My parent-teacher association meetings are well attended, usually by more than one thousand parents. All parents are mandated to attend at least three meetings per year. When the minister of education visited a parent-teacher association meeting, eleven hundred parents were in attendance. I encourage both mothers and fathers to attend. McBride and Rane (1997) purport that the importance of fathers and other male role models is often overlooked in efforts to increase parental involvement in children's schooling. These researchers call for educators to identify and target these men for parental involvement initiatives. I find that the parents from Central Village and the inner-city communities are very supportive and cooperative, contrary to popular opinions that parents of low socio-economic status rarely attend parent-teacher association meetings and contrary to Kahlenburg (2006) who suggests that children from low-income households are largely from family environments that do not support academic achievement.

The Role of Personal Qualities

I deal with parents based on their personalities. I am approachable to children, teachers and parents alike. I seldom wear white because the students are always hugging or holding onto me. I love my job and I do my best to ensure that I perform at my optimum level. I believe that what I do and where I am defines me: I cannot and will not settle for mediocrity. Not all parents are fond of me and sometimes they make unkind remarks, but at the end of the month, I know that I have earned my salary and imparted justice and my conscience is clear. The bottom line is this: I am not here to be liked, I am here to do a job and I am going to do it well.

I believe in leading by example. I am the principal who waters the plants. I walk into the bathrooms and if they are not fresh, I will freshen them. Many principals would not do that. There are times when I will prepare lunch for my teachers in the canteen and serve them. On Teachers' Day I will cook for them. I see my role as a leader. I do not say to my teachers "get here early" and then arrive late myself. I practise what I preach. I do not walk with a cell phone. I cannot tell the children and the teachers not to use their cell phones while on the job or while walking along the corridor and then do so myself. I try to lead by example and to be totally involved.

Conclusion

The motto of Kensington Primary School, "If you can dream it, you can achieve it", embodies all that transpires at the school. The theme embraces the high expectations, the quality of leadership, the supportive learning environment, the high levels of collaboration and communication, the high levels of parental involvement, all of which are hallmarks of an effective school (Bergeson 2007).

The last National Education Inspectorate report rated this school as "exceptionally high" overall (Ministry of Education 2013). This means the following:

- The leadership is dynamic and often inspirational. The board makes a significant contribution to the leadership of the school and its successes.
- Systematic and rigorous self-evaluation is embedded in the school's practice at all levels.
- The performance of most students is very high in relation to similar schools.
- Almost all students make excellent progress and achieve very well in relation to their earlier attainment.
- The teaching methods are effective. Lessons are often imaginative and consistently stimulate and challenge the students to achieve as well as they can.
- Almost all students understand and appreciate the defining characteristics of Jamaican society and of the region's tradition and culture. They have a high level of spiritual understanding.
- Almost all students understand the importance of securing Jamaica's economic progress and are equipped and willing to contribute to it.
- Almost all students understand the importance of securing a sustainable environment. They take care of their immediate environment and some are involved in related co-curricular activities.
- The staff is very well deployed according to skills needed to teach.
- The school has a full complement of well-qualified staff and deploys them to achieve the best possible standards for students. The curriculum is appreciably enhanced by a wide range of enhancement programmes that are well organized and well attended and which enrich the students' learning experiences considerably.

References

Bergeson, T. 2007. *Nine Characteristics of High-Performing Schools.* Olympia, WA: Office of Superintendent of Public Instruction. http://www.k12.wa.us/research/pubdocs/ninecharacteristics.pdf.

Checkley, K. 2000. "The Contemporary Principal: New Skills for a New Age". *Education Update* 43 (3): 4–6.

Johnson, S.M., and S.M. Kardos. 2005. "Bridging the Generation Gap". *Educational Leadership* 62 (8): 8–13.

Kahlenbery, R. 2006. "The New Integration". *Educational Leadership* 63 (8): 22–27.

McBride, B.A, and T.R. Rane. 1997. "Father/Male Involvement in Early Childhood Programs". *Early Childhood Education Journal* 25 (1): 11–15. doi:10.1023/A:1025625713166.

McCann, T.M., L.R. Johannessen and B. Ricca. 2005. "Responding to New Teachers' Concerns". *Educational Leadership* 62 (8): 30–34.

Ministry of Education. 2013. *National Educational Inspectorate Report.* Kingston: Ministry of Education.

Sammons, P. 1999. *School Effectiveness and Equity: Making Connections. A Review of School Effectiveness and Improvement Research-Its Implication for Practitioners and Policymakers.* Berkshire, UK: CfBT Education Trust. http://repositorio.minedu.gob.pe/bitstream/handle/123456789/1561/2007_SAMMANS-school-effectiveness-and-equity-full-.pdf?sequence=1&isAllowed=y.

Stipek, D. 2006. "Relationship Matters". *Educational Leadership* 64 (1): 46–49.

CHAPTER 5

STRENGTHENING LEADERSHIP CAPACITY
The Journey Continues

GARTH GAYLE

ANGELS PRIMARY SCHOOL, BY VIRTUE OF being a new institution, has several structural advantages. It is located in an upscale community and so some of the challenges faced by other schools did not exist at Angels. There is a perimeter fence and spacious classrooms with proper walls, and so I made good use of that. There were however, programmes that needed to be implemented. We discovered that notwithstanding the good infrastructure, there were challenges with academics.

Making a Difference in Student Performance

When I took on the role of leadership at Angels Primary, the academic challenges were an eye-opener. A child can be well dressed, from a stable background, but not a hungry learner. I employed various approaches. First, I conducted base assessments of the children using the Grade One Individual Learning Profile. Second, with the assistance of the guidance department, I had the students assessed through the Mico Care Centre. Each year, we discovered that we had a cohort of approximately 25 per cent of students who were operating below their grade level.

Supervisory management plays a critical role in motivating and mobilizing teachers for effective work. We must understand the role of the school organization in preparing students to become corporate, self-serving citizens. Along the way, there are various tools that must be utilized. You must allow middle managers to do their job. You, as principal, must maintain the focus. People must be allowed to manage where they ought to manage and be taught to manage where they are not. You allow for development. You must not allow mismanagement to stall your programmes, therefore, you must make staff rotations where they are necessary. At the end of the day, you have to give account for your stewardship.

Administrators must find the necessary coaching and mentoring mechanisms to make a difference and, where those fail, find the hardcore, truthful stance to say, "Shape up or ship out." Teacher appraisal, as suggested by the Ministry of Education will not work in all cases. Students, the parent-teacher association and the school board must be brought into the accountability matrix. They are the customers. Teachers cannot be allowed to get away with poor and mediocre performance. We know that in our Jamaican context, it is very difficult to dismiss a teacher, but it can be done if leaders follow due process and practise proper documentation. After all avenues have been explored to assist the teacher, leaders must not be afraid to recommend dismissal. It is not a pleasant job to dismiss a teacher, but the development of our education system far supersedes the individual's needs and interests. Leaders, however, must be fair and practise equity in their dealings with teachers.

I have found during my interactions with teachers that I am able to use the art of persuasion to get my teachers to improve performance and to build their capacity to continuously make a difference. As the National Comprehensive Center for Teacher Quality (2007, 6) posits, "One way a principal can improve teacher quality is to support staff development needs. Teacher-leaders can help principals support professional development by identifying teacher development needs, offering professional learning experience, developing and delivering opportunities, and evaluating the outcomes of staff development." You cannot always throw the book at teachers, as they might just throw it back at you.

Leadership Style

My leadership style is mostly democratic, but I am not averse to being autocratic nor am I against taking a laissez-faire approach in some situations, although this would hardly work in Jamaica. Research suggests that a democratic leadership style may have a better effect on student achievement than an autocratic style. The democratic leadership style means facilitating conversation, encouraging people to share their ideas, and then synthesizing all the available information to formulate the best possible decision. The democratic leader must be able to communicate that decision back to the group to bring about unity and commitment to the cause of the school. The emphasis is on how the leader communicates with followers, on gaining the followers' trust, and on influencing and persuading them to follow (Riggio 2012). Lunenburg and Ornstein (2000, 126) state that an effective leader should possess a little of all the leadership styles. However, of the three styles, subordinates prefer a democratic style that is "more consistent with supportive and collegial models". The style of leadership is also predicated on the climate and culture of the school. At Angels Primary, I could practise mostly a democratic style. However, transitioning from Angels to Charlie Smith I had to change my style of leadership. I had to be less open and more autocratic. The staff accepted that style of leadership as there was the need and a hunger for leadership.

I am a go-getter. Life has never been particularly kind to me, but I have used each opportunity as a stepping-stone. This has helped mould my personality and make me humble and grateful, but it is important to understand that one cannot be too humble or too overly grateful, or one may be stepped upon, ridiculed or taken advantage of. There comes a time when you have to become autocratic in order to rule effectively, having discovered that there is a dishonest intent among some of those in the school community. You also have to be clear, try to remove ambiguity and, where a misstep is made, not to be afraid to apologize. I am that type of leader. When you have a job to do, you must do it. I use myself as a benchmark. I do not know whether the psychologists or behaviourist theorists will agree, but my approach is to be prepared to do that which I am asking others to do. To pick up a piece of paper on the ground is not beneath me: if I pick it up, I can ask a child or a staff member to do the same. I believe in truth, fairness, honesty and punctuality, which are the keys to success.

Relationship with the Ministry of Education

From the time I was in training, I learned and understood the importance of respect. If you make a strong effort to adhere to the guidelines of the Ministry of Education and if you develop a good rapport with them you will get more support. You therefore have to build a good relationship. Maintaining open communication is crucial in fostering such a relationship. It makes the job of leading a school easier and facilitates quick action. Reese (2004) notes that good state leadership and good local leadership partnerships can coexist and lead to a cohesive system. Further, when a culture of high expectation leads to changes in behaviour, it is important to sustain that achievement. And the job of the effective leader is to ensure that all stakeholders are accommodated in a culture that emphasizes collaboration, networking and teambuilding.

Income Generation

Raising funds at Angels was not a problem. We had a very successful enterprise. We had good support from parents and we were able to complete some basic infrastructural development, such as grilling, tiling and painting, without asking the ministry for financial support. We had challenges with the vendors. Their numbers grew and it was a major drain on the capacity of the tuck shop to make a profit. We struck a compromise in that they did not come during school hours or in the mornings. Now, at Charlie Smith High School, we have only two main vendors and we try to keep students inside school grounds. One of the challenges I inherited was poor management of funds. I had to put accountability measures in place to monitor sales, check inventory, and provide checks and balances. A finance committee was also established.

Challenges in Administration

One challenge I faced in the primary school system, unlike in the secondary system, was the lack of administrative support and resources. I got the board to buy in with a clear vision to develop and expand the school's administrative operations. With the board's approval, I used available resources to employ an accounting clerk and an administrative assistant. I was able to use these individuals with the aid of a clerical assistant provided by the ministry to implement the various administrative structures necessary for curriculum development. I also altered the physical spaces, procured equipment and put structures in place to facilitate students' records and other files.

There is the tendency for educators to overlook the role of school boards in effective schools. This may be due in part to the fact that some school boards are seen as powerless, especially in our Jamaican context. However, the role of school boards must not be taken lightly as they can be powerful engines in ensuring effective schools. Effective school boards can expand their influence in the educational environment if they undertake aggressive policymaking and leadership for education reform within their communities (Hansberger, Kirs and Usdan 1992, quoted in Kansas City Consensus 2001). We did not have to rely much on the board. The school was able to procure the necessary financial resources through the school's tuck shop. However, the Code of the Regulations and the Financial Administration and Audit Act suggest that funds raised on the compound belong to the ministry. Although there were some missteps at Angels Primary, the audit trails and other monitoring systems allowed us to correct and streamline to meet the requirements.

We followed clear guidelines and budgeting. I have developed accounting skills along the way (I did not enter the job with that skill set). I cannot say I am an accountant, but the experience made me aware of the requirements and that a certain course must be followed to be in compliance. Angels benefited greatly from good financial management. As a result, we developed sports programmes, students participated in Jamaica Cultural Development Commission activities, and clubs and societies were introduced. If schools manage their financial resources well, they can achieve a great deal.

Maintaining Discipline

I took a multifaceted approach when it came to discipline. It entailed engaging and reminding members of staff of their role in maintaining discipline and setting high standards for student behaviour. We emphasized good parent-teacher relationships, student-teacher relationships and relationships among staff. My teachers had to be professional and had to understand that they were not in the job only to be liked but to do a good job. Teacher behaviour was therefore critical in setting the tone of discipline. According to Lunenburg and Ornstein (2000), effective teacher behaviours include verbal and non-verbal communication, teacher expectations and teacher characteristics. The interactions of these behaviours establish the climate of the effective classroom practice and outcomes.

Parental support was very strong at Angels Primary. It must be noted, however, that most of the students came from stable homes and close to 70 per cent of parents were professionals themselves. We did not have to send out a lot of circulars about school activities because word-of-mouth helped to publicize them. Parental involvement played a major role in discipline at the school. Regular parent-teacher association meetings were held at which parents were updated concerning the rules and expectations of the school. We kept parents abreast with the Ministry of Education's guidelines, schools programmes, the dress code, homework policies and how students should speak to teachers. Parents were also carefully reminded about how to deal with matters pertaining to students.

The guidance programme provided support for students with disciplinary problems. There was of course the odd misbehaviour problem which was dealt with at the general or specific level. Middle managers played a critical role in effecting discipline. The principal as the chief leader must understand the importance of delegating and building leadership capacities. A principal does not always have to be at the centre of everything but must allow middle managers to assist. We must rely on the structure or system. We must take into account what happens when we are absent. Lambert (2003) contends that leadership capacity is the organization's capacity to lead itself and sustain that effort when key individuals leave. Delegation therefore becomes critical. Open communication is also crucial in managing and in maintaining discipline. Once something is reported, it must be dealt with expeditiously. Communication is essential to a school's effectiveness.

Transitioning From Primary to High School

It was not very difficult for me to transition from Angels Primary School to Charlie Smith High, even though research has shown that differences exist in how principals in secondary schools and principals in primary schools carry out their instructional leadership function. The differences result from the organization and structure of secondary schools as compared to primary schools. Principals in secondary schools usually delegate most of their instructional leadership functions to middle managers. The principal in turn facilitates and develops the instructional leadership competency of these middle managers. Principals in secondary schools reflect the indirect instructional leadership model since they are not directly involved with what goes on in the classrooms but, rather, ensure that the resources and other conditions are in place for good teaching and learning.

On the other hand, principals in primary schools reflect the direct model of instructional leadership since they are directly involved in what goes on in the classrooms, in terms of quality of instruction and students' learning. However, it is about the person and his or her leadership capability. It is important for you to bloom where you are planted, instilling best practices and setting up accountability structures. We must also pay attention to evaluation, which must be data driven. My theme is "setting goals to achieve success". One must set goals and implement them and then review the process. Most importantly, we must not be satisfied with mediocrity. I am resolved in making Charlie Smith High School a top-performing school by working with all stakeholders in moving the school forward.

Conclusion

I am grateful for the opportunity to serve at the primary level for nine beautiful years. I am now in the second sojourn at the secondary level and I pray God continues to guide my steps. I told the boards in all of my interview panels to "judge me for what I did, see what I leave. Judge me there". I enjoy teaching, and a friend told me once, "Garth, you are not a bad manager, but lead, learn to lead." I am learning to lead. Effective leadership in schools allows for the creation of productive organizations whose productivity is measured by the quality of learning and behaviour in the school setting. There is a strong connection between the leader and the environment. Principals must therefore be equipped with the appropriate knowledge, skills and attitudes to carry out their leadership roles effectively.

References

Kansas City Consensus. 2001. *Steer, Not Row: How to Strengthen Local School Boards and Improve Student Learning.* Kansas City, MO: Kansas City Consensus.

Lambert, L. 2003. *Leadership Capacity for Lasting School Improvement.* Alexandria, VA: Association for Supervision and Curriculum Development.

Lunenburg, F.C., and A.C. Ornstein. 2000. *Educational Administration: Concepts and Practices.* Belmont, CA: Wadsworth/Thomson Learning.

National Comprehensive Center for Teacher Quality. 2007. "Key Issue: Enhancing Teacher Leadership". http://www.gtlcenter.org/sites/default/files/docs/Enhancing TeacherLeadership.pdf.

Reese, S. 2004. "Effective School Leadership". *Techniques: Connecting Education and Careers* 79 (6): 18–21.

Riggio, R.E. 2012. "What Is Charisma and Charismatic Leadership?" *Psychology Today*, October. https://www.psychologytoday.com/blog/cutting-edge-leadership/201210/what-is-charisma-and-charismatic-leadership.

PART 2

TRANSITION
Primary to Upgraded Secondary Schools

CHAPTER 6

EFFECTIVE PRINCIPALSHIP
Innovative Leadership Skills

O'NEIL ANKLE

I HAVE ALWAYS BELIEVED I COULD make a worthwhile contribution to the education sector as a school leader, having spent some time in the classroom at G.C. Foster College. If asked whether or not teaching was my first choice or my first love, I would say no. Essentially, teaching chose me. I ended up in teaching and fell in love with it.

Making a Difference in Student Performance at Green Park

When I arrived at Green Park, the school had been selected to participate in the New Horizon Project for primary schools. It was a low-performing school. Nobody wanted to send their children there. When I had my first senior teachers' meeting I remember saying, "God, I have never been a principal before (the only senior or supervisory position I have held was to be in charge of the evening programme at G.C. Foster College), but You sent me here so You will have to give me words." When I looked around the room all the persons except the guidance counsellor were older than me. That meeting must have lasted for three hours and I said to them then, "I am going to give you three years then we are going to change the perception of this school." I also said to them, "For the next five years I am not going to allow you to invite anybody from outside to be guest speakers at graduation, I will choose the speakers." They asked me why – I had a strategy.

Indiscipline was at an all-time high on the junior high side. Boys were fighting teachers and we had to deal with the "fish belt" students and the "cane belt" students. Additionally, the literacy rate was at 28 per cent, hence, the school's participation in the New Horizon Project – a participation with which everyone seemed happy. The more I got involved in the project and listened to schools, including the Jericho Primary and White Marl Primary and Junior High, making presentations about how these schools were progressing under the project, the more I wondered what was happening at Green Park. I realized that despite the fact that we were getting all the resources, nothing was being done. The physical resources were underutilized and the teachers were not challenged to use them.

I believe in using data to transform students' performance. Some members of staff were upset that I was implying they were not performing and some were even embarrassed at the results. But, at times, we have to be embarrassed before we can be happy. I can recall when the New Horizon Project ceased supporting schools that had improved their overall performance. Our school overperformed by two points and therefore was not qualified for continued support from the project. I told my staff that I was happy, because I wanted the school to get off the programme. It meant that we had to raise the bar in literacy. What I did was to start with grade 1, where the teachers had to give me monthly reports on students' performance and attendance. It also involved visiting the students' homes to ensure that parents supported the students. I designed tests for grades 1 and 2 which were similar to the Grade Four Literacy Test. These tests were administered each term, and feedback and strategies for improvement were provided by teachers.

I realized that to increase literacy, a library was needed. We were also participating in the Reform of Secondary Education programme and so I wrote to the ministry and solicited permission to use some of the funds from that programme for the library. I identified an area of the school and transformed it into our school library, now known as one of the best school libraries in Clarendon. I wrote to the ministry and requested a librarian. The librarian hired was a graduate of the Mico University College and not only had library skills but also literacy teaching skills, and so she was charged with assisiting grade 3 students with literacy. The students who passed the grade 3 literacy tests were accelerated to grade 4, but those who did not pass were put into an intervention programme facilitated by the librarian, who would provide monthly reports on their progress. I certified my grade 3 students as literate and made a ceremony of it by inviting the parents and handing out certificates. Hence, prior to the ministry mandating schools to have grade 4 students remaining in grade 4 for an additional year, I had in place an intervention programme to assist students and get them ready for the Grade Six Achievement Test. The results over time were remarkable, as in 2012, the literacy rate was at 92 per cent and numeracy was at 84 per cent.

I would leave my house on Saturdays and visit the students' homes and interact with the parents. I held parent-teacher association meetings in the community, even with the knowledge that some areas were considered volatile. When I arrived at Green Park, only one child met the minimum requirement in the Grade Six Achievement Test to attend Glenmuir (a traditional high school). Most of them would return to school the next year as junior high students. However, at the time of my departure, only a few did not advance. One year in particular, none returned. All went on to a high school. This achievement was really a landmark event.

Another initiative I undertook was to improve the infrastructure of the school. We solicited funds to paint the exterior of the school and give it a fresh look. Murals were added, the floor was paved, and benches and chairs were repaired and repainted. Through the Reform of Secondary Education programme, a perimeter fence was installed. These improvements helped to change the culture and climate of the school. Significantly, the students were also affirmed. They had to repeat the following affirmation every morning, "I am born to be great." This affirmation allowed them to understand that where they are from should not define who they are or who they would become.

Working with Students at Jonathan Grant

My wife was apprehensive about my going to Spanish Town to work. I arrived at Jonathan Grant with a predetermined view of how I would proceed. I had spoken to my colleagues who were in the high school system and had got some pointers as to how to progress. When I went to Jonathan Grant High, indiscipline was a major concern. But after three years of working at getting my teachers and all stakeholders to understand that indiscipline and high academic performance cannot swim in the same sea, things have changed and we are beginning to see the full potential of our students. I had to take some drastic measures just to get things right; some even landed me in trouble.

Today, however, I can say without contradiction that the school is a far safer place, the attitudes of the students and teachers are different and, by and large, the community is happy with the changes that have taken place. More importantly, the school is a more productive and orderly place. At present, children at Jonathan Grant want to soar; they want to learn and excel. The data have indicated that changes are taking place. Slowly but surely we are getting there.

When I arrived in January 2012, bleaching (skin toning) was a major problem. It was a culture shock for me. I felt I was in North America. Students, in no uncertain terms, were asked to go and not return until their skin tone returned to its original state, as I would have none of it. Today, we no longer have to deal with that issue.

Student dress was another area that had to be addressed, particularly, the wearing of tight pants (spangy) and short dresses. The dress code of the school was violated in every shape and form. I gave students one month to conform to the dress code. After that, the boys who failed to comply were given "tailored skirts". The hems of the girls' skirts were slit all the way around to give the uniform a "shredded look". After many challenges, that problem no longer exists and today students are wearing their uniform with pride and loving it. In fact, many students have echoed the sentiment that this change was needed long ago. Whether we want to believe it or not, children want structure in their lives; if you fail to provide it, they will be more likely to demonstrate undesirable behaviours.

Another shock to me upon arrival in 2012 was the small number of students who were actually sitting in class as opposed to staying outside during class time. What was happening at the time was that if a student came to school to learn, he or she would go to class, sit down and learn what was being taught. On the other hand, if you felt that school for you meant remaining on the outside for the duration of school, most of the time occupying the lazy benches, then that was where you would stay. Sadly, most of the students who found themselves in that position were the boys of grades 10 and 11.

Many teachers, it seemed, were afraid to address these students. For me that had to change – and quickly. I had come to Jonathan Grant High School with several goals and one of those goals was that of making the school a better place. I was not going to be sidetracked or derailed. Green (2000, 11) postulates that "it is very important not to be deflected from your goals; your vision is sacrosanct and every day you will find there are many pressures and siren voices that seek to deflect you from your purpose".

Against such understanding, I met all grades 10 and 11 students in the "Dome" (kind of an auditorium) to let them know, in no uncertain manner, what my thoughts were and who was going to be in charge of the school. I made it clear that I was not about playing school with anyone. I told the students that afternoon that if they come to school they must be in class. If they did not want to be in school they were advised to stay home. Today (three years later) there is no longer a problem and all are on board.

Graffiti was another matter. This too was a culture shock as I only saw this ugliness on television, in American schools. The classrooms were filled with explicit drawings and scribbling. During the summer, I had the classrooms repainted and went to devotion the following September morning of 2012. I issued my warning and the rest is history. Three years have passed and all that I have done each summer is to repaint the walls where the backs of the chairs had scratched them. For me, schools are effectively run by those who are called to education – individuals who are passionate about education, who are fearless, who are risk-takers and who want to make things happen. It is that simple.

Before I went to Jonathan Grant High, Wednesdays, I was told, were designated as fight days. There were usually seven to ten fights involving weapons. I have zero tolerance for indiscipline. All I did at the time was to make an announcement, "If you fight, you go; wrong or right", and that settled it. It was a risk I took, but it worked. Of course my dean of discipline was put to work and she was given the support needed to carry out her job. Today we have few fights among students. The community and safety officers who were attached to the school in earlier days are no longer needed. The truth is they rarely come to our school anymore.

Students were often unpunctual. On any given morning, approximately 150 students would be late. I told the students that they needed to adjust their clocks because I would not tolerate tardiness. Likewise, I told them that they needed to get to school by 6:30 a.m. and by 11:30 a.m. for the first and second shifts, respectively.

I believe that corporal punishment has its place; however, much of it is not used at Jonathan Grant, because I instituted a "black book" into which students' names would be entered for poor behaviour. Upon my arrival at the school I realized that a uniform behavioural system was in place; different colours were used for different offences. All I did was to strengthen this system. A "ticket system" was also instituted, whereby students would receive a ticket for misconduct. After three tickets, students would be referred for counselling. One thing that I often used was motivation; I also practised an open-door policy. I would be available to any student at any time, unless I was otherwise occupied. I believe that I am a servant – without the students I do not have a job. I give all the parents my phone number so that they can be in touch me with me at any time – even at night. Parents are encouraged to communicate their challenges and report student behaviour and that impacts student discipline. The film *Lean on Me* was instrumental in how I did things. I would watch the film every morning before coming to school and that acted as motivation for me.

Gender Diversity

I did not have any special programme for boys, despite the fact that research has revealed that boys learn differently than girls. Boys generally do more poorly in academics than girls, and for Brozo (2006) this notion is embedded in the popular consciousness which leads to a perception that boys will not become thoughtful accomplished readers. It begs the question as to what we are doing wrong and whether we are ill-preparing our boys. Research on the male brain versus the brains of females suggests that boys' brains are made up differently and as such, they will learn differently. King and Gurian (2006) suggested that verbal and spatial differences, a less active prefrontal cortex, neural rest states, and natural aggressions are some of the differences. However, Brozo (2006) advanced the idea that we can narrow the achievement gap by building on the resources boys bring to school. Conversely, Perkins-Gough (2006) contended that we should not panic, as the boys are doing fine and we should first be concerned with other gaps besides gender.

The boys at Jonathan Grant are not doing badly despite the fact that the girls are outperforming them on tests. I have an honour roll system. One boy has got a scholarship to Germany. I try to motivate boys by sharing my life story with them and by getting them to believe in themselves. I believe that the male teachers' presence in school makes a difference. I am a role model to the boys; they do not fear but respect me. A young man who is now attending the evening programme told me that if I had been at the school two years ago he would not have taken only four CSEC subjects. The male vice principal and I have recently rolled out a programme called "Power 60" to help motivate the boys. This programme is aimed at spending sixty minutes with the boys at different times. Motivational speakers are brought in to address and to share with them, and already we have seen growth. These boys are exposed to a variety of influences, and so it is my job along with the team to work at diffusing anything that would stunt their growth, be it intellectually, morally or otherwise.

Making a Difference in Student Performance at Jonathan Grant

When I got to Jonathan Grant, the school average was 21 per cent in CSEC mathematics and 56 per cent in English language. I met with the senior staff and gave each a goal. In fact, I created a goal wall. The school goal was that student performance would reach at least 90 per cent in mathematics and English language by 2016. The students were here and they had the ability. I pulled all the data and disaggregated the results and allowed teachers to see where we were as a school. I developed an accountability matrix. Each teacher was given a target and had to report whether he or she met the target and if not, why. Each person had to say how they contributed to the school's target. In fact I provided incentives for teachers who were doing well. I used my parent-teacher association to provide a monetary incentive and developed a Teacher, Supervisor and Form Teacher of the Year competition. Additionally, I created the same programme on a per-term basis in an effort to motivate staff.

Today, much of the morale and attitude have changed and each teacher is working towards meeting the established targets. It is significant to note that since data analysis has become a critical part of the teaching-learning process, teachers are more aware of what is taking place in the classroom. It has become the talk among teachers: "The data will speak hence I must do what is required." For me, data are the foundation on which to build student outcomes. I must work the data, and I am pulling the teachers along so that they too can work the data and understand their importance to the entire process of teaching and learning; furthermore, focusing on data helps to raise expectations. Green (2000, 156) intimates "that raising expectation is one of the most important aspects of the job of the school leader because it has been found that it is one of the most critical of all factors in school improvement".

Working with Parents

Working with parents must be part of the equation in any school system. I use motivating strategies with parents. I tell them that if they give me the support, I guarantee that I will have each child leaving the school with at least five CSEC subjects and a vocation. In fact, graduation is not held in June but in November, and a criterion for graduation is that students have to pass at least four subjects, be it CSEC, Human Employment and Resource Training (HEART) Trust, or city and guilds examinations. If parents are not invited to become a partner in their children's education because of socio-economic or educational challenges then they will not be motivated to get involved. It is therefore important that educators recognize that parents must be involved, regardless of their status. However, Comer (2005, 39) remarks that "even when schools expect and encourage parent participation, many educators do not understand how it is supposed to work". Parents must be seen as leaders in their own right and be invited on that basis. Lambert (2003, 66) adds that "talking about parent as leaders is different from discussing parent involvement. The latter term conjures up images of parents volunteering at school, showing interest in their own children, fundraising, and reading the latest newsletter".

I have also broken down the amount of money parents spend on their children for the five years in high school so that parents are able to see how much money they were investing in their children. That allowed parents to see that they must hold their children accountable and responsible. In presenting the characteristics of effective schools, Creemers, Peters and Reynolds (1989) cite parental involvement and a sense of community as characteristics of an effective school.

Working with Stakeholders

Two months after my arrival at the school, I had an idea to host a stakeholders' cocktail party. We invited all the individuals with whom we did business as a school – the parent-teacher association, the past students' association, the police, the business community of Spanish Town and the member of parliament. They were feted and then I addressed them. I shared my vision for the institution, including the short- and long-term goals. Of course, I sought not only their moral and physical support but their financial support as well. We exchanged business cards and today I am still reaping the benefits of that initiative. Green (2000, 16) suggests that "the heart of management is the capacity to get things done using whatever resources or lack of them that are available to you". I believe that finding creative ways of building stakeholder partnerships – especially with those who possess the requisite skill set, knowledge and financial resources – is critical to the growth of any school.

Working with Teachers

Most of the key decisions that are made are related to teaching and learning, and these decisions are first taken at the senior management level before presenting them to the general staff. This senior management staff meets once each month. The decisions that are made at this level are then taken to the senior staff meeting for further discussion and following that, ventilated at a general staff meeting after which a final decision is made. I have found this to be a most effective way of taking decisions and conveying to the team what will be done. It also gives the team an opportunity to buy into what you hope to achieve. Furthermore, it makes sense to involve all persons, as it makes for a smooth operation of the organization.

Collaboration facilitates and engenders high expectations and performance. It is therefore important for me, in most cases, to garner the support and opinions of the team, especially from those who may have the requisite knowledge. Hersey, Blanchard and Johnson (2001, 361) propose that "facilitative decision making is a cooperative effort in which manager and followers work together to reach a shared decision". It is definitely better when the leader can share the decision-making process. Additionally, I have discovered that cooperation promotes a sense of ownership, shared responsibility and more camaraderie among colleagues. However, there are some decisions that the board of governors will have to sign off on before they are filtered down to the general staff.

Communication

I know the importance of communication and how it makes or breaks an organization. For that simple reason, communicating with my team members is critical to the school's growth and development, and I do not take the function for granted. I decided immediately upon my arrival at Jonathan Grant that I would create and e-mail to staff and all members of the team, a bulletin every Monday. The bulletin keeps all members of the team – academic, administrative and ancillary – updated on what is happening, on what will take place and on what is to come. The bulletin also focuses on new trends in education and on strategies to aid teaching and learning. This mode of communicating with the team is most important, as hosting general staff meetings on a regular basis can be disruptive. My academic staff complement is 106 and I run a shift school with a population of over two thousand students. Having general staff meetings on a monthly basis means I would have to disrupt the flow of school too often. It also means asking one shift to arrive late and, possibly, dismissing the other early. All this takes away from the already limited contact time I have to offer to the students.

Electronic mail is part of the new dimension of communicating with individuals in a quick and efficient way. Green (2000, 114), in making reference to the different media of communication, suggests that "the methods available are changing, but this is one of those personal areas that help you to define yourself as head of your community". He further states that "you have to choose the most effective way to tell people about events, children's progress and school's progress". Consequently, general staff meetings are held basically once per term, hence, the importance of the weekly communiqué.

Supervisory Leadership

Davidson (1979) advances the notion that while principals would like to think of themselves as supervisors, many do not understand what being a supervisor entails. Sergiovanni and Starratt (1990) propose that an education supervisor's work is primarily in the area of instructional improvement, hence, the need for it to be given prominence over any other function the principal has. The term "instructional supervisor", therefore, sums up the primary role of the principal in the quest for academic excellence in education. In essence, the instructional supervisor focuses on student learning and student success.

I have more than one hundred staff members; hence, the staff is not easy to manage. However, I use my middle managers to help me. I have a lesson-plan matrix and each middle manager is accountable to provide reports of what is happening. They also have to provide a report as to what they have done to help the situation. Of course, you have some persons who are afraid of reporting because they want people to love them; but I have told them that they will be logged as having failed to execute this aspect of their duty if they do not make such reports. Winter and Dunaway (1997) assert that the job of principal might be the most challenging administrative position in public education, as school reform initiatives mandate greater emphasis on instructional leadership. The Jamaican Education Regulations (1980, 58), which is the only legal document that guides the education system, clearly outlines a number of duties and responsibilities of principals. These duties and responsibilities underscore the importance of the role of the principals in instructional supervision and include

- formulating, in consultation with members of staff, the curriculum of the institution within the general educational policy laid down by the minister and by the board;
- planning and administering the day-to-day educational programme;
- ensuring that the curriculum gives proper significance to national emblems and makes provisions for the observance of respect for them;

- supervision of the instruction in the institution and, assisted by the vice principal, heads of department and other persons holding posts of special responsibility, giving advice, guidance and professional assistance to the teachers and other teaching personnel; and
- recommending to the board the appointment and promotion of members of staff and the demotion or dismissal of such persons whose work or attitude is unsatisfactory, but only after warning the member of staff in writing, giving guidance and assistance, and allowing a reasonable time for improvement.

Despite this however, many principals spend most of their time focusing on the mundane and routine exercises and not enough time on the instructional component.

Monitoring

In an effort to ensure that teachers stay and remain on task, here are a few of the things I have implemented:

- *Walk-through rubric.* Here the grade coordinators, senior teachers and vice principals have to visit the teachers under their care at least three times per term and report at the end of term.
- *Lesson-plan rubric.* Each head of department is given this instrument to use as a guide when marking the plans. The heads of department have to submit a report on lesson planning, and copies of the marked rubric on each teacher must be submitted with the report on a monthly basis. A teacher who fails to submit his or her lesson plans must be given a memorandum, which must be attached to the monthly report. If the head of department fails to do that, he or she will be given a memo. It may sound harsh but I find that it works, as I take planning very seriously. Additionally, each teacher has to conduct a self-reflection at the end of each term. The reflection is not on student performance per se but on the teacher's pedagogy.

Using Data to Drive Performance

I walk data. I talk data. Likewise, I use data to drive every decision I make. I have instituted a looping system whereby a teacher moves up with his or her classes. I did my research and shared ideas with staff, showing them the advantages and disadvantages. I also compared each year's data for the teachers to see the value added. Looping has many benefits. I use the data to qualify the need to continue the looping. I also noted that the children on the morning shift did better academically than those on the afternoon shift; hence I changed the shifts once per year so as to maximize performance. I also shared data that I had researched so that teachers can be kept up to date. We know that sometimes data can be faked, but they are difficult to fake all the time.

The Role of Personal Qualities in the Principalship

I believe that we have to love what we do. We must be passionate about the growth of other individuals. One has to think creatively in order to accomplish more than would be possible by following the rules of the ministry to the letter. I am also at risk. Most importantly, I enjoy what I do. I get up every morning knowing that some child would be coming to me for a hug or with a problem that I would have to help them to solve. Education is not a job, it is a calling, and nobody can take that away from you. Individuals should understand that principalship involves more than paper pushing, managing paper or staying behind the big desk. Principalship is all about changing lives and one cannot lose that focus once he or she has taken on the role of principal.

Significant Progress

Since coming to Jonathan Grant High there are a number of achievements I would consider to be significant. Here are six:

1. the construction of a new classroom block (twelve rooms; the cost for the building was J$55 million and this was undertaken totally by the school)
2. moving mathematics from a 15 per cent pass rate of those who were recommended to sit the subject in 2011 to 65 per cent in 2015

3. introduction of our sixth-form programme in September 2014
4. introduction of a programme in automotive engineering technology in September 2013
5. regional recognition, for the first time, of three students in CXC for their outstanding performance – first and tenth place in mechanical engineering and third place in agricultural science double option (we do not have a farm as such, just a plot)
6. overall attitude and behaviour of our students significantly improved since arrival in January 2012; tremendous change across the board

Areas That Still Need to Be Addressed

While the school has shown significant improvement, some areas still need work:

- Data application: the need for teachers to understand the role data plays in driving instruction and the whole matter of teaching and learning. (While the utilization of data is far better than three years ago, there is still room for improvement.)
- Parent involvement: the need for parents to play a greater part in the education of the children. (Many parents still have not recognized the importance of sound education; they do not seem to understand the significance of their investment.)

Conclusion

Leadership in schools is a tough job, and people have to realize that it is especially hard work if you are interested in the students and their success. Anyone assuming a leadership position in a school must leave his or her desk and be visible in the classrooms. Every member of staff, ancillary or otherwise, is important. I do not treat my staff differently. I try to make them comfortable because I want them to perform and remain at the school. Darling-Hammond and Berry (2006) opine that just paying teachers more will not suffice; the conditions must facilitate their success.

I use the team approach to get things done. According to Lezotte (1994, 1), the study of leadership in effective schools suggests two conclusions: first, effective schools and school districts are led by individuals who have the vision that learning in a democracy must be inclusive – learning for all; second, these individuals have the ability to communicate this vision to the others in the district and in the school so that they share the vision and accept the mission of making it happen. A leader's vision will lack endurance unless he or she is able to garner committed support from among those who will help execute a plan to sustain it.

References

Brozo, W.G. 2006. "Bridges to Literacy for Boys". *Educational Leadership* 64 (1): 71–74.

Comer, J.P. 2005. "The Rewards of Parent Participation". *Educational Leadership* 62 (8): 38–42.

Creemers, B., T. Peters and D. Reynolds, eds. 1989. "The Future of School Effectiveness and School Improvement". *School Effectiveness and Improvement.* Amsterdam: Swits and Zeitlinger.

Darling-Hammond, L., and B. Berry. 2006. "Highly Qualified Teachers for All". *Educational Leadership* 64 (3): 14–20.

Davidson, F. 1979. "Teachers' Perceived Leadership Behaviour of Principals and Morale in a Selected Sample of Schools". Master's thesis, University of the West Indies, Mona, Jamaica.

Green, F. 2000. *The Head Teacher in the 21st Century: Being a Successful School Leader.* London: Pearson Education.

Hersey, P., K.H. Blanchard and D.E. Johnson. 2001. *Management of Organizational Behavior.* Upper Saddle River, NJ: Prentice Hall.

King, K., and M. Gurian. 2006. "Teaching to the Minds of Boys". *Educational Leadership* 64 (1): 56–61.

Lambert, L. 2003. *Leadership Capacity for Lasting School Improvement.* Alexandria, VA: Association for Supervision and Curriculum Development.

Lezotte, L. 1994. "The Nexus of Instructional Leadership and Effective Schools". *School Administrator* 51 (6): 20–23.

Perkins-Gough, D. 2006. "Do We Really Have a 'Boy Crisis'?" *Educational Leadership* 64 (1): 83–84.

Sergiovanni, T.J., and R.J. Starratt. 1990. *Supervision: Human Perspectives.* 4th ed. New York: McGraw-Hill.

Winter, P.A., and D.M. Dunaway. 1997. "Reaction of Teachers as Applicants to Principal Recruitment Practices in a Reform Environment: The Effects of Job Attributes, Job Satisfaction, Job Information Source and School Level". *Journal of Research Development in Education* 30 (3): 144–53.

CHAPTER 7

TRANSFORMING LIVES THROUGH EDUCATION

BRADLEY ROBINSON

WHEN I STARTED AS PRINCIPAL, I had already served twelve years as an educator. My experience had spanned the spectrum of educational framework in Jamaica and had even extended beyond local boundaries to cover a stint in England. These experiences underpin my personal belief system – that of a deep-seated belief in people and the desire to see them do well – and my infectious love for children, greatly aided my overall effectiveness. I have been empowered by my humble upbringing, which gave me the foundation in putting others before self and a desire to live for some cause which was or would amount to be much more than self. I was also driven by a promise I made to my deceased mother to become an educator.

I emerged as a school leader at age thirty-two. There were a number of factors that were pivotal in preparing for my career. My personal abilities also aided my success. I had a good command of the English language, and I am naturally a good listener. I had been seasoned as a leader in all areas of my development prior to becoming principal. I served as academic course, option leader, assistant hall chairman and hall chairman at the Mico College; I was prefect and deputy head boy at Titchfield High School and assistant supervisor in my first job as an accounting clerk. I also held supervisory positions at Superdrug in the United Kingdom. All these experiences contributed to me becoming one of the youngest principals in Jamaica during my tenure.

Making Learning Your Priority Objective

One of the challenges I faced as principal was in transmitting a set of beliefs which explain what school was all about. Erkiliç (2008) advises that our philosophy is what is going to drive change. Therefore, if I was to make teaching and learning my priority objectives, I would have to change the philosophy of the community regarding the central role of teaching and learning in improving student outcomes.

In my first year as principal, I successfully recruited four volunteers to aid with teaching. Additionally, through skilful advocacy, we were able to get a National Youth Service Volunteer from the community to assist with clerical work as, based on its size, the school was not eligible for a clerical assistant. We then set about to restructure the programmes so that they represented first-class examples of teaching and learning. Through fundraising and support from donor agencies and other companies, we were able to get a multimedia projector, twenty-four computers, a laptop and a multipurpose printer/copier/scanner, telephone and Internet services and some used AlphaSmart mini computers.

We structured the programme to reflect continuous assessment. As an instructional leader, I undertook a number of measures, inclusive of regular walk-throughs and feedback from the teachers. We created monthly teacher rating profiles which reflected a tiered system of measuring effectiveness. Other measures were monthly planning sessions with individual teachers, as well as groups, demonstration lessons, and team and weekly planning and feedback sessions. A reading and numeracy coach was brought into the framework. We crafted a policy for literacy and identified a school-based literacy coordinator to run all the programmes relating to literacy in the school.

We held regular meetings with senior management staff; appraisal of middle managers and teachers was instituted and a rigorous review of what worked and what did not was conducted.

We instituted a mentorship programme for teachers to expose them to best practices from other professionals in the field. This led to a massive improvement in the performance of the teachers. They were afforded access to first-class practices and thus gained practical working knowledge which also brought out strengths and qualities that they did not know they possessed.

Teachers were thus able to twin their own experience with that of more seasoned contemporaries, which helped them to hone their skills significantly. That redounded to the performance of the students in a series of required national examinations.

Within two years, we moved from being a school that was performing far below the national average in all external exams to being in the top three schools in the corporate area and among the top 5 per cent of schools in the country in literacy and numeracy. Additional reinforcement of teaching excellence through a "Teacher of the Term" initiative was also well received. There was also an incentive programme introduced for teachers and other non-teaching staff in which rewards were given each term. This significantly improved performance and impacted the overall effectiveness of the school. In fact, in 2013 the school had the highest average in mathematics in the Grade Six Achievement Tests in the country.

In 2009 when I started as principal, donkeys, cats, dogs and cows roamed the school yard. Additionally, the bathrooms were some distance away from the school. Consequently, the students, teachers and other workers alike, had to walk for about five minutes through open air in order to get to the bathroom. The community is located in the hills of St Andrew and thus is exposed to torrential rainfall. This affected the children's ability to function because whenever it rained (which was every day) they had great difficulty getting to and from the bathrooms. The open school yard presented a serious security dilemma and also militated against attendance and punctuality. Members of any organization need to feel safe to perform at their optimum level.

We had to decide to either build a covering to get to the bathrooms or build a bathroom attached to the main school building. With regard to the fencing, we knew we had to seek sponsorship or engage in fundraising. Within two years, we were able to fully fence the school compound, with four gates (based on the shape of the school compound). We identified a room on the main building that could be converted into a bathroom. We went on a massive campaign to raise funds and were able to construct a bathroom for the students with thirteen stalls (eight for the girls and five for the boys), urinals and showers. Three bathrooms with showers were constructed for the teachers.

Building and Maintaining Relationships

School Community and Alumni

An integral part of my initiatives at the school was forging relationships with key stakeholders. The main stakeholder group (parents) had to be exposed to the vision, with the hope of getting them to buy in. According to Ciulla (2004), once the leader demonstrates the kind of behaviour which stimulates trust, then stakeholders will buy into the vision. This proved difficult initially, however, as the main stakeholder group had "fallen out of love" with the school. What was good was the fact that the majority of the adults in the community were past students; therefore, the children who attended the school hailed from those very homes. In response to the low level of performance at the school, the community created two preparatory schools which most of the children attended. This intervention helped to stem the literacy and numeracy deficiencies which were challenges to learning for those entering the school.

In an effort to integrate the main stakeholders into the mix of the operations of the school, three main groups were created to ensure efficiency: a robust parent-teacher association, with a full slate of executives; the establishment of a past students' association, and a school advisory committee. These groups were apprised of the kind of support the school would need and they were also expected to participate in setting performance targets for the school, with the principal leading the effort. Based on the needs of the school, it was critically important that other stakeholder groups be engaged.

The Role of the School Board and Regional Office

The board was mandated to undertake two major tasks each year which would form a part of the school improvement plan. Additionally, a finance committee, formed by the board, would oversee the financial operations of the school. The principal and his staff would be held accountable if pre-established performance standards were not met. The regional office was aware of what was happening at the school and through the school improvement plan became knowledgeable as to how those areas would be treated.

The Role of the National Education Inspectorate, National Education Trust and Jamaica Teaching Council

The National Education Inspectorate was instrumental in my formative years as principal. They helped me establish the platform on which my foundation regarding what was expected of a principal was built. The National Education Inspectorate then provided a buffer, through their recommendations, meetings with me to iron out the way forward. It was instrumental in providing support through an intricate network of human resources. Additionally, it assisted me in providing wonderful examples of best practices in areas in which our school was weak. The National Education Inspectorate helped me to liaise with other school leaders, who cradled my leadership while it was still in the embryonic stage, and to develop a critical network which also enhanced my growth.

The Jamaica Teaching Council also provided support to me as a school leader. Its staff was always open and available to answer questions, clarify areas that were unclear and intervene when such interventions were necessary.

Making a Difference in Student Performance

Any educator who is worth his or her salt knows that the *raison d' être* for school is student outcome. Hence, irrespective of the plans and initiatives, a leader cannot be deemed to be successful if he or she does not eventually steer the school towards monumental student attainment and success. People learn through the behaviours and attitudes of others. According to Bandura (1977), quoted in Myers (2012), most human behaviour is learned observationally through modelling. I therefore encouraged teachers to exemplify the sort of decorum they would expect to be replicated in the children. Our teachers should always be shining examples for the children.

We recognized that our school did not enjoy the support of an affluent community. We needed the resources to develop a comprehensive feeding programme. What we did have at our disposal was a farming community which had most of the material resources we needed to develop such a programme. We also had willing parents who contributed their time. So we developed a breakfast programme and a feeding support for lunch. Research shows that schools with breakfast programmes share marked improvements in attendance and punctuality after such programmes are established. There is also the additional benefit of ensuring that the children were provided with the right kinds of foods that would aid brain development and contribute to overall better health. Children would be more alert and better able to maximize the experience of being at school. This proved to be the case at Woodford.

I describe myself as a transformational leader – one who motivates his staff to do more than they expect to do (Lunenburg and Ornstein 2004). Most of my leadership practices are geared towards positive change in the persons I lead. I am very passionate, enthusiastic and driven to elicit the best. So my teachers, my students, my parents and other chief stakeholders all benefited from the warm infectious way I would go about dispensing my duties. An important part of my leadership practice was identifying talents in an effort to validate potential and utilize vision and mission strategies to achieve long-term goals.

I also used internal structures and systems to reinforce overarching values and goals. I was for the most part a democratic or participative leader, although there were times when I exercised my executive authority to have the final say or stamp on any decision taken. However, whenever this modality was utilized, it was done in such a way that those involved did not feel disenfranchised in any way. In fact, it was always a matter of policy that at some point prior to implementation, all stakeholders had a say in all major decisions. Group members were encouraged to share their thoughts and this led to better ideas and more creative solutions to problems. Key members of the school community became involved and committed to projects; this made them more likely to care about the end results and ultimately led to higher productivity among the constituents.

Conclusion

One of the greatest compliments ever paid to me as an educator came from a student when I was about to transition from Woodford Infant and Primary to my current assignment. The compliment still resonates with me. In a tribute, the student sang the song made popular by Lulu, "To Sir, with Love", then he turned to me at the end and said, "You will no longer be around us, and life, as we know it, will never be the same." That comment, as simple and innocent as it may have appeared, is the single most significant moment of my career thus far.

If the intent of the educator is not to totally transform lives, influence change and foster growth in all spheres, then the option of being a teacher is being practised as an exercise in futility.

Woodford Primary School, upon my exit as principal, was on a sustainable path of success, fulfilling its core mandate of providing quality education and affording all the persons who are a part of the organization equitable access to an environment in which they can grow and thrive. The school moved from a multigrade school with just over sixty students and four teachers (including the principal) to a school that now boasts a student population of well over two hundred and just over eleven teachers (excluding the principal). An infant department was added to expand the range of students for which it caters. Additionally, the education product in terms of quality has grown tremendously. It has become a school of choice, excelling in local, regional and national examinations. The school now boasts a rich co-curricular programme, which caters to the holistic development of each student. In five years, the school's transformation has been revolutionary, the level of dynamism is first class, and the growth it has experienced is palpable and has continued long after my sojourn there.

Reflecting on my time at Woodford, I think if I had it to do over again, I would have worked a bit harder on succession planning. That is one area where there could have been a little more improvement, even though when I left, there was a clear-cut successor identified who could, and did, assume the reins of responsibility of running the school. With a little more precision and diligence, that process perhaps could have been even more refined and had more time and effort been placed on it.

References

Ciulla, J.B. 2004. "Ethics and Leadership Effectiveness". In *The Nature of Leadership*, edited by J. Antoniakis, A.T. Cianciolo and R.J. Sternberg, 302–27. Thousand Oaks, CA: Sage.

Erkiliç, T.A. 2008. "Importance of Educational Philosophy in Teacher Training for Educational Sustainable Development". *Middle East Journal of Scientific Research* 3 (1): 1–8.

Lunenburg, F.C., and A.C. Ornstein. 2004. *Educational Administration – Concepts and Practices*. 4th ed. Belmont, CA: Wadsworth.

Myers, J. 2012. "The Effects of Lesson Study on Classroom Observations and Perceptions of Lesson Effectiveness". *Journal of Effective Teaching* 12 (3): 94–104.

PART 3
UPGRADED SECONDARY SCHOOLS

CHAPTER 8

BEING PRINCIPAL
The Experience of a Lifetime

EVERTON WALTERS

IN 1983, I GRADUATED FROM TEACHERS' COLLEGE quite immersed in the idea of creating an impact on the Jamaican educational landscape. I was trained in the areas of mathematics and science. I took up teaching duties at Alston High School and after two years I was advised by a mentor to focus on mathematics because there was a shortage of teachers in that area. I taught from grade 7 through to grade 11, preparing students for the CSEC examinations. It was an exciting experience working with students and seeing them improving. The notable success that was seen throughout the school attracted many community members to join the evening institute, which I was asked to supervise.

Transforming the School

In 1996 I took up the principalship at Aenon Town All Age School. On arriving at the school on the first day, I was appalled at the level of vandalism and disrepair. Animals were allowed to roam the compound because there was no perimeter fencing. Having done an audit of the school, I discovered many weaknesses. There were inadequate classrooms and certain programmes, such as home economics and agriculture, were abandoned because the school was unable to provide the necessary facilities and equipment for students to successfully complete these courses. Some business subjects were also impacted negatively because the school did not have a typing machine or a duplicating machine. The buildings needed painting and the yard needed paving. The aesthetics were far below an acceptable standard. According to the World Health Organization (2002, 12), a healthy school environment is one that is in a complete state of "physical, mental and social well-being".

There was no designated area for a tuck shop to operate. Vendors sold their goods everywhere on campus. The school did not have a guidance counsellor and this was critical for proper development of the students. There was no specialization of content or grade level. All teachers taught all subjects from grades 1 through 9, which I thought unwise. I met with the board of management and shared my vision for the school. I solicited their support in getting the proposed programme on stream. I later met with my senior staff and then general staff to chart the course. Everyone was enthusiastic about the plans for the school and pledged to support them as we moved forward.

The first order of business was to get the plant in a state of readiness for the beginning of the school year. This was a primary focus because it was necessary to create an environment in which students could feel comfortable. The buildings were given a facelift and that alone changed the general tone of the school. The next thing was to put in place a structured timetable to operate an effective school. Subject teaching was introduced and persons were now able to operate in their areas of expertise. Research has shown that students who have teachers who are able to perform at a high level of competence in their area are more likely to succeed than those students who have teachers who are less qualified to teach a particular subject (Whitehurst 2002). The dismantled home economics room was renovated and I sought assistance from the Ministry of Education and the business community to provide the requisite tools and equipment for the area. Agriculture was now on the timetable and we introduced a tutorial farm that provided a canteen with fresh vegetables. A small poultry project was also undertaken.

Within months the parent-teacher association grew, with 80 per cent attendance of parents at meetings, and became involved in many projects. On Teachers' Day, it would give special treatment to the staff – for example, sponsoring them on an excursion. The school integrated itself well with the community. This group assisted the school to erect the perimeter fencing. No school can function effectively without the involvement of the home and general community (Epstein and Sheldon 2002), so I paid attention to improving this relationship.

The school had virtually no systematic way of recording information on student performance, so we created special forms to enter the grades of students. A file was generated for every student so that useful data could be accessed and used to inform improvement plans. The school later received a duplicating machine from the Ministry of Education, which significantly assisted the school in preparing documents and test items. I later sought sponsorship from the business community to assist in purchasing some computers. The response was tremendous. The school received fifteen computers. This paved the way for us to introduce computer studies in the school. Hence, I sought permission from the Ministry of Education to modify a classroom to create a computer lab. Permission was subsequently granted and computer science was taught from grades 4 to 9. Teachers who were not computer literate capitalized on the opportunity to learn computer skills. A major part of transforming a school is encouraging the staff to expand their skills and knowledge base (Bryant 2003). This improvement of the staff eventually positively impacted the students. A general sense of accomplishment and possibility permeated the entire school over a matter of a few years as changes and improvements were seen right across the board.

We focused on sports. The school participated in football competitions and track and field events. We produced quality athletes who went on to perform at the National Stadium in the competition sponsored by the Jamaica Teachers' Association. I later lobbied the Culture, Health, Arts, Sports and Education (CHASE) Fund to donate a multipurpose court at the school, which they did. In 2004, the school, in collaboration with the citizens' association, lobbied the Jamaica Social Investment Fund to construct a two-storey building to ease overcrowding in the school. After completion, the space was configured into classrooms, bathrooms, a staff room and a storage room. The entire roof of the old building was redone by a banking organization. The school later received a container building, and this housed the guidance counsellor's office, the tuck shop and a book room.

Relationships

As an educator, my main goal is to impact human lives in a positive way. As a principal, I endeavour to maintain the highest standard of equity and justice. No one has ever had any reason to doubt my veracity or, indeed, my integrity. I display a serious attitude towards work and enjoy a commanding respect from both the school and the community. In all my deliberations, I endeavour to be the teachers' teacher, guide and instructor. One of my most distinctive features is the ability to harness the teachers' efforts without sacrificing their professionalism, dignity and decorum. Sergiovanni (1991) suggests that the principal should seek to create an environment that is warm and supportive to staff, students and the wider community. With this in mind, I employ a meticulous and firm approach, ensuring that this is done with respect and love. I consider it my responsibility to support and guide those for whom I am responsible. My strong work ethic inspires those around me and even encourages them to achieve their goals.

School Achievements

One of the proudest moments in my career came recently following the results of the 2012 Grade Six Achievement Test results. One of my past students of Alston High, who teaches at a prominent preparatory school in western Jamaica, had the responsibility of coaching a group of students, one of whom earned a government scholarship with an outstanding one hundred per cent score in mathematics. He was very elated and attributed his mathematical prowess to the knowledge gained under my influence.

In 2007, I took up the principalship at Edwin Allen High School. At the time, it was the second largest high school in Jamaica. Edwin Allen High School is nestled in the cool hills of Water Works, Frankfield, in north-west Clarendon. It caters to students from diverse sociocultural and economic backgrounds. Students are offered the opportunity to advance their personal, intellectual and cultural fulfilment through multifaceted approaches to learning – that is, involvement in academic pursuits and vibrant clubs and societies.

My first course of business was to meet with all the relevant stakeholders, where I shared my vision for the school and solicited their support. We focused on all areas of the school. We renovated using borrowed tools and equipment and increased the number of classrooms. Liethwood et al. (2006) posit that the principal is responsible for setting directions and developing people – core practices of successful leaders. Setting direction involves working with the staff to create the mission, vision, values and goals that support shared purpose and student learning. Developing people requires the effective employment of the knowledge, skills and attitudes that support people in making changes to the way they practise as professionals.

With the support of its affiliates, the school has managed to continue to generate funds for economic survival. For instance, the school has received donations from past students, the endowment fund, private organizations, the parent-teacher association and the member of parliament for North-West Clarendon, government assistance, and students' miscellaneous fees. In addition, with the growing number of students and the phenomenal development of sports and academic programmes, the school now welcomes the support of the Edwin Allen diaspora in generating funds for the longevity of these admirable programmes.

The school has a well-structured sports programme in which emphasis is placed on areas such as football, basketball, netball, cricket, and track and field. The girls' track and field team has performed phenomenally over the years, climaxing when it became the champion school at the Inter-Secondary Schools Sports Association Boys and Girls Championships in April 2012.

The school has undergone many changes over the years. Its infrastructure, employment configuration and educational level have significantly improved. The educational programmes have extended beyond the walls of CAPE and CSEC. The most recent programme for school leavers is the Career Advancement Programme. This is a government-initiated programme, whose aim is to provide young people with life-coping skills. We are particularly committed to this programme as students have gravitated towards the skills training that is offered.

There are several projects that have been undertaken to enhance the quality of life at Edwin Allen High. First, the River Water Project was introduced to allow for the pumping of water from the Rio Minho to the school for cleaning purposes, hence, reducing the school's water bill. Second, the Bio-digester

Project was introduced to allow the school to produce cooking gas from its effluent and at the same time provide water for irrigation while protecting the aquifer. Third, the Bee Project was recently re-established, with the acquisition of new hives.

Like any other social institution, the presence or the threat of acts of violence is of grave concern. However, Edwin Allen is at the threshold of eradicating the scourge of violence that sometimes impacts the lives of the minority within its environs. We have worked very closely with civic groups and the police to forge strong bonds between community and school to promote good values and attitudes. Hoy and Miskel (2001) speak strongly of the importance of stable relationships within a social system to secure support and unity among stakeholders. It is important to note that the school has managed to keep a firm grip on acts of violent conduct, given its size and population.

Children who are exposed to school violence need assistance from adults. Parents, educators, administrators, school mental health workers, police and other health and safety providers have a responsibility to children to provide them with the safest possible learning environment and keep themselves informed about violence issues and experiences that children face every day. Our school has adopted a zero-tolerance policy against school violence. Anti-violence interventions at the school may include conflict resolution, good citizenship instruction, peer-mediation training for children, and early-warning-sign and crisis-response education for adults.

The Teachers

Edwin Allen High has always managed to have a highly motivated and qualified academic staff. Most teachers have successfully attained a first degree in the field of education; others have achieved their second degrees while some are striving towards completing other studies. It is difficult to have better student achievement without working on teacher capacity (Whitehurst 2002).

The school has positioned itself as a learning institution on the cutting edge of technological advancement. There has been significant improvement in the use of technology for learning instruction. With the assistance of the e-learning programme, the school has received added computers for teachers and students. Hence, the computer laboratories are more efficient and students can readily access information via the Internet. The teachers have also benefited from the availability of Internet service in the staff room for research and lesson-planning purposes. Students' end-of-term grades and reports are electronically documented and generated, respectively, via the school management system. Finally, the Teacher Incentive Programme, which had its genesis during the current administration, has received strong support from members of staff. Following evaluation from teachers and students, a teacher would be selected as teacher of the month and appropriately awarded with an incentive.

Overcoming the Challenges

When I took over the leadership at Edwin Allen High School, there was room for improvement in academics. The main goal of any school is to enhance student learning. At this school, students are required to work diligently to achieve an education. Naturally, this is not as easily achieved as one would hope. The core values speak to hard work, commitment, dedication, honesty and integrity. Teachers and administrative staff are always monitoring students to ensure they are doing their part to provide meaningful educational experiences. Hence, we have seen marked improvements in most subject areas. For example, at the last sitting of the CXC examination the school's overall pass rate at the CSEC level was 81 per cent and 89 per cent at the CAPE level.

Leadership is regarded as the single most important factor in the success or failure of institutions such as schools (Hoy and Miskel 2001). Most schools struggle with maintaining student discipline. At Edwin Allen High School, great emphasis is placed on this aspect. The school's handbook provides a guide to students on the required standards of behaviour. There are measures in place to assist students in conducting themselves in an acceptable manner. Punishments such as detention and suspension are given to those who violate the rules of the school.

The disciplinary system which prevails in a classroom will be influenced not only by the educator's behaviour and expectations but also by the expectations learners bring with them and, importantly, by the prevailing ethos in the school. In schools where it is recognized that there are a number of learners with marked emotional or academic difficulties, applying relevant teaching techniques can ensure that effective delivery of the lessons will become the norm. Importantly, it is desirous for parents and guardians to play an integral role in the affairs of the school. Throughout the years, the school has received tremendous support from the parents. This is evident in the support of the parent-teacher association of many projects and programmes undertaken by the school. The parent-teacher association has contributed books to the library, purchased machines for the vocational education department and sponsored the expansion of the sick bay.

The school has a continuous student assessment policy. There are different modes of assessment and teachers are required to record all data garnered from assessing the students. School records comprise both quantitative (attendance, test and examination results) and qualitative data (perception of the school by community, parents, teachers, present and past students, and the board of management). The risks are too great for school decisions to be left to hunches, intuition and guesses. The use of data allows the school to address real issues, set realistic goals and track progress to support continuous improvement. Data assists in teacher deployment and student placement (Fullan 2001).

Given the historical focus on instructional processes, it is understandable that many current supervisory practices look primarily at curriculum and instruction – what the students are learning and how they are learning it. This focus is evident in the typical pattern of supervision and evaluation: a new goal at the start of the school year; periodic classroom observation, with formal and informal feedback; mid-year and end-of-year meetings to discuss progress towards the goal; and the supervisor's end-of-year evaluation report that comments on the teachers' accomplishments and perhaps lays the groundwork for next year's focus.

The school provides an incentive for outstanding teachers. At least three teachers each month receive the Teacher of the Month award. There is also a Teacher of the Year award; the recipient of this award receives a valuable gift – for example, a weekend for two at a hotel. There are also many activities throughout the year that cater to the welfare of the teachers, such as a welcoming party for new teachers, a luncheon for all categories of staff, a weekend at a hotel during Education Week for academic staff and an excursion for administrative and ancillary staff. In situations in which staff members have deaths in their families, an independent wake is held for the deceased and a financial contribution is also made towards funeral expenses.

As a principal, I aim to be an instructional leader and assessment expert with a working knowledge of curriculum as it aligns to content standards. I also consider myself a disciplinarian, community builder and public relations expert. In addition, I am a budget analyst, facility manager, special programmes administrator and guardian of various legal, contractual and policy-mandated initiatives. It is the principal's job to get everybody in the school involved and invested in a new vision for the school and to demonstrate to them that their input is valued. More collaboration contributes to a more vibrant culture which allows the kind of innovation and vision to which we all aspire. Great ideas are going to be generated, and sometimes the smartest thing a principal can do is provide support for a teacher who has a good idea and then get out of the way and let him or her implement it.

The principal should be a transformational leader. Transformational leaders are people who can create significant change in both followers and the organization with which they are associated (Griffin 2003). The transformational leader helps to bring about change by making a convincing case for it. I achieve this by involving all staff in the shaping and reshaping of the school and departments' strategic plans on a regular basis. I lead the change process. A sense of urgency must be instilled. Finally, change needs to be embedded. This is achieved, for example, by monitoring progress, changing appraisal and reward systems, and hiring staff with a commitment to collaboration. Together these should also empower followers to help achieve the organization's objectives.

In conclusion, I believe a highly effective principal should

- demonstrate awareness of and have experience with the knowledge, skills and attitudes needed to effectively lead teaching and learning which is appropriate to the needs of all students in the school;
- have successfully completed the requisite training programme which builds the knowledge, skills and attitudes to effectively lead people, lead learning and manage school operations;
- engage in continuous professional development, utilizing a combination

of academic study, developmental simulation exercises, self-reflection, mentorship and internship;
- demonstrate the capacity to lead in establishing and maintaining a professional learning community which effectively extracts information from data to improve the school culture and personalize instruction for all students to result in improved student achievement;
- demonstrate knowledge of youth development appropriate to the age level served by the school; and
- demonstrate the capacity to create and maintain a learning culture within the school which provides a climate conducive to the development of all members of the school community.

My experience as a principal has helped me to grow as a person. I have learned to appreciate people and their varying personalities. The job has taught me tolerance and patience. It allows me to be optimally rounded. It allows me to accept the role of a servant-leader. Indeed, this occupation has positioned me for life, and I am grateful for the gains I have made and the challenges I have faced along the way.

References

Bryant, S.E. 2003. "The Role of Transformational and Transactional Leadership in Creating, Sharing and Exploiting Organizational Knowledge". *Journal of Leadership and Organizational Studies* 9 (4): 32–44.

Epstein, J., and S. Sheldon. 2002. *Improving Student Behaviour and School Discipline with Family and Community Involvement*. New York: Sage.

Fullan, M. 2001. *The New Meaning of Educational Change*. 3rd ed. New York: Teachers College Press.

Griffin, D. 2003. "Transformational Leadership". http://desgriffin.com/leadership/transform.

Hoy, W.K., and C.G. Miskel. 2001. *Educational Administration, Theory, Research and Practice*. 6th ed. New York: McGraw Hall.

Leithwood, K., C. Day, E. Sammons, A. Harris and D. Hopkins. 2006. "Seven Strong Claims about Successful School Leadership". http://dera.ioe.ac.uk/6967/1/download%3Fid%3D17387%26filename%3Dseven-claims-about.

Sergiovanni, T. 1991. *The Principal: A Reflective Practice Perspective*. 6th ed. Boston: Allyn and Bacon.
Whitehurst, G. 2002. "Research on Teacher Preparation and Professional Development". White House Conference on Preparing Tomorrow's Teachers. Washington, DC.
World Health Organization. 2002. "The Physical School Environment: An Essential Component of a Health-Promoting School". http://www.who.int/school_youth_health.

CHAPTER 9

THE IMPACT OF TRANSFORMATIONAL LEADERSHIP

CYNTHIA PEART

PAPINE HIGH SCHOOL STARTED AS A typical upgraded secondary school which faced challenges related to students' performance, discipline and lack of resources. While the challenges at times seemed insurmountable, I was committed to making Papine High a model for similar high schools and even some of the traditional high schools. I realized that the task would take a long time to achieve, especially because of the weak academic background of many of the students who attended the school. I was convinced that by enhancing the academic programmes and increasing the opportunities for students to have more choices in their preparation for the world of work, it would make a difference for the school and students alike. I can say that we are satisfied with our achievements thus far; however, there are many more strides to be made. With effective leadership and a committed staff, Papine High will continue on the path to success.

The Road to Becoming a Principal

My involvement in education started at a technical high school where I learned to see each student as a unique individual with different capabilities and needs. After leaving that institution, I started working at Papine High, which in my opinion was not on the path to progress. The leadership was poor. Many of the tasks and duties which were to be carried out were neglected, resulting in poor academic results and a lackadaisical culture overall. As a senior teacher, I was able to take on some leadership responsibilities. Shortly after, I was offered the opportunity to lead and I saw this as a chance to use my skills for the advancement of the institution.

Early Years

Papine High School, like other simliar schools built in the 1950s, provided limited developmental scope for students in the secondary system. The school was constructed to accommodate four hundred students. However, when the school was opened, six hundred students were admitted, thus, immediately putting a strain on the resources that were available. This situation was even more challenging as areas designated for extracurricular activities were converted into classroom space. In 1974, the curriculum was expanded to include technical vocational education and there was the addition of two grades. This expansion of the curriculum resulted in the construction of two blocks specifically to accommodate the technical vocational programme. Throughout this period, no new classrooms were constructed. The school population continued to expand, and so administration had to devise a solution which would temporarily ease the overcrowding. The shift system was introduced to ease the strain on resources and students were separated into different streams based on grades.

Over the next two years, the school population grew to over two thousand students and an academic staff of a hundred, inclusive of two vice principals. The requirements for entry were mainly based on age. The cohort that was accepted came mostly from those who did not attain placement in the traditional high schools from the then Common Entrance Examination. The students who had a number of academic challenges as a result were labelled failures and non-readers. This issue compounded disciplinary problems. In addition to students' academic performance, other problems included space constraints, lack of adequate furniture and teaching aids, and the strain on sanitary facilities, which were inadequate for the number of persons who had to use them. The matter of classroom space was a significant problem since the school then had to rely on off-campus facilities to accommodate the students.

Preparation for the Journey of Transformation

Armed with my philosophy and based on my knowledge and experience, I conducted a SWOT analysis which helped to determine my way forward. The result convinced me that with the right leadership in place, the school culture could be changed. Second, the analysis made me cognizant of the fact that change in itself could create a plethora of problems. With little reservation and much determination, I was going to create a difference. There was no other way that this school would progress and create the required impact on its charges, the community and the society. There had to be a change in the status quo. For this journey of transformation, I developed a strategic plan which included performance targets as well as a vision and mission statement for the school. The main aim of the plan was to guide my daily thoughts and actions.

Papa and Baxter (2008) suggest that the shaping of a school's vision requires the right people and a principal who is able to identify and mobilize the right resources to achieve the expected outcomes of the school. Realizing the vision of the school required a concerted effort on the part of many – I had to rely to a great extent on others. Hence, a review and re-examination of the management process was necessary. An agenda was set and the goals and objectives prioritized. Networking would be a priority. One of the strategies we employed was building and maintaining relationships and partnerships with the Ministry of Education, the school board, all categories of staff, students, parents, the community, service clubs, funding agencies and other interest groups. We paid attention to the physical facilities, security, discipline, financial resources and, more importantly, human resources, staff morale and school and student performance. In fact, the whole social life of the school was examined and reordered.

Staff-Development Initiatives

The incorporation of human resource management is integral to the strategic management of people and to the effective management of educational institutions as these entities are more people-oriented than other types of businesses. Young (2008) identifies the functions of human resource management which include the management of policies, examination of practices affecting staff, such as recruitment and performance evaluation, and the development system to respond to the human resource needs of the organization. In addressing the human resource needs of the school, I first reflected on the morale of the staff. According to my observations, they approached their jobs with some level of ambivalence because their training had not adequately prepared them for the task at hand.

We took a number of measures to improve the training of teachers. We referred some teachers to Vocational Training Development Institute programmes. Others were allowed study leave to institutions of their choice to improve their knowledge base and teaching skills. We held development seminars in which persons with specific skills from within the school were asked to present on their strong areas. In addition, external individuals were invited to make presentations and share their expertise. Teachers were also encouraged to be a part of associations created specifically for staff development. These associations hosted subject workshops in science, Spanish and so forth, and teachers were allowed to attend.

Danielson (2006) emphasizes the need to develop a collaborative relationship with colleagues as this inspires all to become a part of the journey of providing education of the same quality to all. Staff members were therefore encouraged to share ideas and teaching strategies with each other to promote their own development and to improve learning. Team teaching was promoted: teachers who were strong in one area were encouraged to help those who were weak. This was done through mini-workshops within the school and in other informal ways. In some cases, the more-skilled teacher was allowed to go in and teach a specific topic in the syllabus if the assigned teacher was weak in that area. External collaboration developed as joint meetings were held with other schools in an attempt to share new ideas and learn new approaches to teaching.

In the past, the teachers had displayed a lack of interest in the students. The teachers displayed no interest in organizing structured co-curricular activities, and this impacted students' participation. It is vital for teachers to show interest in their students and their responsibilities in general, as a lack of interest can significantly impact the performance of students. According to Tella (2008), teachers' interest in the teaching of a particular subject and their attitude towards their students play a significant role in the performance of their learners. In an attempt to improve teacher interest, teachers were given the opportunity to be leaders. This had a positive impact on the school and on the teachers themselves. As Katzenmeyer and Moller (2001) state, teachers who are given opportunities to lead are able to inform and effect reform, which makes a significant difference in the depth of school change.

My Approach to Leadership

School is a business and the leader or principal is the manager. Miller et al. (2007) define leadership as "the activity of influencing others to strive willingly for group objectives". Management, on the other hand, involves ensuring that the functions of planning, organizing, staffing, leading and controlling are implemented (Koontz 2010). For both leadership and management, it is imperative that a clear vision and mission be developed.

In my quest to lead the school along a richer, more productive path, I used what is described as transformational as well as instructional leadership. According to Basri, Rusdi and Samad (2014), a transformational leader is one who has the ability to persuade staff members to pursue specific objectives which describe values and motivations, desires, needs, aspirations, and expectations of leaders and staff. Through transformational leadership, the staff can perform beyond expectations. Transformational leaders motivate their staff, have high ethical and moral standards, have a deep insight into the future and strive to improve and develop the organization. Therefore, transformational leaders are visionary leaders.

And in the case of instructional leadership, Hallinger and Murphy (1991) emphasize the need for framing and communicating school goals, supervising and evaluating instructions, coordinating instruction, developing high academic standards and expectations, monitoring students' progress, promoting the professional development of teachers, protecting instructional time and developing incentives for students and teachers. The challenge that I face is how to be an effective instructional leader while at the same time perform all the tasks related to management. Leadership and management are often viewed as separate roles, but I was convinced that there had to be a blending of both roles in order to be an effective principal. In virtually all of the more dominant theories, there exists the notion that, at least to some degree, leadership is a process that involves influencing a group of people towards the realization of goals (Wolinski 2010). Though the problems and challenges in this school appeared insurmountable, I was convinced that the school had potential and could be transformed into an excellent performing institution with the right leadership in place.

Addressing Discipline

The issue of discipline was not just a problem encountered with students. I had to address this problem among staff. Rules and guidelines had to be implemented before any measurable change could take place. In an attempt to curb staff indiscipline, we created a handbook which outlined the activities that were prohibited and the various consequences for engaging in prohibited behaviours. I ensured that each member of staff received a copy of the handbook. In addition to this, we conducted sessions to brief individuals on the contents of the handbook. Staff members provided input as to whether the guidelines were realistic, fair and implementable. After consensus, we implemented the policy. This led to changes in overall staff behaviour. Punctuality improved significantly and it was clear that teachers began to take their jobs more seriously.

Student discipline was a greater challenge. It is important to note that a majority of the students came from communities commonly associated with gang violence and various other illegal activities. The environment which was familiar to them was one in which crime and violence were condoned. Derzon (2009) asserts that a child growing up in a home where crime is condoned and practised is more likely to display similar behaviour. It is also important to realize that generations of children differ. During my tenure, students communicated facetiously and were not hesitant to backchat teachers and administrators alike.

Societal and household problems significantly impacted student actions, performance and behaviours. At times, the actions of society were clearly reflected in the school. On one occasion in my absence, a group of students were reprimanded, and in an act of anger and protest they blocked Gordon Town Road (the main road used to access the school). Upon my return, I spoke with those involved and was surprised to find that I had to explain why their actions were wrong. They felt justified in blocking the road because this is what they are accusomed to in their community as a means of protest. I then realized that the school had to play an integral role in shaping the values and attitudes of the students because, without that, some would not be able to distinguish between acceptable and unacceptable behaviour.

In order to have a general point of reference, a student handbook was also created. The student body, student council representative, prefects, teachers and the principal all provided input into the rules included in the handbook. All the rules were broken down and explained to the entire school community. What I found was that by including the students' opinions into the rule creation process, students were more inclined to accept and follow the guidelines outlined. Additionally, as principal, I ensured that I talked with the students and maintained a balance between confidante and disciplinarian. In the event of a breaking of rules, depending on the offence, a certain disciplinary process would be followed according to a hierarchy. The home-room teacher would be responsible at the basic level. A more serious situation might require the attention of others, in which case a supervisor would be involved. A dean of discipline and/or vice principals would be called in if needed. In some circumstances, the principal would be involved. I ensured, however, that most problems were brought to my attention so that if parents became involved I would be able explain reasons for disciplinary action being taken. In the event that a situation required the direct involvement of the principal, I gathered the information as to what went wrong and explored with the offender what could have been done differently. I also explained the punishment for such actions, making reference to the handbook.

Plan for Effective Results and Outcomes

The intention of the school is to work with the community, parents and students to promote discipline and good behaviour. Once this was under control, other programmes were put into place to promote academics as well as students' involvement in sports, music and other areas. We formed links with adjoining institutions, which significantly influenced the success of the transformation. The University of Technology, Jamaica, provided much-needed expertise to the staff. In addition to providing technical advice to students, the university allowed them to visit the campus, thereby exposing them to their technical labs, workshop equipment and the general environment of the campus. The Vocational Training Development Institute sent instructors from their institution to share knowledge with our students and teachers. Students were also allowed to visit and use the facilities available on the campus. There were also a number of interventions from the University of the West Indies, Mona. These actions allowed the students to be exposed to areas in the sciences and to administrative leadership, among other things. Additionally, during the summer, our students were invited to be a part of a number of programmes hosted by the University of the West Indies.

The School and Its Immediate Environment

The school is offering a service to the community; hence, it was important for me to be informed whether the school was achieving the desired impact of service contribution to its clientele. I conducted an assessment of the dependability of community support and patronage for the school. Regarding success criteria, it was noted that the school enjoyed a high level of patronage, community support and service contribution. This was exemplified in the construction of a perimeter wall and an upgrade of the physical facilities. The school sits on ten acres of land and is completely fenced and gated. Supervision and construction were undertaken by the skilled and other labourers in the community. They benefited from employment while labour and security costs to the school were minimal. The school's guards and security officers are from the community. They value and respect the school; hence, problems of break-ins and destruction of property are not condoned by the community. It sees the school as a beacon in their community and as an interest that must be protected. In developing the strategic plan, I remained cognizant of the need for the school to grow in its capacity to meet the needs of the community and the developmental changes in the society. Plans were also developed to ensure that the image and reputation of the school remained favourable with the stakeholders.

Strengthening the School Facilities and Systems

Central to the development of the school was ensuring that adequate and appropriate systems were in place. Schools and, in particular, upgraded secondary schools are not usually involved in income-generating activities that will make a difference in the plans they have to implement. In addition, these schools do not have the type of alumni with the resources to make meaningful financial contributions. It was therefore necessary for me as principal to work alongside my team to acquire funding from a variety of sources. Financial health strategies were developed to ensure that the school was kept in good financial health. A part of my preparation was the completion of a basic accounting course to ensure that I was knowledgeable on accounting procedures, records and the management of funds.

Alliances and partnerships were formed with funding agencies, such as the CHASE (Culture, Health, Arts, Sports and Education) Fund, service clubs, the Jamaica Social Investment Fund, the Sports Development Foundation, the Canadian Green Fund, the US Agency for International Development, and with other companies and businesses around the school. I was able to access grants and funding for some of our projects, such as upgrading and refurbishing of our buildings, the construction and equipping of a music and performing arts facility, and the road leading from the main roadway to the school was paved and sidewalks were built. Most significantly, a school bus was acquired on the fiftieth anniversary of the school. This was a historic milestone for our school and it became the foundation for its transformation.

In the area of computer technology, rooms were expanded and fitted, again through partnering and sponsorship. The school library was refurbished and a research room was added and fitted with computers.

Interest in sports grew at a rapid rate. Having attained high school status, we were now able to participate in all Inter-Secondary Schools Sports Association competitions. The playing field was upgraded, returfed and fenced. We obtained a multipurpose athletic court through the Sports Development Foundation. New sporting activities were introduced and, with more areas for play, resulting in greater enthusiasm and involvement among students.

My strategy to get the students on board and to buy into the vision of transformation was to be proactive and use a positive approach. They had no option but to change their way of thinking and to "aim for the heights" (school motto). The students were involved in the decision-making process. They agreed to the changes and made the transition for their personal development.

The school board was a source of support in the transformation process. The board assisted in getting sponsorship and funding for the various improvement ventures. It was essential to get stakeholders to buy into this notion of change and the support of the board was critical to this. Each year, they met with staff members to discuss what was expected.

Developing Engaging Leadership

The transformation experience was fulfilling, the staff, students and community had hope and a positive self-image which I know gave them strength to face the challenges of the transformation process. To keep up the momentum, special programmes were introduced through mentorship, guidance and counselling, peer counselling, student leadership and parenting workshops. The curriculum, though challenging, was engaging and was geared to teach them responsible behaviour. We developed a safe, orderly and trusting environment. Teachers and supervisors built a climate that encouraged strong parental support and a strong sense of family.

Leading this transformation was a tremendous responsibility. At times, I became so bogged down and burdened that I had feelings of isolation. I had to create opportunities to communicate and commiserate with my fellow principals about issues on the job. This was a rewarding experience, just having persons to bounce ideas around with, sharing daily practices. Sharing experiences and ideas helped to relieve some of the feelings of isolation as I learned that others had similar experiences. I tapped into every available resource. I attended all relevant conferences and workshops. I even visited other school plants to get ideas as to how to organize instruction. When ideas came, I was able to modify and create new ways of dealing with similar situations in my school. I joined professional organizations such as the Jamaica Teachers' Association and the Principals' Association. I found opportunities for growth and for sharing professional knowledge that helped to create a positive and supportive school environment. Teamwork was critical in the process of working together and cannot be overemphasized. My team took the vision and implemented it. They gave support both to me as a person and to the vision itself. Accepting their critical role allowed me to better acknowledge my individual responsibility as part of the process of change and development. While I was observing and critiquing my team members, I was also being observed. I had to be careful about my public image as well as my image in the school. I found that there were some areas that are invaluable – being a lifelong learner; remaining current; nurturing talents, being compassionate, and building and maintaining partnerships.

Challenges to Overcome

There were a few areas where more could have been done to improve the school. The shift system posed a major limitation in terms of the time available for non-academic activities. Ideally, all students need to be involved in the extracurricular activities but most were not able to remain at school. The limited space on the school grounds contributed to this challenge as well. More could also have been done as related to discipline and academic performance. I strongly believe that if there had been more emphasis on sports and other non-academic activities, discipline would have been less of a problem and academic performance would have improved greatly. In addition, there was no facility where students could be trained in basic social graces, etiquette and decorum. A major contributor to these challenges was the lack of support from the Ministry of Education and other external sources of funding. Often, students were invited to participate in competitions based on arts or sports but it was not financially feasible to do so. This was because parents did not see the value of spending on such activities and, in most cases, could not afford the expense. As such, the responsibility was solely on the school to provide food, transportation, equipment and medical attention, if necessary.

Concluding Points

Today, this school is a monument in its community. It has grown into a highly rated and sought-after institution based on its development, infrastructure and physical facilities; academic success; performance in sports; growth and development; and meeting the needs of the community. Its overall impact in producing talented and skilled graduates for society is commendable.

My advice to anyone who is placed in the capacity of principal can be summed up in two important points:

1. Ensure that you love and enjoy your job.
2. Attend to the supervision and administration of all facets of the school community. The role of principal is not limited to the curriculum; it also includes providing guidance and support to parents and the community at large (including past students) and ensuring the financial and social stability in the school.

As one author puts it, "Principals are the linchpins in the enormously complex workings, both physical and human, of a school. The job calls for a staggering range of roles: psychologist, teacher, facilities manager, philosopher, police officer, diplomat, social worker, mentor, public relations director, coach and cheerleader. The principalship is both lowly and lofty. In one morning, you might deal with a broken window and a broken home, a bruised knee and a bruised ego, a rusty pipe and a rusty teacher" (Trail 2000, 1).

References

Basri, M., M. Rusdi and S. Samad. 2014. "The Effects of Transformational Leadership on the Teacher Performance at Senior High School, Maros Regency". *International Journal of Academic Research* 6 (5): 61–66.

Danielson, C. 2006. *Teacher Leadership That Strengthens Professional Practices*. Alexandria, VA: Association for Supervision and Curriculum Development.

Derzon, J. 2009. "The Role of the Family in Crime and Delinquency: Evidence from Prior Quantitative Reviews". *Southwest Journal of Criminal Justice* 6 (2): 108–32.

Hallinger, P., and J. Murphy. 1991. "Developing Leaders for Tomorrow's Schools". *Phi Delta Kappan* (March): 514–26.

Katzenmeyer, M., and G. Moller. 2001. *Awakening the Sleeping Giant: Helping Teachers Develop as Leaders*. Thousand Oaks, CA: Corwin Press.

Koontz, H. 2010. *Essentials of Management*. 8th ed. Nagar, New Delhi: McGraw-Hill Education.

Miller, T.N., M. Devin, and R.J. Shoop. 2007. *Closing the Leadership Gap: How District* and *University Partnerships Shape Effective School Leaders*, Thousand Oaks, CA: Corwin Press.

Papa Jr, F., and I. Baxter. 2008. "Hiring Teachers in New York's Public Schools: Can the Principal Make a Difference?" *Leadership and Policy in Schools* 7 (1): 87–117.

Tella, A. 2008. "Teacher Variables as Predictors of Academic Achievement of Primary School Pupils Mathematics". *International Electronic Journal of Elementary Education* 1 (1).

Trail, K. 2000. "Taking the Lead: The Role of the Principal in School Reform". *CSRD Connections* 1 (4): 1–9.

Wolinski, S. "Leadership Defined". Blog post, 6 April. http://managementhelp.org/blogs/leadership/2010/04/06/leadership-defined/.

Young, I.P. 2008. *The Human Resource Function in Educational Administration.* 9th ed. Upper Saddle River, NJ: Pearson.

CHAPTER 10

CHALLENGES OF A SCHOOL ADMINISTRATOR

MONICA McINTYRE

MY INTERVIEW FOR PRINCIPAL WAS SOMEWHAT different from a traditional interview session. The chairman recognized the need to address the new curriculum and my capability to undertake the transition. He noted that the school was more focused on the vocational training and the population at the time was mostly male. As a result, he was hesitant to employ me because of my gender. However, my response directed him to focus not on the factor of gender but on the competence I would be bringing to the job. When I was appointed to the post of principal, I was inexperienced. Rather than allowing this to be a hindrance, I used my inexperience in a positive way. The school was also new and this allowed me to start from scratch and so create a positive school culture.

My first mandate was becoming an effective transformational leader. Thompson (2013) posits that in order for us to be able to transform something, we have to do more than reform. The focus is not only on what is done but also on how the process is introduced. To me, a transformational leader takes time to understand what is happening at every point in the organization and uses that finding to chart the way forward. This requires working from the inside out and making use of all available resources to show confidence in what exists. Initially, the leader must assess the employees' understanding of where they are, how they feel about their image and what they would want to change. The leader must impress upon the employees that they will have to be the change. The employees must also be given unconditional support to overcome all the challenges that will be encountered during the process. The leader must display genuine interest in each person.

During my second year, I created a developmental plan which served to outline the direction of the organization which provided all stakeholders with a description of the path that would be undertaken. Lunenburg and Ornstein (2008) contend that strategic planning is needed because changes in the social and economic conditions must be taken into consideration in order to achieve goals. The implementation of a plan requires stakeholders to become cognizant of the factors involved in school administration. The structure that is adopted must be one that reflects the most effective means of achieving the growth and development of the school. This allows the leader to implement the programmes that would otherwise be rejected by stakeholders and to communicate properly to ensure that all members of the team are working towards the same goal.

During my second year, in August 2003, a complete development plan was unveiled. The goals and objectives were derived from information garnered from interactions with stakeholders, my observations during year one and my vision for the school. "Repositioning and Renewing Our School" greeted everyone on "September Morning", prominently displayed on an attractive banner. This mantra was at the centre of everything that happened for the better part of the next five years. It was our rallying cry and rudder. By the end of the second year, my vision and leadership style had caught the attention of the stakeholders. This is borne out in a poem that was written by a teacher and published in our first revived yearbook of 2003/2004 entitled "This One-Woman Band", dedicated to Monica McIntyre.

Throughout the third year, the focus changed from implementation to the analysis of what had been implemented. This provided much-needed information as we were able to determine which aspects of our programmes had yielded the best results and which required more work. This analysis also highlighted the challenges and what would be required from external sources.

Reflecting on My First Chair

Looking back on my first assignment, it would seem as if the three years were rolled into one. I had to hit the ground running. There was little established culture and no history or experience to draw on. In fact, as a new principal leading this school in its second year of existence with an unknown brand of education labelled "Vocational" with no clear policy, it was a real case of trial and error. I had to learn fast. You cannot successfully lead what you do not know and understand. I assessed my own personal situation and analysed our strengths, weaknesses, opportunities and threats. Using my previous experience, consultations with staff, the help of colleagues in the other two similar schools, the Ministry of Education and the support of the school board, I put together a development plan to guide our operations.

Mobilizing and Motivating Teachers

The motivation of staff is integral to the performance of students and the willingness of staff to go beyond the call of duty in the execution of their duties. Leithwood et al. (2006) recognize the need for leadership in providing the right influence on student achievement. An administrator has to create the ingredients that will initiate school improvement. This involves empowering the staff to take responsibility for their respective areas or departments and to operate as the most important asset of the organization. In every meeting or discussion with the staff, I always identified with the area or department by saying, "Where are we now?" or "What are we going to do?" These questions became even more important when the plan did not meet its expected goal.

I gave recognition to any form of achievement. Thompson (2013) recognized the need to incorporate recognition and appreciation to the people who serve. This, he suggests, builds the self-esteem of the individual and provides the leaders with a better relationship with the people who are an essential part of the plans becoming reality. Another strategy I employed was to socialize with staff and students and to give support whenever necessary. There was a high level of trust, as they could confide in me and still maintain their pride and dignity. This allowed for the smooth transition and implementation of new curricula, as teachers were more willing to embrace the changes when administration provided the requisite support.

The Ministry of Education established the school's programme as a vocational one in order to get students from neighbouring all-age schools. However, these schools represented fewer than expected students accessing the programme. Some years there was the need for approximately one hundred additional students to meet the minimum requirement. This resulted in the school having to recruit from external areas, such as those leaving all-age schooling and those who were under twenty and without formal training. Despite the programme which was instituted by the ministry, we opted to make amendments that would allow for an extension in the age range of the cohort to which we would offer our services. This brought about a rigorous recruitment drive to attract students who could be accommodated in the programme.

The facilitation of these changes proved to be challenging to the staff, as these new recruits were not literate and numerate. In addressing this challenge, the staff members were required to obtain additional training to meet the needs of the new students. We had to integrate a number of programmes that would improve the level of our students relative to those in mainstream schools. The curriculum was adjusted to meet the needs of the populace by educating them using a more skills-based approach to learning. This was a success, as many of our graduates acquired jobs in the hotel industry, a direct result of the quality of expertise our students were able to obtain. Students were also encouraged to develop their innate talents as they got the opportunity to showcase their talents in cultural folk forms. These enhanced social programmes also assist in improving school attendance.

Making a Difference in Student Performance

Eight years later, the transition came and the school was upgraded from a vocational secondary school to a comprehensive high school. The cohort of students that we were now accepting had better competencies in numeracy and literacy, as we were now able to accept students who sat the Grade Six Achievement Test and Grade Nine Achievement Test. Despite this new influx of students, we did not abandon our traditional recruitment process.

The new enrolment of these students highlighted a staffing issue, as the current staff was not adequately trained to deliver the formal curriculum. As the leader, I decided to address this matter by ensuring that the teachers obtained the training needed to upgrade their qualifications. This was met with some reluctance; however, the teachers soon realized that the training was necessary to provide for these students. The new category of students now being accepted resulted in an increase in the school population and a need to upgrade the students' school uniform.

Relationship with Community

The development of the cultural programmes created a new popularity for the students, and they were often invited to a number of events in the community. Additionally, students from other schools were allowed to utilize our workshops and labs. The developmental sessions held were also open to community members. Annual school events such as graduation and sporting events (for example, Sports Day and football matches) created new opportunities for a strong relationship to develop between the institution and the community. The community also became more interested when the team started defeating rival high school teams.

Developing and Valuing Discipline as an Ingredient for Improvement

The discipline of the students and teachers played a key role in the development of the school. Focusing on underachieving students resulted in the school attracting students with aggressive, passive or nonchalant behaviours. We therefore had the challenge of showing them the appropriate behaviour to be displayed at school. Punctuality was an issue for both teachers and students. The school's location contributed to the tardiness, as the area did not have adequate transportation to facilitate the number of individuals who had to commute to the school. The problem was addressed by meeting with the transport operators to implore them to help by adjusting their schedules. Additionally, an arrangement was made with an established bus company from outside the area to transport staff and students commuting in the mornings and afternoons. I made it my obligation to visit the route used by the students and observe their conduct while on the streets. The conduct of teachers was also examined and where they displayed an inability to adhere to the rules, a memorandum was sent to address the situation.

The Initiative of Best/Good Practices of This School

Many of the things that have become best/good practices are as a result of observation over time. In this way, you can identify those areas which need improvement and strategies which will improve the process. The school subsequently became a trailblazer in secondary education in both the parish and the nation. Persons wanted to know what we were doing to make such positive changes. This positive change was evident in the discipline of the students and staff. On one occasion, a member of the Ministry of Education Panel Inspections was at pains to ask the principal, "What kind of pill have you given to the students that resulted in them behaving so well? There were no students hanging outside classes, and the noise level was frighteningly low." After five years, the over three hundred parents seeking to have their children transferred to the school, as against the over one hundred who took away their children at the beginning, bore witness to this transformation. Several schools copied many of our best practices such as staff-development seminars, grade dinners, annual yearbook, principal's honour roll, single-sex classes, cooperative planning, vibrant student leadership and beautification of the plant.

Inclusive Classroom with a Focus on Mixed Abilities

The strategy of mixed classrooms was adopted to encourage students to be more participative rather than having them streamed, or tracked, and separating the top performers from the students who presented with challenges. The initial responses from the teachers were not positive, as most of them were accustomed to having the best students in their classes. Most of the resistance came from the longer-serving members of staff, as they would now have to embark on practices that were outside of their comfort zone. With this reaction, I took the decision to closely supervise the process.

At entry, students were placed randomly in their classes. This measure ensured that the various talents and abilities of the students would engender a harmonious relationship. In addition, students remained in their classes for their entire school life. At mathematics and English sessions, the timetable was blocked to facilitate students working at their performance level. This was to ensure that no student was left behind as there was no guarantee that teachers would do multilevel teaching. They also stayed within these groups throughout their school life. The teachers stayed with their assigned form classes and subject groups through to grade 11. In this way, there was better accountability for student performance. There was a burden of responsibility on the teachers for students' learning. Team teaching was practised so that students and teachers got the required results.

Improving the School Timetables to Facilitate Student Improvement

I believe that a school timetable is the engine that drives the teaching and learning process. To make it dynamic, the six-day rotating scheduling was introduced. Instead of scheduling classes by the chronological day of the week; classes were scheduled over a six-day cycle with eight periods daily. Other activities such as devotion, clubs and house meeting were held on chronological days. The blocking of the timetable was also used to facilitate the grades 10 and 11 subject options and grades 7 to 9 resource and technology classes. At the end of grade 9, all students are exposed to career development seminars. They are then given the responsibility, together with their parents, of choosing the subjects that are necessary for their chosen career path. Some teachers were not pleased with this system, as the so-called bright students were choosing what was seen as subjects fit for students at a lower academic level, such as music, plumbing and carpentry. It took much patience to drive home the point that students are more likely to excel in areas of their choice. In addition, we must never lose sight of the fact that every industry or skill set needs "bright" people so that the consumer can get the best product or service. The fact is that one of the roles of the school is preparing students for life. This policy creates an environment in which students are socialized to accept and appreciate each other unconditionally; this will transmit to better relationships at work and in the community. It is important to note that students have different strengths from which the class can benefit. I have seen many instances where a student who is weak academically is embraced by his or her classmates because of his or her skill.

Single-Sex Classes

Closely related to de-streaming, or heterogeneous grouping, are single-sex classes. If ever there was resistance to any change, it was to this one. Bearing in mind that Jamaica is a homophobic society, most teachers wanted to have nothing to do with that arrangement. Some parents were somewhat uneasy with the idea but somehow gave us the benefit of the doubt. Their main concern was the impact on their children's education. I had reviewed some literature and was convinced based on the reported impact that it would make a big difference, especially for the boys. "While simply separating boys and girls doesn't guarantee success, schools that use best practices for gender-specific teaching may be more successful at teaching to boys' and girls' strengths" Novotney (2011, 1). I challenged staff to do their research and find documentary evidence to disprove my claim of the benefits to be gained from single-sex classes.

Implementation of same-sex classes had its own challenges. Teachers had to develop a new mind-set and employ new teaching strategies to reach the students and, in particular, the boys. One immediate benefit was that boys got the opportunity to be boys. They were not overshadowed by always playing safe around the girls. One major positive effect was the fact that both boys and girls had more opportunities to be placed in the top ten of their classes; the scale was now more balanced. Therefore, at prize-giving, there was a balance in the awards for academic performance. The boys got a confidence booster, and many boys were propelled into leadership positions.

Principal's Honour Roll

To motivate students at every grade level to excel academically, any student with 80 per cent and above was placed on the honour roll. The photographs of these students would remain on display until the next set of awardees were announced. These students were also featured in the school's yearbook, the achievement is noted on their report cards and they receive the coveted badge at prize-giving. It was heart-warming to see the pride and joy of both teachers and families of students who achieved that academic milestone. In the first year of the award, seven out of the approximately twenty-four hundred students made the roll. That number grew steadily to twenty-five over a five-year period. After the introduction of single-sex classes, the number of boys increased greatly. Many schools quickly adopted this practice.

Grade Dinner

This was a deliberate move to strengthen the social skills of both staff and students. The original idea was for us to have occasions wherein students and staff shared at a different level. It was an opportunity for us as a group to interface with the wider community and enjoy some of the facilities that exist for recreation and entertainment. Students were given guidelines in dressing for the occasion, in dining manners and other social graces. Once again, it was challenging to have teachers buying into the idea. As the years passed, the students came to look forward to this event.

Community Service/Work Experience

To kindle the spirit of voluntarism, every student, starting at the end of grade 9, is required to give fifty hours of community service before the end of grade 11. In addition, grade 11 students are required to complete three weeks' work experience in their vocational skill. These activities are requirements for their certification and are printed on the reverse side of their certificate.

Empowering Students

School is charged with the responsibility to educate the total person to be a productive member of society. Therefore, every aspect of their development must be addressed. Students nominated and voted for their leaders. Our student council, within five years of my tenure, was so strong that they controlled both the regional and national bodies, with our president representing Jamaica at the UNESCO Youth Forum in Paris. We were the only student council to construct its own office and wear a special uniform. In fact, on club day, students were allowed to wear their related uniform. (It was on the nudging of the student council president that the school revive its yearbook.) There were student energy wardens to monitor both light and water. On Teachers' Day the school is managed by students, with the head boy or girl as principal.

Staff Development

A lot of time and energy was spent in getting staff to be in a strong position to facilitate the teaching and learning process. One way to ensure that students are not left behind is to expose teachers to relevant training that will inform their instructional strategies and hopefully make a positive impact on student learning. The first seminar topic was "Thinking Outside the Box". From then onwards, when we approached any task, the punch line was "think outside the box". The workshops also lent themselves to personal development of the staff. There were sessions ranging from relationship building, to financial management, to protocol. The sessions were not confined to classrooms. We had luncheons, socials, beach picnics, tours and hotel stays. These occasions allowed us to meet and share at a different level and, to some extent, break down barriers.

Making Learning a Priority through Teaching Strategies

We found the following teaching strategies useful:

- Seizing the moment. Teach topics that are current regardless of position on the syllabus. For example, if a hurricane hits, hurricanes are discussed in class.
- Educational tours locally, nationally and internationally. Tours act as a vehicle of socialization as they expose students to the outside world.
- Cooperate planning. Time is allotted for all teachers to plan simultaneously. It allowed departments to collaborate on the theme and reflect on their work.
- The project or research method. Students are given the topics to research and do presentations or projects; their work is also displayed in prominent areas.
- Test and retest. At the start of each year, students take grade assessment tests. The results show the teacher their strengths and weaknesses and thus inform what needs to be taught. At the end of the school year before end-of-year exams, this same test is repeated. Then the teacher is able to conclude what difference, if any, the teaching made on the student.

Improvement of the School's Plant and Environs

When I arrived at Ocho Rios High School, I had already garnered ten years' experience in administration. I was alarmed to see the poor condition of the plant. The compliance rate of fee payment was 52 per cent. In the interim, we focused on low-expense projects, which included clearing the school grounds of derelicts. The students' bathroom and the staffroom were the first areas to be renovated. When the teachers complained that the renovation would encourage students to spend more time in the bathrooms, they were encouraged to make their lessons too interesting to be missed. The staffroom was painted and new desks, swivel chairs and a refrigerator were installed. Over time, the entire landscape was transformed. New areas were constructed through our efforts and the School Enhancement Fund. These areas included a sick bay, book rental room, cafeteria, technical drawing room, plumbing workshop, additional classrooms, senior staff room, bursar's office, gazebos, guard house, games field, auditorium and a park. Our attractiveness was further advanced by painting the buildings and the outer perimeter walls in the school colours. We paved the parking area.

Put Your Critics to Work

Judging from personal experience and sharing with colleagues, it is safe to say that the teachers can be the most difficult set of workers to lead. Many who criticize initiative are either inept or lazy. It is the duty of the principal to find opportunities to get staff involved in doing something that will not jeopardize the programme but will cause them to need your support. For example, there was a teacher who was a loafer; he did very little to engage the students. His pastime was to challenge the administration. When a number of projects were being officially opened, including the park which was created by his department, he was asked to chair the programme. He was very astonished when he heard and later returned to inform me that he was nervous because he had never done anything like that before. I assured him that I would work closely with him to ensure success. He was so intimidated that I had to stand next to him throughout the ceremony. Consequently, he became an ally. The principal also has a responsibility to support the timid and the shy in building their confidence and helping them to take charge in small steps. This way, everyone has equal opportunity to become involved, to lead and to participate at varying levels. No position should be made to seem inferior. As a result, the staff will develop trust in your judgement and resistance will be lessened. When your staff seeks your involvement to settle disputes, it is consolidating your power. Tread carefully.

Discipline at Ocho Rios High

At this school, with two shifts and approximately twenty-four hundred students and 130 members of staff, indiscipline was the order of the day. It was a rough place in attitude, behaviour and physical appearance. Frequent fights occurred on and off the campus. Weapons were plentiful and could be found in students' bags, on their person and hidden on the campus. Gangs operated internally and externally. Consequently, the school was invaded whenever there was a dispute. Sometimes, relatives would join in the attack.

A zero-tolerance approach was implemented. At my first parent-teacher association meeting, parents were informed of the unacceptable state of indiscipline of their children or wards and were asked for their cooperation in bringing order, love and respect to the school community – while being reminded of their responsibility to inculcate good moral values in the children. Underperforming teachers who used the students' poor behaviour as an excuse were placed under the spotlight. With everyone understanding that the principal and the board were serious in achieving zero tolerance regarding indiscipline, they were ready to work to tame the monster.

School rules were revised and all stakeholders brought up to date with rewards and penalties. Parties signed off, acknowledging acceptance. The police visited frequently and addressed students, carried out searches and patrolled the school zone. Student leaders were installed and empowered to stem acts of indiscipline while celebrating achievements and developing qualities such as trust, acceptance and competitiveness.

It was an uphill task to make the change. The school board was a tower of strength. Without its support, it would be impossible to function effectively. We became one of the most-talked-about schools. As indiscipline diminished, students' academic achievement soared. The school outperformed many of its counterparts and became ranked among the top ten and top fifteen schools for passes in CSEC English A and mathematics, respectively. Integrated science and social studies saw quantum leaps in the number of passes. As a result of the large numbers of qualified students leaving school, we were determined to start our own CAPE programme. Despite the fact that the Ministry of Education withheld official recognition, we were not deterred. We raised the bar when one of our students passed fourteen subjects in one sitting.

The Role of Personal Qualities and Competences in Effective Performance

Anyone seeking to occupy a principal's chair must do so with a conviction that he or she can make an indelible mark on everyone within the institution. I learned valuable lessons in my experience as a principal. If the principalship is effective,

- every child will become a productive citizen;
- the community will feel a sense of pride in relation to the school;
- parents will be confident that children are being taught and groomed; and
- staff will be engaged, have the feeling of self-worth and be prepared to develop their brand of pedagogy that produces successful students.

The Role of the School Board and the Ministry of Education Regional Office

The school board and the principal must be on the same page. In the case of a new principal, the board must be able to provide guidance as the principal discovers and establishes a format for the office. There should be no power struggle between the parties. The principal should feel safe sharing or expressing the challenges in administering the programme. Therefore, ideally, the board and the principal should not be novices to school management. Where there is lack of experience, they need to acknowledge the deficiencies and seek the support of successful colleagues or the regional office. The difficulty arises when there is incompetence in the regional office or the principal lacks expertise.

It is my view that the regional office operated on the principle of "catching the school administration doing something wrong". During the period 1991 to 2001, it offered no special training for novice principals. Most of the officers' visits were in response to complaints from staff or parents. I got the impression that they delighted in getting negative reports about my effectiveness. As a result, most of the conversations were interrogative in nature.

As the product developed and the school gained recognition from the business community, performance in external examinations, and participation in sports and cultural activities, officers sought to reposition their relationship with the principal.

There is no doubt that the success of Ocho Rios High School between 2002 and 2010 was due to the solid support and backing of the board. After working two terms with this board, I was confident in meeting any challenge both from staff and students alike. Things became easier once I was well established; all the programmes were making a positive impact and the stakeholders bought the vision. Mendels (2012) suggests that effective leadership begins with the development of a schoolwide vision of commitment to high standards and the success of all students. If as an administrator you are able to give that direction to the managers of the organization, it will allow the team to understand the importance of a system that fosters student development which leads to the success of the institution.

References

Leithwood, K., C. Day, P. Sammons, S. Harris and D. Hopkins. 2006. *Seven Strong Claims about Successful Leadership*. London: Department for Education and Skills.
Lunenburg, F., and A. Ornstein. 2008. *Educational Administration: Concepts and Practices*. 5th ed. Belmont, CA: Wadworth/Thomson Learning.
Mendels, P. 2012. "The Effective Principal". *Journal of Staff Development* 33 (1): 54–58.
Novotney, A. 2011. "Coed versus Single-Sex Ed". *Monitor on Psychology* 42 (2): 58. http://www.apa.org/monitor/2011/02/coed.aspx.
Thompson, C.S. 2013. *Leadership Re-imagination: A Primer or Principles and Practices*. Kingston: Herald Limited.

CHAPTER 11

DEALING WITH CHALLENGES, SUCCESSES AND SETBACKS

JOAN WINT

HAVING HAD THE OPPORTUNITY TO LEAD a non-traditional Jamaican secondary school for some twenty-five years, observation and experience have repeatedly confirmed that there is a direct link between the quality of leadership and the level of performance of the school. I go further to say that the level of success leaders achieve directly relates to how well the leader handles the challenges he or she encounters. For me, successful leadership revolves to a great extent around the leader's ability to see challenges as opportunities and how well she uses these opportunities to advance the institution. In my view, the most successful leaders are those who commit to seizing every moment to develop and implement the strategies that will redound to the advancement of the institution. Too often leaders wait for things to happen. Successful leaders make things happen in order to effect change and influence growth.

Achieving Successes in the Educational System

Meeting the needs and challenges of the twenty-first century requires leadership of a special kind. This is true in every area of enterprise but particularly so in the area of education, especially as it relates to leadership of educational institutions. In the context of the changing role of the school leadership, Gamage (1990, 99) posits that it is necessary for a principal to understand where he or she stands along the leadership continuum in leading and managing a school towards improving student achievements.

One strategy I utilize is what I call deliberate intentional indoctrination; that is, using words and phrases that became a belief system, such as "the Denbigh Family" – signifying a sense of community among all academic, ancillary, administrative staff and students. Another phrase I use is "being the best and giving of your best" – calling for and embracing a culture of excellence which takes into account where you are, who and what you have, noting also that excellence is a moving target. It was necessary to address the problem of absenteeism and drop-out among students. Oram-Sterling (2009, 128) writes that "many students did not see Denbigh as a viable option for schooling". I will add, neither did parents, the community nor colleague educators who should demonstrate faith in the future of Denbigh. Along with senior members of staff, I made visits to the homes of former students who had a skill (for example, netball players). They were encouraged to come back and help the school in their area of competence, while at the same time complete their schooling. This enabled us to meet the parents individually, sell the school's vision and solicit their support for the then-defunct parent-teacher association which was now being rebuilt. The result was that apprehensive curiosity gradually grew into interest, which translated into improved attendance and participation by students and parents, respectively.

We attended the parent-teacher associations of neighbouring schools in a bid to influence both colleagues and parents of the renewed focus and vision of the school. Strategies relating to the improvement of the school plant and changes to the curriculum were embarked upon. As the teachers became more involved, showing individual interest in their students, general interest level and attendance increased and improvements in learning began to take place, painstakingly slow at first, and soon we made significant strides with satisfying results.

As the students' performance improved, the word spread that "something" was happening at the school. This had the effect of encouraging the teachers to do even more, which also helped improve student attendance. According to Steltz (2010, para. 11), "A teaching staff that gets to the point of trusting and sharing can then begin to make decisions as a team, a collaborative effort, to make the school the best possible place for our students." This became our reality. Additionally, a staff-recruitment policy was developed guided by the Total Staff Concept (which sees the organization as a total system existing in a specific environment with essential parts which are interdependent). This means that every effort would be made to have, residing in our staff, the skills and abilities needed for the total growth and development of the school. As time progressed, the school could boast a fine blend of personalities, skills and competencies and an enviably low attrition rate. Focus on value added was a major factor in determining our success. Staff was constantly reminded to focus more on "how well" than on "how much". Targets should be realistic. At times this was not consistent with expectations of the Ministry of Education or the nation. This means we were celebrating our successes even when nationally we would be classified as failing. However, we stuck to our guns, refusing to be defeated by the distance yet to be achieved or by how others saw us. Braun (2005) suggests that value-added analysis is a more accurate and fairer method to measure the impact of a teacher (and by extension the school) on student learning, as it takes into consideration where the student commenced and their academic growth. Today our school ranks among the top-performing schools nationally.

In one subject at a particular time, a look at the profiles of students' performance at the CSEC level of the CXC examinations, showed that high scores were received in "knowledge" but extremely poor scores for "application". This led to new ways and methodologies to structure teaching strategies, beginning from the lower grades. Significant improvements, internally and externally, resulted. We increased the use of data in all aspects of our planning as more were collected for both academic and non-academic areas. We were better able to allocate resources and staff – making a better fit between competencies and needs. Through improved ways of tracking student progress, we were able to identify students who needed special help and relate more meaningfully with parents regarding their children's progress.

Moral suasion; in-house seminars; publicly highlighting the successes of both students and teachers (at school functions, in corporate devotions, on notice boards, in letters of commendation); increased supervision; staff development (which also addressed their personal development); sharing best practices from within and from other schools and cultures; and of course, taking corrective action when and where necessary were among the strategies used to achieve success.

Student Discipline

Indiscipline was not a major problem in the early years, as classes were small and the general breakdown of discipline in society was not of the level seen today. However, the successful leader must be proactive. A philosophy, as it relates to discipline, was hammered out. Many teachers favoured punishment-focused supervision, where detentions and suspensions and the like are meted out. However, while acknowledging that this had its place, I felt it should be subordinated to strategies that fostered self-discipline. Here students are taught to take responsibility for their behaviour rather than exhibiting behaviour that is influenced by external rewards or fear of punishment.

We recognized that punishment-focused discipline is immediate and results in compliance, and self-discipline takes longer. As a result, much time was spent on the following strategies: educating students and parents as to what was required; development of written and "unwritten" rules – which were constantly communicated to parents and students; early parental involvement – parents were brought in when a potential problem was identified rather than after the problem manifested itself; and community involvement (so involved were they that it was not unusual for them to report on students' good or poor conduct). Additionally, students were also often encouraged to analyse their own course of conduct and prescribe how it should be treated.

Resistance came from both parents and teachers. Parents often questioned why they needed to come in and teachers wanted quick action. However, before long, we began to see benefits. Parents began to appreciate the preventative approach and staff members could often be heard remarking, "This could not happen at Denbigh" when incidents of indiscipline in other schools came to the fore. While other factors have contributed to the high level of discipline the school enjoyed and still enjoys, it is my belief that our guiding philosophy was the major contributing factor.

The School Plant

Some of the best adjectives to describe the school plant were "severely vandalized", "dilapidated", "disrespected" and "grossly unattractive". Equipment in some areas was totally absent and one building was designated "no man's land", as it was used as a night haven (bathroom and bedroom) for persons who ran afoul of the law. "Inadequate", "non-functional" or "non-existent" aptly described the school's furniture and equipment inventory. This was probably the most formidable challenge of all in the process of transforming the school.

According to Douglas (2012), schools fail because of their inability to cater to the needs of the students. This is especially so when one takes into account Denbigh's surrounding community. The article reported that these schools were typically located in communities with high rates of poverty, unemployment and crime. All three characterized the communities which surrounded the school. In addition, the school was in the middle of two opposing politically tribalized communities. Small wonder, therefore, that the school was mercilessly preyed upon. Theft of everything that could be removed and vandalism of most of what could not be removed was the order of the day. Buildings in some areas had no doors or windows; furniture for staff and students at best was inadequate and in poor condition. Landscaping was impossible, as community-owned cattle occupied not only the grounds but also the corridors at nights, taking shelter from the elements. Perimeter fencing was non-existent in one area (though a few areas bore signs of being fenced in the distant past). Electricity was non-existent in nearly all classrooms.

That was the reality and there was no time for tears or placing blame – the leader must respond. Along with some students and their teacher from the woodworking department, I visited a nearby saw mill and solicited materials which were used to make windows for the windowless auditorium. Removing a huge logwood tree from the front lawn immediately made the school more visible and sent the message that something new and different is taking place here. Indeed, small initiatives can have tremendous impact: community partnership, collaboration, ownership, industry and increased visibility in addition to the improved appearance of the building were some of the benefits derived.

The school grew. The construction of additional space was necessitated in order to accommodate an increasing population, new programmes, changes in existing programmes, as well as space to enhance the administrative function and incorporate the use of technology. There can be no question that a safe, healthy, attractive school environment stimulates creativity and positively impacts behaviour and conduct. Hence, with great urgency, a plan of action had to be formulated.

Forging Partnerships

Initially, support of any kind was slow in coming and when it did, it was limited, especially when compared to what was given to nearby traditional high schools. Initiatives were many times flatly ignored or given negative responses. As the leader, every opportunity was used to sell the school's vision and its potential to become "the education hub" of the community, while at the same time, highlighting the gains made. Over time, general support in kind, commendations and visits saw much improvement. The greatest challenge in forging partnerships was getting the surrounding community to respect, appreciate and protect the school instead of preying on it. Informal talks proved most successful. On the street or on the compound, as their animals grazed or as they walked through, I would engage people by telling them to own the school, explaining how it would build and enrich their community, assuring them that the school would be there for generations to come.

The vision was shared with excitement and each project that would affect their "use" of the school was shared with them. For example, the cattle owners and their herd were gradually moved further and further away from the buildings until they were finally off the compound. We re-fenced the most urgent portions of the perimeter fence after it was cut open a few times. We dialogued with persons from the adjoining housing complex, asking for their help in protecting it. Workdays were planned, spearheaded by the school, to assist in painting and cleaning projects. The burgeoning parent-teacher association in the early days did not have the clout to inspire the needed response. However, this was completely reversed over time. Getting help from the Ministry of Education was often a long and frustrating process and a bureaucratic nightmare. The ministry, however, was helpful in providing expertise, especially in building and construction. I soon learned how to navigate my way, to bargain, to negotiate, to challenge, to offer alternative approaches and, above all, to be persistent and knowledgeable regarding the ways, means and projects that could benefit the institution. It is always useful for leaders to align themselves with persons of influence. This can prove very beneficial at times and was used to good effect, when possible.

Self-help was probably the most significant strategy utilized (the strategies had varying levels of success and some even downright failed). They included fundraising activities at the school and class levels, classes taking responsibility for the care and upkeep of their classroom, while the school retained responsibility for the exterior; and other income-generation projects, such as the tuck shop which became the financial enabler, facilitating much of the refurbishing and building projects. In addition, vocational departments were mandated to generate income and they responded adequately. For example, the machine shop supplied hurricane straps to hardware stores; welding provided grilling for the school; cabinetmaking provided furniture manufacturing and manufacture of louvred windows (this failed as importation of louvred windows began and we could not compete); clothing and textiles made physical education gear; electrical installation rewired portions of the school (this department even got the contract to rewire the Milk River Bath building).

Beautification of the compound became a personal project of the principal, and it was done with strong support from the agricultural department. As the years went by, the school benefited from the skills and generosity of a professional landscaper – a past student. The school became known, and is still known, as one of the best-kept, cleanest and most beautiful schools in the island. Not to be taken for granted was the commitment, motivation and dedication of the support staff in its development and maintenance. The construction phase saw the building of the tuck shop, classrooms, rooms to accommodate the University of the West Indies Distance Education site, science and computer laboratories, and later the first floor of an administration building and a new classroom block. Only those who saw what the physical plant of the school was like in the 1980s could truly appreciate the magnitude of the transformation in this regard. With minimal financial assistance from the Ministry of Education and comparatively modest help from the community, the school plant is beautifully expanded, well laid out, well equipped, technologically outfitted and functional.

The Curriculum

At first, the major focus was on mastery of basic literacy skills in reading and mathematics, with much emphasis on higher-order skills – thinking, reasoning and problem solving. Every teacher was required to embrace these in their planning and implementation. This significantly influenced students' performance.

The school began to see increases in student enrolment of the fifteen-year-old cohort who had by then exhausted their time in all-age schools and who had experienced failure at Common Entrance, the technical school examination and Grade Nine Achievement Test and had been rejected for special entry into the more attractive schools. Our focus must now include vocational training. Rebuilding, repairing, retooling and providing additional space proved to be the way forward. Community needs and opportunities for employment within the community were a major push factor in determining what vocational areas would be addressed. Of course, the financial costs and affordability would be a factor. Current needs and accommodation for future growth and development led to the resurgence of areas such as carpentry, cosmetology, art and craft, home economics, machine shop and welding, electrical installation, plumbing and agriculture.

Success in one area encourages success in others. As the vocational areas thrived and the students bloomed into literate, disciplined, skilled, qualified, certified graduates finding their place in the world of work or moving on for further training and education, "better" students, academically, were attracted to the school. This necessitated the expansion of the curriculum to respond to fresh needs – namely, the natural sciences (physics, chemistry and biology) were added to integrated science, technical drawing, Spanish (to all grades) and computer science. We now had new laboratories, redesigned classrooms, new equipment and machinery. Eventually a sixth-form programme was added.

After many frustrating attempts to get the blessing for the sixth-form programme from the ministry, the school, having done careful due diligence including visiting and assessing sixth forms in a number of schools, charted what has now become a sixth-form programme of choice, unable to respond to the demands by applicants from traditional and non-traditional schools alike.

Successful schools ought to be places that provide a series of pleasant experiences. Hence, co-curricular activities were an integral part of the curriculum offerings. There were always active, vibrant clubs and societies which provided an outlet for students' varied needs and interests, stimulated and fed their creativity, reinforced formal tuition, exposed and developed talents through competitions at home and nationally, regionally and even internationally. We purposefully carved out a niche in football, especially at the local level and later at the national level, in the junior teams and with individual players who made it to national teams. Netball was a major success. It brought the school to national prominence at every level. Success in sports gave the school wider recognition, developed a loyal following of fans and sponsorship to help with further development. Successful leaders must be astute and quick to recognize, develop and capitalize on their school's competitive edge. This we certainly did, not only in sports but in several other areas.

As the school progressed, the population threatened to outgrow the physical facilities and its ability to meet curriculum needs. The response came in the form of tighter and more creative timetabling as well as the reorganization of the school day to operate as an extended day. Flexibility was required in accommodating the sixth-form programme which placed limitations on the number and type of courses that were offered. Very soon, however, a sixth-form block was constructed. Worthy of note is the fact that the level of commitment to the school, its programmes and its successes was so high that teachers willingly accepted additional workload, without remuneration, to make the sixth-form programme work. Truth be told, there were times when teachers initiative and drive forced me as principal to pull out all the stops to provide the resources needed. Every successful leader must be a facilitator. Oram-Sterling (2009) observes that when members of staff present ideas and show that the goals can be realized, the principal will certainly support them, even if she does not agree with them.

Other Initiatives

While some strategies to develop the human resource were mentioned earlier, there is a need to highlight the tremendous impact the University of the West Indies Distance Education Centre, sited on our compound, had on the school. Even though physical space was limited, we saw the potential benefits and grasped the opportunity, enduring short-term discomfort for future gains. The school "compound" was more often than not referred to as "campus". Students became visibly aware that another tier of educational achievement was literally within their grasp and this expanded their horizons and served as a catalyst for improved performance. Parents saw glimmers of hope as the presence of the centre meant, as the member of parliament often pointed out, that a child who lives in Denbigh can move up the educational ladder through to tertiary level without having to leave the community. Community persons who, prior to this, had been unable to access tertiary-level courses and degrees because of family and work-related constraints were now facilitated. The academic and administrative staff benefited. They were cajoled, encouraged, persuaded and even mandated to utilize the opportunity to upgrade their qualification at the centre.

Hosting of the site aligned the school with the university. As a result, the school's status rose. Its visibility improved and resulted in increased respect for and ownership of the school. The impact, as the university's vision transitioned (now the University of the West Indies Open Campus), has not diminished even though the university has outgrown the physical accommodation that the school could afford them.

Strong alliances with the Ministry of Education is both necessary and required. Residing in the ministry is a large pool of expertise, information and power. The leader must use these to his or her institution's advantage. The academic innovations were oftentimes made possible because the ministry honoured requests for additional staffing. Of course, the rationale and plans had to be satisfactorily documented. Alliance with the political representatives proved extremely helpful. Building projects were enabled, support staff was augmented, University of the West Indies Distance Education Centre was made possible (the idea and funding came directly from the member of parliament), sports programmes were supported in cash and kind. Strong alliances developed with past students and with other educational institutions. Sharing of best practices, successes and even failures with colleagues and their institutions proved advantageous.

Leaders must accept the responsibility to guide, support and train others to take over and continue to move the institution forward. At Denbigh, four classroom teachers moved up the ranks to serve as vice principals of the school, several other members of staff have gone on to serve as principals of other institutions and there is still much leadership talent among the middle managers.

Through hard work, dedication, caring for students, developing team spirit and having a vision of what one wants to accomplish, a principal can make change happen, and non-performing institutions can be revitalized and become successful corridors of learning.

References

Braun, H.I. 2005. *Using Student Progress to Evaluate Teachers: A Primer on Value Added Models*. Princeton, NJ: Policy Information Center. http://www.ets.org/Media/Research/pdf/PICVAM.pdf.

Douglas, L. 2012. "Failing Schools Must Address Community Needs to Improve, Experts Say". *Sunday Observer*, January 22, 5.

Gamage, D.T. 1990. "Changing Role of Leadership of the Australian High School Principals". *Perspective in Education* 6 (2): 95–108.

———. 2006a. *Professional Development for Leaders and Managers of Self-Governing Schools*. Dordrecht, Netherlands: Springer.

Oram-Sterling, J. 2009. "The Joan Wint Story: Biography of a Principal Whose Transformational Leadership for Social Justice Transformed a Rural Jamaican High School". PhD diss. Illinois State University, Illinois.

Steltz, J. 2010. "Leaders in Education: Five Essential Characteristics". 28 April. http://jsteltz.wordpress.com/2010/04/28/leaders-in-education-five-essential-characteristics/.

CHAPTER 12

SETTING CHALLENGING GOALS
Achieving Inspiring Performance

PAULEEN PAMELA REID

I HAVE ALWAYS KNOWN THAT MY role as an instructional leader was going to be very crucial in creating the story of Holland High School. Consequently, I have always been careful to lead the charge in ensuring that the curriculum caters to the needs of our students. This has led to a continuous revision of the curricula for all subjects. We have centralized curriculum planning. Teachers of all levels come together in the summer to reshape the curriculum to ensure that it is responsive to the needs of the students. The execution of the curriculum is heralded by the termly (quarterly) distribution of course outlines to parents and is carefully monitored through common planning sessions and standardized monthly tests followed by the preparation of monthly report cards. This is a permanent part of the Holland culture and it enables us to track students' progress and provide timely feedback to parents.

Teachers of classes which are below par have to meet with the principal, vice principal and heads of the department to agree on a course of action to effect improvement in lesson delivery. The controls on the curriculum are later expanded as the lesson plans are scheduled for collection at a certain time each week. These plans are properly vetted and documented by the head of department, and each plan book passes across my desk at least twice per term for my scrutiny and vetting. This system of control ensures accountability. The document used for lesson-plan vetting is very detailed and is an innovation of a subject teacher. Each department gets a new plan book each year. At the end of the term, teachers in each department sit together and analyse the performance of their students. Another document used to track performance is completed with a plan of action. These forms are forwarded to me and are part of the teachers' continuous assessment.

At Holland, each department head visits two classes each week to offer clinical supervision. This is to ensure that the teachers are getting the necessary support required to perform at their best. As DiPaola and Hoy (2014, 26) state, "The purpose of supervision is neither to make judgements about the competence of teachers nor to control them but rather to work informally and cooperatively to improve their teaching." To ensure objectivity in the grading scripts, we practise table marking at the departmental level. This allows for equity and adherence to standards. After assessment, the teachers analyse the students' performance. This role of the reflective teacher cannot be downplayed, as it is my belief that if, by way of systems, teachers are forced to reflect on their practice then this will evoke the desire for improvement. When students do well, we are sure to reward teachers in a tangible way.

Another strategy in the promotion of student learning is allowing for students to retake a test. Students apply for a retake, and with valid reason a retake is granted. The overarching desire is for all students to gain mastery, and so students should not be deprived of an opportunity to perform at their best. They must be supported into becoming the best version of themselves. To facilitate this process and retain the integrity of the test, two versions of each test are prepared.

As a part of our wider vision for academics, each grade level has a special mantra. This is a statement of goal that is repeated by each child several times throughout the day. Wrapped up in this exercise is the idea that students must have a goal and that if this goal is properly communicated then it becomes more achievable.

An integral aspect of academic progress is providing rewards for outstanding performance. Levitt, List, Neckermann and Sadoff (2011) note that incentives positively impact student performance. Our annual prize-giving ceremony is like no other. The ceremony is the climax of our celebrations for excellence. Each year a concerted effort is made to make prize-giving a thrilling experience. Every child must have a fair chance of winning a prize. We laud outstanding student performance, applaud exemplary social conduct, highlight outstanding educators and celebrate model parents whose involvement in their children's education meets the Holland standard.

Visioning for us is crucial and so we take our grade 7 students on a tour of the University of the West Indies, Mona, and the University of Technology campuses in order to focus their aspirations on tertiary-level training.

We are the harbinger of collaboration among high schools in the region, and so we have our annual Roylan Barrett History Lecture named in honour of the late custos of Trelawny. The chosen topic is always from the CSEC syllabus and this has been engendering great support from high schools in the region. Our annual culture quiz has also attracted media coverage and corporate sponsorship and continues to spark the interest of high schools in the region. It must be noted that excellent work attracts excellent people. We make it a point of duty to teach our students to recognize and honour the hard work of others and to be aware of their cultural heritage. This prompted the development of a first of its kind in a Jamaican High School: a Nation Builders' Park, Heritage Haven and Culture Corridor. These three areas have been helping to influence our students' cultural awareness and national pride.

Instructional leadership is crucial in the success of any school. I am therefore very careful not to hire or retain shirkers. The students' lives are on the line and are in my hands. I must exercise care in recruiting qualified, competent and efficient staff. We have a structured mentorship programme for new teachers and are known for transforming inexperienced educators into outstanding and exemplary educators. The newspaper carried a report entitled "Great Things Are Happening at Holland". The "great things" at Holland have resulted in Lasco teacher and principal of the year titles, several Jamaica Teaching Council Excellent Teacher awards and several other recognitions from the Ministry of Education.

Making a Difference in Student Performance

We have always been working with students with a low academic profile from the Grade Six Achievement Test, and so it was clear to me that I would need to focus on incremental success rather than large gains. There is a senior teacher assigned to ensuring that academic successes are highlighted. One of the central things to the academic celebrations is the master sheets with students' scores. This is crucial to identifying value added and to establish advancement to academic clubs. At Holland, students are placed in academic clubs based on grade ranges. I ensure that the report cards are printed on metallic gold and silver cards for those students who attain grades in the respective grade ranges. However, the students who do not attain these grade ranges are celebrated openly if they move from one grade range to a higher one; this serves as motivation for students to strive to achieve their academic goals.

As part of the mandate to improve the national average in numeracy, we opened our math lab and we schedule sessions for students to work on their weak areas on a one-on-one basis with an assigned teacher. This continues to have a positive impact on our mathematics programme.

At various times throughout the school year, there are several academic competitions. These include the math and business quiz, debating competitions, and essay-writing competitions. The competition was supported with prizes and surprises to keep students interested.

The report cards are so designed that students' progress can be tracked term by term. There is a column labelled "value added" which highlights the performance of each child in comparison to the last immediate report card. This policy accords with my belief that incremental change is important.

Using Data to Make a Difference

While we thrive on innovation at Holland, these are all within the context of data collection. We base our decisions on the data that are gathered by a key group of persons within the organization. We make data collection everybody's business, but the analysis and interpretation are done by a few key persons. These people make up the data team. They have the rudder that steers the ship of Holland. This team meets on a regular basis to share findings and to strategize on the methods of collecting the desired data.

The effective principal knows which ones are to be utilized for short-term changes and which data are for future policies. Being able to make this distinction enables the principal to make decisions which are relevant and effective.

Teacher Professional Development

Ongoing professional development is crucial and so every staff meeting has a staff-development component. Teachers are exposed to best practices and next practices so that they can continue to positively impact the lives of students. Most times the person conducting the staff-development activity is another member of staff. Guskey and Yoon (2009) recognize the value of conducting professional development at the school. First, this approach will allow for better focus on the performance gaps which have to be addressed, and second, it will ensure a more efficient coordination of professional development activities. Schools are better able to take on this task because more persons have relevant training and are more knowledgeable about the local performance problems. At Holland, we acknowledge with some pride that collectively we are endowed with much expert knowledge and strengths.

Mobilizing and Motivating Teachers

It is my firm belief that teachers must be motivated and empowered. Each Monday morning at 7:45, administrators and middle managers meet for a "Pow Wow". At this session we reflect on the activities of the past week and agree on our course of action for the week ahead. It is my belief that my middle managers must be empowered with the responsibility of running their individual areas of responsibility with a clear picture of the overall vision. These weekly sessions are in addition to coaching of middle managers. I make a deliberate effort to ensure that all middle managers are exposed to effectively operating the different dimensions of school. It is my belief that we must teach our team to fish (Jones 2004).

Connors (2000) highlights the importance of keeping staff motivated. Not only are staff fed knowledge from my expertise and that of each other but they are also literally fed at our annual Christmas luncheon. I prepare a three-course meal for the entire staff and I express my gratitude for their support and encourage them to be faithful stewards. They are also very literally fed at Easter, at our monthly staff socials and on our special times spent together. As such, teachers must be allowed to feel that they are important and that their efforts are being recognized.

At Holland we issue letters of reprimand, but we also issue frequent commendations for the roles that our teachers play in keeping the "Holland spirit" alive. The Holland Trail Blazer award is given to any staff member who comes up with a novel idea which can be implemented to make the school more successful. I keep a record of everybody's birthday. Baby showers and wedding anniversaries are celebrated at Holland. We celebrate these so that the members of the staff know I am interested in their joys. When a relative dies we go in groups to the remembrance service to offer support. When teachers feel that a principal has his or her best interest at heart, the teacher will work relentlessly to ensure that the school continues to operate successfully. Additionally, we operate with "out of the box" ideas, and so we have been spearheading and organizing an annual joint Staff Development Day for members of all categories of staff in the high schools in Trelawny. This helps our staff to gain confidence and also to expand their network.

The effective principal has a high level of emotional intelligence. This allows for discernment of the right people for the right job. This ability to match people with tasks allows for maximum productivity and causes the staff to be more interested in contributing to the school's success. This high level of emotional intelligence accounts for the many teachers we have at Holland who are outstanding professionals and who continue to challenge the status quo.

The Role of the School Board and Regional Office

We have deliberately created a family setting at Holland, because school development has to transcend petty differences and personality traits. There is an urgent need for stakeholders to be united in the bid to ensure "improved student learning" with the goal of educating the "whole child". I therefore ensure that we involve the school board and the regulators in all our projects and programmes. We have had the board represented at all school events; its members are not just cheerleaders but active participants. I also ensure that the school is compliant with all requirements from the regional office and that there is ongoing and open communication.

I have always felt that the National Education Inspectorate would have been far more effective if it had conducted an administrative and academic audit in all schools (Triple A). They would have been able to identify the deficiencies and then use this information to recommend training and scaffolding for school leaders. With the inspection, many school leaders who were appointed without the requisite training and governed by an untrained board are now being perceived as incompetent and inefficient.

Dealing with Student Discipline

At Holland, discipline is not only for our students but also for every person who comes onto our campus. As for the visitors on the campus, there are a set of guidelines with which the security guards and office staff must comply. All visitors must get clearance, a visitor's pass and an escort to traverse the blocks. If there are breaches on the part of the security guards then the security manager is called and a replacement is found for that worker. To complement the security control of the school, no student is admitted without an identification card. In the event that it is not available then a temporary pass is issued.

Students are further kept in line on campus. There is a system that requires students to have either a hall pass or clinic pass if they are seen outside of class during scheduled sessions. This is reinforced by the block monitors system which is led by several junior teachers who are responsible for checking students throughout the day for these passes. Those without a pass are given a detention or a warning at the discretion of the junior teacher. I only intervene if requested, since I believe that responsibility must be spread and workers must be given autonomy.

The clubs and societies are timetabled activities which are regulated by teachers and a club president. A senior teacher, on a termly (quarterly) basis collects the documents for these clubs. These clubs are monitored for meaningful engagement so that discipline and order are maintained. Students and teachers who miss clubs without a proper reason are identified by the block monitors and are reprimanded appropriately. These systems help us to have minimal occurrences of indiscipline.

There are several social intervention programmes to assist our students. Those who are recognized to be at risk are drafted into a specially designed programme to ensure that this does not happen. Students who repeatedly are truant are placed on a behaviour monitoring programme in which each teacher records the child's presence and participation at class by using a form provided. I check this form to ensure conformity to instructions and for the parent's signature, indicating parental involvement in the process.

Working with Parents and Guardians

We take parental involvement seriously at Holland. Our first parent-teacher association meeting each year is a cocktail party, which enables the teachers and parents to interact and bridge the gap between home and school. For monthly meetings we do not engage in the mundane activities of discussing challenges and all the perceived ills of the system; instead, we offer parental training, invite experts to address relevant and pertinent issues, engage in school improvement projects such as painting and road patching, and student mentorship. Parents are also encouraged to visit the school during the school day to observe their child at work.

There are several interventions to bridge the gap between parents and children. Our counselling department does not shy away from counselling sessions with parents and children when the need arises. At Holland our parents are all on a rewards system. They are each given a total of one hundred points at the beginning of the school year. Parents retain these points if they continue to operate according to the Holland standard. At the end of the school year, the parents with perfect scores are rewarded at the school's prize-giving ceremony.

Challenges of School Administration

The major challenge of school administration is keeping the vision ablaze in the face of prevailing difficulties and sometimes even failures, such as the negative impact of social factors on student conduct, waning parental support, financial challenges impacting attendance, maintaining a rigid system of accountability, and lack of financial support to effectively implement programmes. However, amidst these challenges, we have maintained a school of exceptionally high standards and our programmes are undiluted. This has been achieved by developing a school community that is united in support of the vision of building a school with a reputation for excellence in all spheres of school life at Holland. As Bass and Bass (2008, 629) point out, "the vision is often a collaborative effort of a leader and colleague [which] ties together a variety of issues and problems that are addressed in a coordinated and systematic manner with everyone playing his assigned role".

Relationship with the Community

The school through a number of deliberate activities continuously embraces the community. At the beginning of each school year, a community tour is done. On this trip, members of the academic staff speak with members of the communities from which our students come and share contact information for the school. The parents are included in every aspect of school development. The community members are allowed to use our football field in the afternoons for structured training, supervised by a member of the board of management.

There is a "care box" placed in each classroom in which students deposit non-perishable food items and cosmetics for distribution to people in the community who are indigent. We have endeared ourselves to community members through the level of care and benevolence exhibited by our school family. To avoid many of the challenges experienced by several schools pertaining to vending and public transportation, we have proactively established a partnership with these service providers through our Vendors and Taxi Operators Association. They help us to enforce the school's standards even while our children are off the school's campus.

Conclusion

At Holland, our work and worth have gained great acclaim. Our basketball team made it to the finals in the national competition in 2010. Our guidance department won the most outstanding guidance programme nationally in 2010. Two students have had the opportunity to go to Scotland for a training programme arranged by the British High Commission. Two student leaders spent the summer at Princeton University, accessing leadership training, courtesy of the US Embassy. These trips were a result of our students' emerging as top performers at interviewing sessions held by the embassies of the programmes' sponsoring countries. The junior mayor and deputy mayor trophies for Trelawny seem to have become a permanent fixture at Holland since our students so often cop these titles. There are several national Jamaica Cultural Development Commission awards that our school has earned for ten years. Awards and written commendations from the Ministry of Education for outstanding contribution to education have been numerous.

The principal who strives to be effective must exhibit accountability and maintain a professional demeanour. This professional must respond appropriately to changes, express an interest in collaborating with colleagues and be willing to develop and implement new curricula that will benefit all students. Recruiting and retaining competent and efficient staff is an essential component of effective leadership. Additionally, the principal must share the vision of the institution and find ways to get all stakeholders to buy into this vision.

Essentially, the principal must create a setting in which students and staff feel physically and psychologically safe. There must always be equity and justice in all facets of school life and improving students' learning must be the fulcrum of the institution. As a principal, I have enjoyed every aspect of my career and I believe that true greatness comes not from worldly fame but from simply seeking to serve in Jesus's name.

References

Bass, B.M., and R. Bass. 2008. *The Bass Handbook of Leadership: Theory, Research, and Managerial Applications*. New York: Simon and Schuster.
Connors, N.A. 2000. *If You Don't Feed the Teachers They Eat the Students! Guide to Success for Administrators and Teachers*. Nashville: Incentive.
DiPaola, M.F., and W.K. Hoy. 2014. *Improving Instruction through Supervision, Evaluation, and Professional Development*. Charlotte, NC: Information Age.
Guskey, T.R., and K.S. Yoon. 2009. "What Works in Professional Development?" http://www.k12.wa.us/Compensation/pubdocs/Guskey2009whatworks.pdf.
Jones, L.B. 2004. *Teach Your Team to Fish: Using Ancient Wisdom for Inspired Teamwork*. New York: Crown.
Levitt, S.D., J.A. List, N. Susanne and S. Sally. 2011. "The Impact of Short-Term Incentives on Student Performance". https://econresearch.uchicago.edu/sites/econresearch.uchicago.edu/files/Levitt_List_Neckermann_Sadoff_Short-Term_Incentives_September2011.pdf.

PART 4
TRADITIONAL HIGH SCHOOLS

CHAPTER 13

LESSONS LEARNED ABOUT THE JAMAICAN CULTURE AND ITS EFFECTS ON EDUCATION

ERROL V. JOHNSON

I HAVE SPENT OVER TWO DECADES as principal, and the most important lesson I have learned is the powerful nature of culture. As an administrator responsible for the daily operation of my school, I have found culture to be intriguing, if not a little worrying. Prior to my principalship, the aspects of the Jamaican existence and modus operandus that I found challenging to assimilate, I simply left alone. But now I headed an institution and recognized that culture, and organizational culture in particular, at least was worthy of study.

Finding a definition is an important first step. Fisher, Frey and Pumpian (2012) state that culture is an underground flow of feelings and folkways wending its way within schools in the form of vision and values, beliefs and assumptions, rituals and ceremonies, history and stories, and physical symbols. The Jamaican culture has a background in Anansi stories. Anancy, or Anansi, is the main character in a number of "trickster folk tales; he is a cultural hero" (Bailsford 2009). These stories often send a questionable message about success – that it should be achieved at any cost, even sacrificing family.

I recognized sadly that this folk hero was replicated in our adults, children, institutions, and communities and country at large. We have created a culture of materialism and consumerism that is leading us to ignore totally, the value of hard work, honesty and integrity. The values, beliefs and attitudes of the past are quickly being eroded and "anancyism" has triumphed. A school is a microcosm of the wider society and any ills of society become evident in school both in students and in the very teachers on whom we depend to transmit positive values. If education does not achieve anything else, it must achieve an "A" in inculcating positive values.

Creating a Culture of Client Appreciation

The formation of a positive school climate requires recognizing the student as the prime focus, developing a strong school administration, and nurturing a competent and caring staff who share common goals with students, parents and the community. Hoy and Miskel (2001) suggest that the effectiveness of a school is affected by a positive school climate. A positive school climate includes an identifiable, open and nurturing school spirit which fosters positive self-concept and encouraging high self-esteem in students and staff. Some characteristics of a positive school culture are positive staff attitude and high morale, teamwork and the sharing of responsibilities, a healthy and safe physical environment, opportunities for student involvement, commitment, responsibility and success, high expectations for students and teachers, and the encouragement of risk-taking.

Tertiary Training of Teachers and Its Effects on School Culture

The National Education Inspectorate is responsible for making an assessment of the standards attained by the students in our primary and secondary schools at key points during their education. It is the aim of the agency to report on how well students perform or improve as they progress through their schooling and learning life. The agency is also charged with responsibility for making recommendations to support improvement in the quality of provision and outcomes for all learners (National Education Inspectorate, Jamaica, 2010). I hope this body, along with the Jamaican Teaching Council, is serious about identifying teachers who are unsuitable for the critical profession of teaching and ensuring they never enter the education sector. I dare to say it has become my sincere belief that those who become members of the teaching profession must be endowed with those special characteristics which can transform a child and, ultimately, a nation. Kelly (2011) identifies six keys to being a successful teacher. These include a good sense of humour, a positive attitude and the value of high expectations.

A Good Sense of Humour

A sense of humour is not a quality which can be created in a teacher by external forces. Rather, it is an inherent quality, a personality trait. Humour not only relieves tension and stress, it makes a leader more approachable. My teachers can attest to the fact that even though I could be considered a very stern, even draconian leader at times, I have always sought to soften severity with a sense of humour which never fails to bring about the desired result – a smile and even a chuckle.

A Positive Attitude: A Culture That Is Solution Oriented

The time-worn adage "your attitude determines your altitude" is a universal truth. I have proven it to be so both in my personal life and my administrative life. There has hardly been anything I have set out to do that has not been accomplished. I attribute my success to my attitude. A positive attitude is better than wealth and intelligence. Intelligence without a vision can accomplish so much and no more, but attitude and vision are a dynamic combination.

When I assumed leadership of St Mary High School in 1990, almost all subjects were failing to attain an average of 50 per cent. I knew that this had to change and I also knew that I had to demand greater accountability from all teachers. I was positive it could be done and I knew it would take much courage and consistency, among other important inputs. The school had to be data driven and heads of departments and grade supervisors would need to buy into the idea of data-driven performance. Bringing about this change was a great deal of work at the time (largely due to a lack of technology) and there was some resistance. At this juncture, I must express heartfelt gratitude to my staff who worked hard to make our vision a reality and at the same time realize their personal dreams. I humbly acknowledge that no principal can realize success on his or her own without successful delegation and deployment.

The Value of High Expectations

At St Mary High School, I wanted all employees to set high standards for themselves – standards that could only be directed and driven by data. I wanted staff members to set personal targets, which they themselves wanted to achieve, and targets for the improvement of their sphere of responsibility. Each time standards are reached, the bar should be raised so that, eventually, excellence is achieved by all. This principle was applied to all categories of work at St Mary High and it is this principle which has earned the school the distinction of being one of the most aesthetically pleasing schools in Jamaica and one of the most sought-after high schools for enrolment.

Effects of National Work Culture on School Culture

An article in the *Jamaica Observer* (Brown 2012, 1) read, "The work ethics encouraged by Chinese contractor, China Harbour Engineering Company (CHEC) is the reason the company is able to keep all of its current projects within budget and on schedule." Jamaican workers on a bridge-building project and, specifically those located in the parishes of Portland and St Mary, told the *Jamaica Observer* that their bosses required them to be punctual for work at all times, give a full day's work and be extremely observant of safety measures. The workers, according to the reporter, proudly declared that the measures being taken by the Chinese have assisted in making the workers more disciplined and aware of a proper work ethic. One worker said, "You have to always be punctual and you can't sit on the 'Chinese work' because they start at exactly eight o'clock and if you are not there eight o'clock, you are late and you have to come back from your lunch on time. They are extremely punctual and they discuss things together a lot." Jenifer Armond, the communications manager of the company, affirmed the workers' view by stating that the "Chinese workers are indeed extremely punctual and because of that, they stay on schedule and within budget thus saving the Jamaican taxpayers a lot" (ibid.).

There are two important statements made that are worthy of commentary. First, the Jamaican workers' view the job they are doing as that belonging to the Chinese, thus a change of attitude is necessary; second, all are aware of the crucial nature of accountability. What would have happened if the work had been managed by Jamaicans? I have learned and subsequently underscored to my employees the importance of punctuality and accountability in the equation of excellence. Public sector workers, generally, have much to learn about work ethic. Jamaicans often joke about the distinction between time and "Jamaican time". This humour is suggestive that Jamaica's time differs from that of other countries and it underscores a growing problem among Jamaican workers – an unwillingness to view time as important to productivity. Almost all public sector entities suffer from this malady and my institution is populated by mainly Jamaican workers. I have had to solve that problem the hard way and, even today, that problem has not been solved completely. It is amazing that the Jamaican worker will work in other countries and respect the value of time, yet in our own country, we have to impose sanctions and battle with unions to get workers to value time.

Consistency in Punctuality

Consistency in punctuality is one of the key pillars for a stable, harmonious, effective and efficient environment. All workers must develop positive patterns of behaviour that are predictable and stable. There are a few teachers, for example, who arrive at work so early that their absence is conspicuous. If they drive vehicles, the students will tell you, "Ms Tyme will not be in school today," because they have grown accustomed to seeing Ms Tyme's car by a particular time. Similarly, if the teacher does not reach the class by a particular time the students know for sure that the teacher is absent. Other teachers develop patterns also but negative ones. Students tell you that "Ms Layte will be attending class" but that Ms Layte is invariably late. Alas, in a culture where lateness is fashionable, some workers just cannot understand "the big deal" when they are consistently late. They do not understand that this kind of pattern is counterproductive and only serves to create a negative impression of the member of staff. As a leader, I have been uncompromising in my message of consistency and its rewards, especially where punctuality is concerned. Therefore, some teachers have several letters of commendation in their files while others have letters reminding them of the value of punctuality.

The Value of Fair Play to Motivation

A culture which emphasizes transparency and fair play is conducive to a harmonious relationship born out of trust. Workers who are constantly reminded of *Animal Farm* by George Orwell might rise up in much the same way the animals in the story rose up and overthrew their master. The less extreme reaction is that resentment will fester among the staff. Discontent among teachers impacts negatively on morale and productivity. Students suffer and performance suffers in all areas. It impacts relationships negatively. Frederick Herzberg's motivation theory has thus been explored in an effort to identify motivation factors. Herzberg theorizes that there are two important factors in the workplace that result in job satisfaction. He was careful to distinguish between what he called motivators and hygiene factors. Motivators include challenging work, recognition and responsibility. Hygiene factors include status, job security, salary and fringe benefits (Warrilow 2009). The presence of the latter does not necessarily motivate workers but its absence does. Perhaps more familiar descriptions of motivation include terms such as intrinsic and extrinsic. Extrinsic motivation depends on external rewards while intrinsic motivation is inherent and needs no external reward. Workers driven by intrinsic motivation take genuine pleasure in completing a task and expect no outside incentive (Syptak, Marsland and Ulmer 1999).

The Value of Support

A culture in which students help and support each other is integral if they are to thrive in an academic institution. With this in mind, St Mary High School launched its internal mentorship programme in 2009. This new initiative involved students from sixth form being trained as mentors for students from first through to fifth form. The potential student mentors either volunteer or are selected for training. The training is conducted by the guidance and counselling department in the summer prior to the opening of school. There is also ongoing training during the course of the school year. Mentees in the programme are usually referred by the guidance and counselling department and are students with either academic or behavioural concerns, or both. Some of the areas in which the mentors assist include completing homework, developing good study habits, monitoring academic progress, developing self-management skills and enhancing interpersonal skills. At the end of each school year there is a social event organized for mentors and mentees. There is usually an award for the most improved mentee. The programme has seen some level of success as more mentees are exhibiting positive behavioural changes and improved academic performance. However, weaknesses do exist in the programme as some students resist being referred. Despite the challenges, the school is proud of the service being offered through its mentorship programme.

Self-Esteem and Its Effects on School Culture

Recognizing persons for a job well-done is an effective way of building self-esteem. The institution I manage has used various methods of recognition, inclusive of verbal and written recognition. Workers who are supportive are commended because this show of support by administration is an important motivator. Despite the tangible efforts that must be made by administration to ensure that workers feel valued, I feel that self-esteem should start from within. Therefore, at new staff orientation held by senior staff, new employees are strongly encouraged not just to set goals for the students to accomplish but to set goals for their own personal development.

Another method used to build the self-esteem of staff members was the introduction of a staff mentorship programme. A mentorship system in any organization is an excellent way of ensuring that all workers and, in particular, new workers do not feel isolated or unsure of organizational procedures. A mentor provides guidance so that new employees can feel confident that they are valuable and well supported.

Flexibility and School Culture

Flexibility and leadership types have forged a somewhat uncomfortable relationship. My experience as an administrator is that I have to be as flexible as I can in most circumstances, but any successful administrator will attest to the fact that it is necessary to be inflexible at times. In other words, there are areas in which flexibility will be limited and some cases will prove prohibitive.

It is important to chart the course of the school by way of data. The subject teacher, therefore, must produce the data necessary for analysis. There are some teachers who will be late in producing such data – some invariably, some occasionally. Flexibility is not an option in this case, because allowing teachers to be late in producing data affects the future of students. Timely intervention is paramount to improving student performance. This constitutes the proverbial "stitch in time". The teacher is obliged to find strategies that work for each of his or her students.

How the Community Affects School Culture

Research indicates that there is controversy regarding the origin of the proverb "It takes a village to raise a child". Whatever the origin, everyone seems to know it and, what is even more important, everyone seems to recognize its value. I cannot recall a parent-teacher meeting at which a parent did not report the misdeeds of at least one of our students, and I have always welcomed their concern and the sentiments expressed. The parents consider themselves a part of the family of St Mary High, so when our students do not live up to expectations, the parents view it with similar disappointment as a teacher or parent would. This underscores the village theory. A student who expects the village to scold him or her, or to report inappropriate behaviour, will think twice before embarrassing him- or herself and the school. As a child, my parents gave any adult the right to scold me if I stepped out of line. This community value hardly exists anymore in our individualistic culture.

Effects of Family Values on School Culture

At St Mary High, resocialization has become routine. Students are socialized into the culture of the school. We impose higher standards of behaviour than the society and we try to undo the damage done by family. We recognize the importance of family but sometimes family values are opposed to those of the school.

The parent-teacher association is filled with mothers, aunts and grandmothers who are tired of trying to raise the children on their own. The lack of males signals to us that male guidance is missing and that there is a serious deficiency in the socialization of our boys. This deficiency forces us to question what Jamaica is teaching its children. The fact that many of these are single-parent families is instructive. The subtle lesson that these children are being taught is that the institution of marriage is not sacred. Recognizing that subtle messages are being unintentionally transmitted to our children by families, my school has had to incorporate into its social development sessions (form-time) talks on family roles, responsibilities and values. We have had to emphasize conflict resolution, especially among our boys, and we have had to redefine the image of a "man" for our young gentlemen.

Effects of Economic Culture on School Culture

Another important lesson that administrators have to learn is that they must reject forcefully the materialistic culture that Jamaica has adopted. I am sure we can recall hearing news reports about students owning multimillion-dollar houses via the lottery scam. These students have decided from a tender age that education is not an avenue to wealth. Wealth is conspicuously displayed in Jamaica. Consequently, our youngsters are eager to acquire wealth by any means possible. Unfortunately, schools have had to try to counter the "get rich quick" culture that our students have accepted.

The parish of St Mary is a poor, farming area and many of our students are recipients of aid from the Programme of Advancement Through Health and Education funded by the Government of Jamaica and the World Bank. The programme is aimed at delivering benefits by way of cash grants to the most needy and vulnerable in the society; yet it is not unusual to see parents of these children catering to what their children want in the form of fashion, for example, rather than providing what the children need to achieve long-term success. For many of our poorest, too much emphasis is placed on external appearance and too little on the pursuit of education. The other side of the coin is the strain on the budget of rural schools, whose parent-teacher associations are not wealthy.

My Leadership Style and Impact on Student Performance

Having a positive relationship with students contributes significantly to overall performance. Motivating students through incentives is important. Over the years, various incentive programmes or activities have been designed to motivate our students to be ambitious and to dream big. Students have been commended for an action as simple as being courteous. Even our prefects have devised ways of getting other prefects to give their best. I cannot take credit for all this innovation. In some cases, I have been a mere facilitator; in other cases, I have been in the cheering section of the gallery. Yes, it is important to cheer on the efforts of staff especially when all they ask for is your moral support, thanks to a culture of "I can do it" that characterizes St Mary High.

I take time out every Monday to tell stories to my senior students and even though sometimes they groan, at the end of the day they understand that the stories are like oysters that they have to open in order to discover the precious gem inside. They know that I am uncompromising where rules and regulations are concerned, yet they also know instinctively that they can trust me to be concerned about their welfare. I occasionally sit on a bench under the almond tree facing the grades 7 and 8 classrooms because this is my time to connect in a friendly way with my students. They feel more comfortable here with me than they do in my office. This is where I hear the stories about the goat which died, the mother who is sick, the teacher who is giving them a hard time. They understand that even though I reprimand and punish them at times, even though I am "strict", I still care about their mothers, fathers, dogs, cats and pigs.

The vice principals, grade supervisors and guidance counsellors all understand the importance of tradition and culture, and so I am happy in the assurance that our wonderful oral culture of storytelling will continue even after I retire, because it is through this medium that many of our important values are passed on.

Conclusion

One of the fundamental factors in the success of any institution is building a positive culture. This cultural development provides the foundation for achieving excellence. As a principal, it is your duty to mould the culture of the school as staff members are typically diverse in expertise, beliefs, attitudes and personality. I recognized early on that a negative culture has the potential to undermine the drive towards success. It is also important to remember that the school operates within the wider society, and negative attitudes are easily transferred into the institution.

References

Bailsford, D. 2009. *Confessions of Anansi*. 3rd ed. Kingston: LMH.
Brown, I. 2012. "J'can Workers Laud Chinese Work Ethic". *Jamaica Observer*, 25 June. www.jamaicaobserver.com/.../J-can-workers-laud-Chinese-work-ethic_1.
Fisher, D., N. Frey and I. Pumpian. 2012. *How to Create a Culture of Achievement in Your School and Classroom*. Alexandria, VA: Association for Supervision and Curriculum Development.
Hoy, W.K., and C.G. Miskel. 2001. *Educational Administration, Theory, Research and Practice*. 6th ed. New York: McGraw Hall.
Kelly, M. 2011. "Top 6 Keys to Being a Successful Teacher". http://712educators.about.com/od/teachingstrategies/tp/sixkeys.htm.
National Education Inspectorate, Jamaica. 2010. *Chief Inspector's Report, Inspection Cycle 1: Round 2*. Kingston: Ministry of Education.
Syptak, J.M., D.W. Marsland and D. Ulmer. 1999. "Job Satisfaction: Putting Theory into Practice". *Family Practice Management* 6 (9): 26–30.
Warrilow, S. 2009. "Herzberg Motivation Theory: How Hygienic Is Your Change Initiative (and) Are Your People Satisfied and Motivated?" http://www.strategies-for-managing-change.com/herzberg-motivation-theory.html.

CHAPTER 14

MY EXPERIENCE AS A PRINCIPAL

ESTHER TYSON

I HAD AN INTEREST IN EDUCATION from an early age. As a child, I aspired to be a teacher and more specifically a teacher of English. When the position of principal at my alma mater opened up, I was hesitant to apply. However, I was encouraged by many who knew my qualifications and potential to lead, and so I decided to apply; the rest is history. I attribute my success in leadership to my father, who was a pastor of ten churches. By observing him, I learned how to empower individuals to be leaders.

Personal Philosophy on Education

Educational leadership is the single most important factor contributing to students' growth and development outside of the effect and impact of teaching and the teacher (Marzano, Waters and McNulty 2005). As a leader in education, it is imperative that you identify and understand how children learn and what the expected learning outcomes of this process are. Furthermore, defining the what, how and why of education is also important. This is your guiding philosophy on education.

I felt it was important that I was clear in my own mind on how I would operate as a leader. I am a Christian and, after being offered the job to lead Ardenne High School, I took a personal retreat and studied the life of David as a leader in the Bible. I saw how he depended on God to direct his decisions, enable him to have courage when he needed it and console him in times of distress. I saw, on the other hand, that when he forgot to seek God, his family life started to fall apart. Also, I saw how David dealt with Saul, his predecessor, who was intent on killing him. David honoured Saul and spared his life twice, even when David's life was in danger. David was determined to fulfil God's promise to the Israelites that they would inherit certain territories. David went to war to gain these.

I therefore determined that I would learn from David's life as a leader. I resolved that David's approach would become my approach; for example, I made up my mind not to be involved in negative, critical conversations about those who might want to undermine what I would be doing in the school. In addition, in the same way that David strengthened Israel's position as a nation, I felt that Ardenne could improve in many areas and that we had to plan and execute that plan effectively to achieve our goals – and we did. We built on a solid foundation of discipline, family-like culture and godliness that had been laid by the previous leaders of the school.

Going in to lead Ardenne High School, I held two strong beliefs. First, every child who had been admitted to the institution should be given the opportunity to develop his or her potential, whether through academic pursuits or involvement in a wide range of co-curricular activities. Second, it is important for students to find an activity in which they experience success and can feel good about themselves. This sense of personal mastery would have a positive impact on their academic accomplishments. Darling, Caldwell and Smith (2005) speak of the benefits of co-curricular activities, claiming that structured leisure activities aid students' growth and development. Co-curricular participation could provide a door through which students could move on to academic achievement. I proved this to be true at Ardenne High School.

A Support System

It is imperative to have a support system which nurtures you spiritually, emotionally and professionally. Being a principal can be a lonesome job. In order to be effective, we must practise team leadership and shared leadership

(Morgeson et al. 2009). It is therefore crucial to establish a support system which will provide you with spiritual and emotional encouragement when the job becomes difficult. This support system should include your relationship with God. Through this experience, you develop a practice of communicating with God and, in turn, expect Him to communicate with you. He will guide you each day as you seek to meet with Him first of all. This support system should also include good friends – a very confidential and tight knit circle – in whom you can confide. Make time to unwind with a good book or a movie. This is a good way to replenish your spirit and your soul. If you have a family, develop routines with them to ensure that you keep connected with them and do not become isolated. Isolation will lead to depression when things get difficult at school. Lastly, network with other principals in order to learn from those who are more experienced. Neale and Cone (2013) outline the importance of principals networking, noting that it facilitates constructive engagement and shared ideas. I found that being on Principals' Retreats provided opportunities for this type of sharing. I found these retreats to be helpful and therapeutic. There are professional principals' associations that you can become a part of. It helps when you realize that you are not the only principal going through the experiences. In addition, these organizations also provide ongoing professional development opportunities.

Develop a Vision for the School

Know What You Are Getting Into

Before taking up your position as principal, where possible, try to interview persons who have been involved with the school. Get as much information about what is happening at the school while at the same time maintaining an open mind. In addition, upon being appointed, seek to review pertinent documents that will give you a sense of what has been happening in the school. Some good sources are board minutes, staff minutes, inspection reports and examination results. Upon assuming the post, during the first week in your new position, spend time to meet with important stakeholders and key staff personnel. This is important as it provides the opportunity to break the ice and give your staff a chance to interact with you on a personal level. As much as possible, meet with the middle managers on a one-on-one basis and listen to their assessment of the school. Find out about their areas of responsibility and use the opportunity to share your vision for the direction of the school. Give them a chance to give you feedback on this, and listen.

Respect What Has Already Been Accomplished

I ensured that I showed respect to what was already accomplished in the school. Seyfarth (2008) supports this ideology, adding that administrators should focus on inspiring others to follow a vision and embrace positive ideas and practices that were already established. Do not change what is effective and working well. Acknowledge the work of those who have gone before you. Make sure that retired principals and senior teachers, for example, are invited to functions at the school. Honour past leaders of the school by highlighting what they have done through having their photographs visible in the school and their contributions included in the school's history.

Spiritual Heritage

Ardenne's strong spiritual heritage is renowned throughout Jamaica and I too benefited while I attended the institution as a student. An article on the history of Ardenne on the school's web page (www.ardennehigh.com) reported that the founders of the school were missionaries, who came to Jamaica after the Kingston earthquake of 1907. The school was started in 1927 to prepare Jamaican students to minister the gospel to their fellow citizens; the focus of the curriculum, however, became academic. Despite the academic focus, Ardenne has always maintained a school culture which highlights the value of the students' spiritual development. This heritage has been maintained through daily devotional exercises, whether corporate or in various groupings. In addition, Miss E.M. Claire Gayle, principal from 1969 to 1978, introduced an annual Christian Emphasis Week that was held during the last week before the Easter holidays. This began when I was a student at Ardenne and was still continuing when I assumed the principalship. The Church of God in Jamaica, the proprietors of the school, plays an important part in maintaining the spiritual dimensions of the school's life. This spiritual culture is reinforced by the school's motto, "Deo duce quaere optima – With God as guide, seek the best", and the school song, "Ye Valiant Youth Arise".

Disciplinary Heritage

Ardenne differs in culture from the neighbouring high schools: it has a strong spiritual heritage and a reputation for maintaining a high level of discipline. This attribute was a source of pride to the school during a period of decline in student discipline in other traditional high schools around the late twentieth century into the first part of the twenty-first century.

Prepare to Deal with Change

Change Is Scary

I was externally recruited to the position of principal at an institution that had minimal staff turnover. Even though I was a past student and had taught there for a year, I was still an unknown. Having assessed some practices at the school, I realized that although some changes needed to be made gradually, others had to be implemented immediately for the sake of academic improvement. I went to Ardenne High School in January, at the beginning of the second term. Having become aware that no ongoing teacher evaluations were being done, I announced to the staff that all new teachers would be assessed with immediate effect. This had not yet been instituted by the Ministry of Education, so I adapted an instrument to be used for this purpose. Change which exposes the unknown can bring fear. Hoy and Miskel (2008) purport that new information and ideas create a pattern of basic assumptions which if not thoroughly understood by members of an organization can result in the members being resistant to change. When I introduced the programme of ongoing teacher evaluations there was silence in the staff room and a palpable sense of fear settled over the teachers. Yet the evaluations had to be done. I introduced the instrument to the teachers and then trained the heads of departments in the process. After some years, this practice of ongoing staff evaluations has been institutionalized.

Be Courageous

When you are convinced that what you are implementing is for the good of the organization, you have to be determined and courageous in the face of resistance. On the first day of the school term, I realized that I had walked into a situation: there would be no handing over from the previous head of school and the documents that were needed to provide insight into the current status of the school were not available. After consulting with one of my mentors, I decided to close the school for two days so that I could meet individually with all heads of departments. However, this was not in keeping with the Education Act of 1980, 9(1)a, which states that every educational institution shall provide no less than five school days each week. A parent reported my actions to the Ministry of Education and an officer was sent to investigate why this had happened. I explained the reasons for my actions and the officer appreciated the need for the decision. These two days of meetings were invaluable for getting information, for breaking the ice and for realizing the need for the implementation of certain practices for good academic outcomes. One such example was the need for all heads of departments to make reports on what had been achieved in the department for the previous year to include goals, objectives, methods, outputs, a review of assessment outcomes and ideas for how to improve on identified areas of weakness. In addition, reports were expected to include activities that had been undertaken by the departments for student enrichment, professional development of staff, planning and delegation of responsibilities.

There was resistance to this approach. Many teachers saw this as additional work and a way to show up the departments that had not been doing well. Planning and documentation were being stressed and that meant writing. Many teachers resented this. Yet it had to be done. I was dubbed the "Writing Principal". A few years later, these very practices were implemented islandwide by the Ministry of Education. By that time, these practices were already entrenched at our school.

Educate Yourself on the Various Stages of the Change Process

I was always cognizant of the fact that change is never easy and I read extensively on the change process. One education expert from Canada, Michael Fullan, has researched and written on change in the educational field. I read his book on the topic and this helped to inform my approach. Educating myself on what to expect in the change process was very important in helping me know how to deal with its various stages (Fullan 2002). I realized that the seemingly negative response that I was getting from the staff was not personal but the outcome of uncertainty and sometimes fear. I had to realize that change was not an event but a process, and process required time.

Educate Your Staff about Change

Sergiovanni and Starratt (2007) declare that staff development allows staff to grow in confidence and keeps them excited about their job. I organized professional development workshops to address the matter of change management and other areas of concern such as teamwork (Fullan 1997, as quoted in Glickman, Gordon and Ross-Gordon 2010). These were organized in the week before each school term began. There was resistance to participating in the workshops. Teachers were resentful about being asked to come out before the beginning of the school term to do professional development workshops. This was something that had not been done before. Even though the board of management approved my having these workshops at hotels, there was still resistance. At first, approximately 60 per cent of the staff attended. The presenter for the first set of workshops found the teachers very difficult to reach. Yet professional development and the need for change were a priority. So I persisted. There was a handful of teachers who appreciated the efforts being made and gave me positive feedback. Eventually, the teachers became accustomed to having to come out before the start of the new academic term to participate in professional development workshops. Later on, some teachers who were experts in their areas made presentations to the other members of staff. This practice is now a requirement by the Ministry of Education.

Sometimes Top-Down, Sometimes Bottom-Up. But Make It Happen

I realized that it was important to listen to what the stakeholders had to say. Even when I disagreed with their position, I had to respectfully allow them to present their views on any matter under consideration. It took some time for the teachers to realize that I would not penalize them because they disagreed with me.

Initially, I made some decisions and implemented them unilaterally. One involved requiring that all teachers write daily lesson plans. Egwa (2015) makes reference to the importance of the principals supervising classroom instruction, which I made one of my priorities. When the teachers were told that lesson planning was necessary for all teachers, the heads of departments were given the responsibility of checking them. I began to realize that after a few months that not all heads of departments were checking the lesson plans. I therefore made a decision to call for the lesson plans of individual departments and checked them myself. This created quite a number of sleepless nights for teachers who in November were writing lesson plans for classes that had been taught in September and October. I systematically went through checking these lesson plans and made comments on how they were done. The plans were returned to the teachers in a timely manner. This meant a lot of extra work for me, since there were over one hundred teachers; but it was worth it. After that initial breaking of the resistance of the heads of departments, to insisting that their teachers write lesson plans, and subsequently vetting them, the planning of lessons became a practice, then a habit and, eventually, a part of the school's culture.

Assess, Develop, Improve

Assess what is before you and develop a plan to make improvements where needed. One view that is typical among some of our teachers is that a practice is acceptable because "this is how we have always done it". As an educational leader, it will be necessary to always keep refining the school's practices to keep doing better. This is particularly true in the twenty-first century, when technological change has become so dynamic that knowledge is rapidly changing and increasing. We therefore must educate our students to be relevant in the twenty-first century. This means that some knowledge will become outmoded and certainly almost all methodology will need constant updating. The following observation made by Hess (2013, 30) is most applicable to how we approach the role of principalship in Jamaica in the twenty-first century: "Leadership always entails two complementary roles. One is coaching, mentoring, nurturing, and inspiring others to forge dynamic, professional cultures. This half often absorbs the whole attention of those who tackle educational leadership. Lost in the discussion is the second half of leadership – the cage-busting half, in which leaders upend stifling rules, policies, and routines to make it easier for successful professional cultures to thrive." Each school is different. It is important to look at the school you are called to lead and assess its strengths and weaknesses. From this assessment, determine the outcome that is possible, and then, along with your stakeholders, plan and implement the measures necessary to make the needed improvements. If the school has a school improvement plan, this will help you to do that. If it does not, then it will be necessary for you to begin the process of establishing a plan.

At Ardenne, I had to make changes to the structure and function of middle management. There were senior teachers who were functioning as both heads of departments and grade supervisors. I thought that teachers who had those responsibilities along with a full teaching load could not be effective. I redistributed these positions and brought on additional senior staff that had the potential to do well in middle management. In addition, there were other areas of responsibility that I had to create to address changes that were being made to the school's programme.

One such post was co-coordinator of co-curricular activities. This needed innovation brought about a structured approach to after-school activities. The teacher given this responsibility had a passion to see to the development of the co-curricular programme which would result in the school, in specific activities, being the best in the country. I shared with her what I saw; she gave her own input and came up with a plan that was approved and successfully implemented.

The co-curricular programme grew to entail over thirty clubs and activities including performing arts, sports, academic clubs, service clubs and environmental clubs. The government did not provide funds for such activities, so creative ways had to be found to sponsor each club. For example, the Performing Arts Club established an annual production, the Christmas pageant. The proceeds from the event were used to purchase costumes, cover transportation costs and so on. I also created the post of coordinator of community service to oversee a programme to heighten a sense of volunteerism among the students. The completion of the required hours became a requirement for attaining a graduation certificate.

There was also the post of coordinator of personnel development, to oversee the establishment of this programme from grades 7 through 11. Added to this was a sixth-form development programme, which was introduced to develop leadership capacity in the students and to expose them to national and international affairs.

In addition to the changes made to the middle management structure, I also made changes to academic standards. On reviewing the academic programmes and the students' achievements, I realized that the students needed to be challenged to excel and produce their very best. Therefore, a decision was taken to move the pass mark from 50 per cent to 60 per cent. Furthermore, the practice of having teachers recommend students to be given permission to sit individual subjects in CSEC was eliminated. The students, parents and teachers were challenged to function in a system in which students, having chosen and been given approval at the end of ninth grade to sit eight subjects at CSEC, would be required to sit all eight subjects at the end of grade 11. Screening became a thing of the past. There were teachers who were not happy about this, especially where they perceived that the students did not traditionally do well in their subject. I challenged the teachers to find ways to inspire and help their students to perform well in their subject areas.

Another important area in which immediate change was needed was the administration of the school. When I arrived at Ardenne in 2000, there was only one computer in the administrative office. This resided in the bursar's office. I therefore went on a campaign to persuade everyone of the importance of improving the use of technology in administration. The board agreed to this, but funds were not available. The alumni and parents got on board and they made donations of computers that allowed for each office to eventually have a desktop. Along with this, training was put in place to teach staff members how to use the computers. There were persons who had problems adapting to this change, but overall the process went very well. As a principal, I found that I had to be always thinking about the big picture and I also had to be forward thinking. Furthermore, I learned that the difference between excellence and mediocrity was attention to detail.

Be an Inclusive Leader to Grow Your School

If you develop a team approach and learn to share power, your growth becomes exponential. To do this, as the leader you need to educate your staff on the value of teamwork. If you practise consultation with the staff, especially your middle managers, you will help to develop in them a sense of being valued. They will see themselves as owning the vision and being a necessary part of making the vision come to fruition.

Have an Open-Door Policy

I found that it was important to be available to speak with my staff when they needed me. If I was not in a meeting, the office staff knew that the staff members were allowed to come in to meet with me. In this way, I developed a relationship with the staff wherein they felt comfortable sharing ideas. Seyfarth (2008) puts forward a number of skills that effective leaders should have, which includes interpersonal skills and stability. These skills are essential in establishing a relationship of trust which further facilitates the sharing of ideas.

Identify Competencies and Fit These to Posts of Responsibility

Leaders not only manage but also inspire and ignite passion in others to participate in realizing the vision of the school. One important aspect of making the vision for your school a reality is to identify the passion with which your teachers are endowed. In determining how to fill the posts of responsibility, it is invaluable to know this. For example, the person who has a passion for the performing arts is the best person to be responsible for that area. That is the person who will dream and think about how to make the idea become a reality. Furthermore, you need to determine the competencies of each of your senior staff and other teachers with the potential of joining this cadre. It is your responsibility as the leader to allocate the responsibilities based not on years in the job but on competencies and passion. By doing this, you will ensure that the area will grow and that growth will be sustained.

Establish a Framework for Accountability

Having identified persons with passion and the competencies required in various areas, you then need to establish a system of accountability. As a leader it is essential to share power with those to whom you give responsibility so they feel empowered to carry out their duties and to develop their area. Prior to the "No Child Left Behind" concept, there was no specific means of measuring the performance of teachers and school administrators (Seyfarth 2008). On the other hand, as the principal, it is important that you provide a structure whereby plans and ideas are submitted to you for approval. Furthermore, you must ensure that any major plans or changes are submitted in writing and that approval is given in writing. This protects both you and the teacher in charge. Another important feature to implement to ensure accountability is to provide each senior teacher with a job description. This job description should be agreed upon by both the administration and the teacher. The teacher should then be evaluated yearly, based on this job description.

Another way of helping to maintain accountability is to require that each senior teacher does a termly or yearly report to submit to the principal of the duties that they have been carrying out during the year. It helps if at the beginning of the year each teacher establishes an action plan, setting out targets for the year. Teachers' action plans have become a requirement from the Ministry of Education.

Change Should Bring Positive Results

It is important to understand that further buy-in will come when changes bring positive results. People love success; this I proved over time. When the students started performing better academically and the external examination results started to improve, Ardenne began to attract more students with higher Grade Six Achievement Test averages. In addition, the restructuring of co-curricular activities resulted in improvement in the performing arts clubs, and the school increased the number of gold medals it won in the Jamaica Cultural Development Commission competitions. As a result, more teachers started being willing to assist in after-school activities, even though they were not paid. There was the attendant sense of well-being and pride that came with being associated with a successful school. Resistance to the changes that were made to strengthen the academic success of the students waned. Most teachers were willing to attend the termly professional development sessions that were put in place.

Celebrate Accomplishments

Celebration is important because it motivates both teachers and students to continue to give their very best. Celebration is a public acknowledgement of the recipients' achievements. Sergiovanni and Starratt (2007) suggest that what is rewarded gets done and serves as a motivational tool. It is therefore important to reward both staff and students as this will motivate them to continue to work hard. One way of celebration was developed when grade supervisors were challenged to find ways to celebrate the students in each grade level who had improved, or who were doing well, and whose behaviour was outstanding. These students would not be recognized at the school's annual prize-giving since, with a school population of almost two thousand, the criteria to receive an award catered to only the very best at each grade level and very few students could be recognized under this system. Initiating this idea began with one grade supervisor who started a Grade Awards Ceremony during child's month (May). The teacher solicited help from parents to purchase trophies for various awards, and she printed certificates at the school for different accomplishments. This was a great success. I encouraged other grade supervisors to do the same and the practice caught on. It is now a part of the culture of Ardenne High School that each year in May, the accomplishments of the students of grades 7 to 10 are recognized in their Grade Award Ceremony.

The teachers' contributions were recognized in various ways. At Ardenne, there is a practice which had long been established called Staff Affairs. Each morning before the bell sounds, prefects monitor the students and the teachers meet in the main staff room for notices from the principal and for praying together. During this period, teachers who had assisted in any way in the school, apart from their regular teaching duties, are acknowledged. Furthermore, at the end of a school year, teachers who had gone beyond the call of duty during the year were recognized by the principal and presented with a certificate of recognition. In addition, departments which had excellent passes in the external examinations would be recognized at the beginning of the year and awarded certificates, which they proudly displayed in their departments.

Then there are other forms of celebrations that involve expenditures, such as feting our teachers on Teachers' Day by taking them on trips to the North Coast or to a luncheon at a recognized hotel or restaurant. A teacher proposed a fantastic idea one year for Teachers' Day. A spa was set up at the school and a company was invited to provide spa treatments for the teachers. This proved to be a very successful way of honouring the teachers for their hard work, and they were immensely pleased. What is important is to recognize both staff and students for their accomplishments. This can be done without having to spend a lot of money. Look at your situation and think about ways public recognition can be given to honour the work that students and teachers have done. This will motivate them and improve the morale of the school overall.

Involve Other Stakeholders in Carrying Out the Vision

Involving stakeholders was one obvious change that needed to occur at Ardenne, as our goals could not be accomplished with the school fees that were being paid. I was fortunate to be a past student of the school and therefore had an early buy-in from the various alumni chapters abroad concerning the projects we wanted to undertake. When the focus was on strengthening the use of technology, alumni assisted with the purchasing of the computers. They also raised funds to help build a science block. I was able to get assistance from the parent-teacher association to accomplish some of our goals. There were many fundraisers conducted by alumni, staff and parents. As a culture, we have to engender a closer relationship between home and school. I find that teachers are afraid to do this. They fear being abused by parents or being treated unfairly. I found that the president of the parent-teacher association played a key role in setting the tone of the relationship between school and home.

Strengthen Students' Loyalty and Commitment to the School

Schools are more likely to achieve their goals of improved academic achievement and increased involvement in co-curricular activities when school spirit is strengthened. As a student at Ardenne, we had sung our school song with zeal. On coming back to Ardenne as principal, I found that the students did not know the school song, so I worked with the music teacher to have each class learn the school song. We began to sing it at the beginning and end of the term and for any official functions. The students soon identified very closely with the song. This song became a source of identification for them as it spoke about Ardenne's flame and the responsibility they had to fan it to make it burn brighter.

In addition, the students began to show more and more pride in their school. This pride was attributed to their increased success, highlighted daily in school announcements via the intercom and at assembly. I impressed upon students their role as future leaders of our nation and the responsibility they have to prepare for this, especially in how they conduct themselves at this stage of their lives. This, I pointed out, included their deportment on the streets, which would help to improve or diminish the school's image. The "Ardenne Swagger", a walk that reflected pride in themselves and their accomplishments, was developed among the students.

Respect Every Level of Staff in the School

I knew that for the vision of the school to be realized, all levels of the staff had to buy into it. I established, early on, an open-door policy that would be extended to all members of the staff, including the administrative and ancillary staff. They were free to come into the office to speak with me on any matter that concerned them. Some members of staff made use of this opportunity more than others. I found that it was important to listen to what the support staff had to say and to value the contributions they made. I also held termly meetings with them and other meetings as needed. Furthermore, it was important to let them know that you valued them as individuals, not just as a worker at school. This helped to engender a sense of family in spite of conflicts that would inevitably arise.

Problems sometimes arose because the ancillary staff felt that they were treated poorly by some teachers. The issues were complex. They involved the teachers' view of the ancillary staff and also how the ancillary staff saw themselves. There had to be ongoing dialogue with the two groups to improve this relationship. What became evident was that it was important that all staff members in the school community felt respected by those with whom they had to work. Once I gained the trust of the ancillary staff, they were able to let me know some of the things that were happening on the grounds among the students. This assisted the school administration to deal with matters that had the potential of becoming big problems.

Practice Impartiality–Conflict Management

Raj (2012) outlines a number of conflict management strategies, which, if employed, should aid school administrators in improving their conflict management skills. He focused on managing one's emotions, addressing one's own conflicts, addressing others' conflicts, assertiveness and mediation – all of which have proven to improve in managing conflicts. Any leader who oversees a group of people will realize this very quickly. I learned that when dealing with conflicts, it is important to reserve judgement until all parties involved are allowed to express their point of view and until the truth of statements is verified. It was also essential to document what was being said during a meeting to resolve conflicts. This must be done to assist a leader in evaluating the situation and also to provide the basis for whatever decision that you might arrive at.

In all situations, I found that it was crucial to maintain impartiality. Even where you might be close to a staff member, that relationship must not influence your decisions. If you are seen to be biased or partial to certain members of staff, this will result in the staff losing trust in you and, in some cases, undermining your leadership of the school.

Conclusion

My experience as a principal has caused me to realize the importance of being properly trained before assuming the role of principal in any educational institution. In addition, a process of mentoring for each new principal should be instituted by the board of the school in collaboration with the Ministry of Education. Reflecting on my early years as a principal, I realized that I made some mistakes because I needed to know the Blue Book, the Code of Education 1980, inside out. I also realized that although I made use of the network of principals and persons I knew in the Ministry of Education, I needed to have been better prepared. I am a reader and this helped me to acquire information. The Ministry of Education has now implemented the National College for Education Leadership. This body seeks to prepare educators who aspire to be principals in the system. I encourage all such persons to participate in this thorough and rigorous programme which will better prepare persons to become school leaders and take on their pivotal roles. This process, in turn, will develop a stronger education system.

Above all, school leadership requires courage, persistence, passion and a willingness to be always learning. As our Ardenne High School motto says, "Deo duce quaere optima – With God as guide, seek the best".

References

Darling, N., L.L. Caldwell and R. Smith. 2005. "Participation in School-Based Extracurricular Activities and Adolescence Adjustment". *Journal of Leisure Research* 37 (1): 51–76.

Egwu, S.O. 2015. "Principals' Performance in Supervision of Classroom Instruction in Ebonyi State Secondary Schools". *Journal of Education and Practice* 1 (15): 99–105. http://files.eric.ed.gov/fulltext/EJ1079965.pdf.

Fullan, M. 2002. "The Change Leader: Beyond Instructional Leadership". http://www.ascd.org/publications/educationalleadership/may02/vol59/num08/The-Change-Leader.aspx.

Glickman, C.D., S.P. Gordon, and J.M. Ross-Gordon. 2010. *Supervision and Instructional Leadership: A Developmental Approach*. 8th ed. Boston: Allyn and Bacon.

Hess, F.M. 2013. "Be a Cage-Buster: The Principalship". *Journal of Educational Leadership* 70 (7): 30–33. http://www.ascd.org/publications/educationalleadership/apr13/vol70/num07/abstract.aspx.

Hoy, W.K., and C.D. Miskel. 2008. *Educational Administration: Theory, Research, and Practice*. 8th ed. New York: McGraw-Hill.

Marzano, R.J., T. Waters and B.A. McNulty. 2005. *School Leadership That Works: From Research to Results*. Alexandria, VA: Association for Supervision and Curriculum Development.

Morgeson, F.P., D. Scott and E.P. Karam. 2009. "Leadership in Teams: A Functional Approach to Understanding Leadership Structures and Purposes". *Journal of Management* 36, (1): 5–39. doi:10.1177/0149206309347376.

Neale, E., and M. Cone. 2013. "Strong Principal Networks Influence School Culture". *Journal of the Learning Principal* 8 (3): 3–5.

Raj, K. 2012. "Conflict Management and School Leadership". *Journal of Communication* 3 (1): 25–34. http://www.academia.edu/2251898/Conflict_Management_and _School_Leadership.

Sergiovanni, T.J., and R.J. Starratt. 2007. *Supervision: A Redefinition*. 8th ed. New York: McGraw-Hill.

Seyfarth, J. 2008. *Human Resource Leadership for Effective Schools*. 5th ed. Boston: Allyn and Bacon.

CHAPTER 15

STRONG LEADERSHIP MAKES A DIFFERENCE

DENNIS M. CLARKE

THE SUCCESS OF ST THOMAS TECHNICAL was possible because I was able to attract and recruit some of the best teachers to drive our vision of excellence. When you recruit, you must ensure that you sell your school as one of the best. According to Ezenne (2011), resource managers need to understand recruitment policies and procedures and recognize that the recruitment of suitable potential employees is critical to the education system.

In recruiting qualified staff to transform the school, I did not do a lot to upset the current staff. Instead, I brought in the new staff and put them in charge, without taking away the posts of the current staff. My passion was to transform this newly upgraded technical school, situated in deep rural St Thomas, wedged between sugar and banana plantations, into an institution of academic excellence. I was mindful that many of the current staff were dedicated people who lived in the community. But I also knew that many were not competent to teach the highly specialized subjects that a first-class technical education demanded.

In order to encourage a culture of academic excellence, I issued a policy that nobody would be promoted without having a minimum of a first degree. (I was ahead of the government in that regard.) I initiated teachers' entry into tertiary institutions to upgrade their knowledge and skills. I went to institutions such as Mico, the University of the West Indies and the University of

Technology, Jamaica, and collected application and registration forms for my teachers. What I did not do, which many schools were doing, was allow teachers to study in areas outside of their specialization; if they were teaching science, they had study the sciences. By the time I left in 1999, 80 per cent of the staff had a first degree.

Poor performance of teachers makes the process of instructional supervision tedious and stressful and leads to ineffective schools. Teachers and other staff members have to be made accountable, hence consistent performance appraisals will have to be facilitated by the principal and senior administrative team to determine teacher deficiencies and strengths and facilitate their development through training intervention. According to the US National Association of Elementary School Principals (2002), leaders who work to provide every teacher with the tools they need to improve professionally are more likely better prepared to support the development to the goals of the school.

Empowering Students

One of the challenges we faced was the stigmatization of the technical-vocational programme. We had to rebrand the skills area and overcome the stereotype that these skills were for non-performing students. One of the strategies was to select students who were excellent academically and strategically place them in agriculture (in two streams, agritechnology and agribusiness, where these streams focused on the sciences). When our students realized that the "bright" students were taking these hands-on subjects, it was easier to sell the idea of embarking on these areas. We were aggressively engaging in competency-based assessment. You must understand the context. At that point, STEM (science, technology, math and engineering) was not even a concept driving schools, and the technical/vocational subjects were still seen as "Cinderella" subjects. My being president of the Jamaica Association of Technical Vocation Education Teachers helped to establish vocational training in my school while at the same time encouraging administrators in other institutions to diversify their offerings by blending academic subjects with skills training. Even though many students had quite a few CSEC subjects under their belts, no student graduated from St Thomas Technical without a skill.

Building Leadership among Administrators

For any school to be truly successful there needs to be strong and effective leadership. I was instrumental in building the principals' fraternity in Region 2. All principals in St Thomas were members, regardless of the school they headed. We met monthly over lunch and essentially became our own mentors, watchdogs and auditors. At these meetings we shared challenges and successes, and every meeting would have a presentation from among us as we tried to be on the same page with regard to issues affecting our schools and communities. Our association was light-years ahead of the ministry's Quality Education Circle.

Parental Involvement

I invited the parents to be involved in all aspects of the school. Some parents avoided me because they knew I was serious about getting students to a certain standard. If you are serious about education, and children understand what they are about, then the parents will fall in line. I had to get parents to buy into the vision of excellence and sustainability. Matters of school attendance and punctuality had to be addressed. We had to work together to build confidence and self-esteem. It was not long before parents felt comfortable being active participants in all aspects of the school. I was visible as well. Living in the community allowed for that kind of engagement, whether it was attending church, weddings, funerals, socials. The school and farm belonged to the community, so it was unthinkable for them to plunder or vandalize.

Parental input is critical for proper instructional supervision. Researchers have consistently argued that parents' involvement in school matters correlates positively with academic performance. Brookover and Lezotte (1979, 243), in addressing the importance of parents to the learning process, state that when "educators involve parents as partners in their children's education . . . [the parents] develop a sense of efficacy that communicates itself to the children and leads to positive academic results". That is why Lambert (2003, 68) calls for enlarging the "circle of community to be more inclusive than in the past if we are to develop reciprocal partnerships with parents and the broader community".

Relationship with Community

I made the main entities and businesses that supported the school feel a part of the institution and part of our vision to be self-sustaining. I determined what they required in terms of skill sets and worker competence, and I provided workers (some of whom were graduates of our programme) for their businesses. With these business leaders I established a programme of workplace experience (a customized work experience) wherein prospective employers could select from our students those they needed for permanent employment. The Work Study Programme was compulsory and all students had to complete the work experience by the end of grade 10. While the business community gained from our student workforce, the school also benefited. I received monthly or annual sums of money from Eastern Banana Company or Goodyear to assist with the school because I was able to supply them with the students who were prepared for the workforce. The school therefore became a community school.

I did not have to go to the Ministry of Education to have buildings erected. Once the Parish Council approved the drawings, we went ahead with the construction. We were able to construct a two-storey building to house the vice principal and guidance counsellor and twelve housing flats for teachers. I used housing as one of the incentives to attract young and qualified teachers, especially in areas such as mathematics, science, agriculture, industrial technology and English language. With assistance from Eastern Banana, we expanded our sports programme to include lawn tennis, netball, table tennis and other sports.

One of the most remarkable benefits of community relationship was a banana project whereby we partnered with Eastern Banana. As a result of our thriving school farm, St Thomas Technical became the first school to export bananas and generate money from foreign sources.

Managing Vending

One of the first things I had to address was vending. Before my arrival, the campus teemed with vendors who plied their wares all day. For many of them, this was all they did to send their children to school. Job opportunities were limited. For unskilled workers, the only opportunities are in either a sugar or a banana plantation. I met with them and accorded them the respect I would give anyone who came to my office. After a series of meetings, certain measures were put in place: we had to reduce their numbers. They would have to get a food handler's permit; be in uniform, clean their area, pay dues and select a spokesperson. They were given designated times to sell and could not compete with the school's cafeteria. This enterprise further strengthened the community spirit. I was one of the first to formalize vending.

Dealing with Student Discipline

School discipline entails more than punishment. It is complex and includes developing student self-discipline (Bear 2005). It must be noted that one of our national footballers had been expelled from another school. When he came, he was indisciplined, but I told him that he would not be involved in any football, not even to watch a game, until his behaviour improved. For this particular case, the entire community (the school, parents) became involved in his behaviour modification, as all wanted to see him play. He was not the only one with disciplinary problems; so I put a type of management in place that held everybody accountable.

Another initiative was to institute programmes that valued and validated students for whatever they did. When we rewarded students and invited their parents to be part of the value ceremony, we started seeing students excelling. At the time, our average was somewhere in the region of 45 per cent; by the time I left the school, it was about 85 per cent. Principals in effective schools set goals and learning targets and expect that teachers and students will work to meet these targets. Sweeny (1982) posits that principals in effective schools have high expectations and set goals accordingly for the whole school and monitor to ensure goals are met. The most important thing is to get students and teachers to value themselves. Teachers must see themselves as bearers of good news and recognize that the success of the students lies with them.

As a result of our success, neighbouring schools began losing their brightest students to us because everybody then wanted to be associated with the success. The students started feeling that they were the best and this translated into students' participating in and winning a lot of competitions, including poster and science competitions. Once you can get students to value themselves and get parents and the community to buy into your vision, you can achieve much. As a result of our success, Eastern Banana, Tropicana and other agricultural entities provided all the equipment we needed to enhance our programmes. Consequently, we became first in many things in St Thomas, such as the first to have a computer lab, Internet and other amenities.

Transition to Dinthill Technical

When I left St Thomas, the school was so successful that many established schools and their boards wanted me to head their institutions. But I always dreamt of being at Dinthill Technical High School. In fact, when I was a student at Mico and was asked to write about the institution I would like to head, I wrote about Dinthill because, at the time, it was the premier institution in agriculture. When I went to Dinthill however, I was disappointed. Agriculture was almost non-existent. The staff was below par and even the student body was not fit for a technical school.

I made it clear that all teachers had to have at least a first degree. I remember telling a teacher that I was not a "chicken"; I was an "eagle". I did not look at eggs as mere eggs since even crocodiles laid eggs. I told the staff then that we were going to make Dinthill one of the top institutions and that we had three years to do it. The first emphasis was teacher training and development. The importance of professional development in schools cannot be overemphasized: it is the process provided for teachers and the support staff that ensures that organizational and individual needs are being met. It was important for the support staff to be as competent as their counterparts in teaching. All categories of workers are important.

Another initiative that was pursued by the school was the upgrading of the infrastructure. We began by cleaning, landscaping and planting trees to give the campus a facelift. The success of this initiative inspired the Task Force on Educational Reform to recommend in its 2004 report that schools embark on a programme to rehabilitate their structures to international standards. Such a project calls for a collaborative effort on the part of all stakeholders. There is the tendency for administrators, school boards and communities in

Jamaica to work in very poor conditions, waiting for the government to make the change. I did not wait for the government; I used the available human and material resources to improve the infrastructure, partnering with the Petroleum Corporation of Jamaica, West Indies Alumina Company and Trade Winds Citrus Company.

For me, every area of the school is an income-generating opportunity, meaning that all areas must be sustainable – the farm, the auditorium (for rental), all technology and vocational areas – all must be commissioned and the surplus used for renewal and maintenance. Government's subvention is basically for emoluments. Administrators are therefore charged with the responsibility of being principals as well as school managers.

Relationship with the Central Ministry and Regional Entities

Although I was open to suggestions from education officers, I did not allow them to lead me. At that time, some lacked the requisite training and experience to lead since many of them had just left training institutions and become officers. I knew what the school needed, and the ministry gave me free rein to execute; so it was not difficult for me to get things going. Reese (2004) notes that good state leadership and good local leadership partnerships can coexist and lead to a cohesive system. She adds that when a culture of expectation is shared, it leads to a change in behaviour and that it is critical for all stakeholders to exist in a culture of collaboration, networking and teambuilding. Chrisman (2005) in a study of successful schools, observes that district (ministry) leadership featured among the top three factors which were most likely to improve students' test scores.

Stakeholders' Support

I implemented a strong agricultural programme at Dinthill. I started with a strong animal husbandry division with the assistance of the then Alcan Jamaica Limited. I met with them and told them what I needed, and they donated a herd of red bulls. I also approached a man who was a pan-Africanist, who I heard was migrating to Africa, and told him what I needed. I did not have much money and so for a small cost he sold me a herd of dairy cattle. In addition, I went to Lloyd Haye, a farmer from Guys Hill, and he gave me some pigs. I also got support from past students, most of them engaging and highly supportive. No doubt they heard about my track record and recognized that I was serious about education. I came with a plan, and there was no hindrance in executing it. By the end of three years the school was propelling to the top, and in time, became one of the top performers nationally.

Reese (2004) concurs with the concept of shared governance to facilitate effectiveness, noting that this can foster a subculture in which faculty and others at a school feel empowered to have a voice – and it can go beyond the formal members of the school. One has to employ input and develop meaningful relationships through community and private partnerships. However, for a real partnership to occur, educators must look at ways the school can initiate this involvement. In such a partnership, school and home share responsibility for children's learning; the relationship is based on mutual respect and acknowledgement of the assets and expertise of each dimension.

Making Learning Your Priority Objective

The most critical improvement at Dinthill was student achievement. When I went to Dinthill, the school only received students who came through the Grade Nine Achievement Test. Hence, the quality of students was not high. However, by the end of the third year, I was able to attract some of the brightest students at the grade 9 level because the programmes that were offered were comparable to any of the top high schools. Not very long after, we started a sixth-form programme, and we had some of the best science teachers. Soon after, we started accepting students at the grade 7 level via the Grade Six Achievement Test. Of course, I had been resisting that, but I recognized that if we wanted a good grade 9, we had to begin the process at grade 7. That is partly what helped to make Dinthill a "scholarship" school and a school of choice.

We also did well in sports, and examination results at the CSEC level were encouraging. We had a very qualified staff when I left in 2012; 40 per cent of the staff had master's degrees and others are pursuing their second degrees. The quality of staff and their leadership potential are important ingredients in students' success. I did not worry so much about the teachers' ability to teach as I worried about their ability to lead the students. One of the worst things for any school is to have a well-trained and qualified staff who do not have the ability to lead, guide and control students. The teacher is to the class what the principal is to the school – the positive catalyst, the facilitator and the instructional leader. This new model of teacher leadership recognizes that teachers are leaders in their own right and schools should not look only to administrators for leadership.

While the formal teacher roles still exist according to Ackerman and Mackenzie (2006), more teachers lead informally by revealing their classroom practice, sharing their expertise, asking questions of colleagues, mentoring new teachers and modelling how teachers collaborate on issues of practice. These teacher-leaders, according to them, empowered by their confidence in themselves and their colleagues, hold the key to improved learning and offer new contexts and alternatives for genuine school change – forcing schools out of established frames of reference and towards genuine improvement. From the very beginning and also by our timetabling, we immersed students in a competency-based programme whether in business, engineering, foods and so forth. We need to realize that the main purpose of education is to have a skilled workforce. The tragedy in our high school system today is that many of our students are leaving with up to sixteen CSEC and CAPE subjects and are unable to find employment because they have not been competency-based trained. One policy at Dinthill that accounted for our success is that we did not allow students to sit more than eight CSEC subjects. If students wanted to take more than eight, they had to demonstrate that they could manage the load. We encouraged our students to concentrate on mathematics and English.

At Dinthill we were not concerned about students passing thirteen or fifteen CSEC subjects. Ours was a holistic programme of study that prepared our students for work or further studies. Their core subjects were their competency-based subjects. For example, if you were focusing on engineering, you had to take physics, chemistry, geography, technical drawing and so forth. If you were studying home economics you had to take chemistry or biology. So when our students graduated they never had problems getting into tertiary institutions because they were trained and equipped.

I do not believe there is any child who is untrainable: you just need to know his or her weaknesses and strengths. I did not pull any student from the mainstream classes. If a child was studying home economics, for example, and was having trouble with chemistry, I might encourage the child to take integrated sciences; however, he or she must *attend* the chemistry classes. There is the tendency, for example, for schools to place students who they believe are not academically inclined in courses of cosmetology and foods and deny them the benefit of taking chemistry or biology, which are critical for the job. You must train everybody for the workforce. We do not laugh at students who may have difficulty reading and yet want to study medicine, because there are many jobs, besides being a doctor, which require knowledge of medicine. These students may pursue jobs as nursing assistants, porters and so forth.

We were more engaged in teaching to the students' strengths. In support of such teaching, Moran, Kornhaber and Gardner (2006, 23) prescribe orchestrating multiple intelligences. They purport that embracing a "multiple intelligences approach can bring about a quiet revolution in the way students see themselves and others". They suggest that instead of students "defining themselves as either 'smart' or 'dumb', they can perceive themselves as potentially smart in a number of ways". This approach fosters collaboration, provides rich experiences and builds active learners. All children must be exposed to the sciences. I believe one of the reasons our students are doing poorly in mathematics and sciences is not because of their inability to grasp these subjects but because of poor teaching and a poor primary school foundation.

The government and many tertiary institutions are now focusing on science, technology, engineering and mathematics (STEM). Our students fail because the teachers at the primary level were not adequately trained in science and mathematics. That is the problem. If you train people they will be able to perform. The Ministry of Education's mantra is "Every child can learn, every child must learn", hence the need for proper training of teachers. We currently train teachers as primary school teachers, special education teachers, science teachers and so forth, but I believe there should be a core of subjects that all teachers must be exposed to, at all levels, after which they can specialize. I do not believe we are training teachers adequately to teach science and mathematics.

Gender and Diversity

I believe that all students have the capacity to perform well regardless of gender. Students will perform well if given the right support, teaching and encouragement. Our students are failing, not because of gender but because they are ill-prepared. Notwithstanding, research and standardized tests worldwide reveal that on average girls outperform boys. In fact, a study by the US Agency for International Development which examined the performance of boys and girls in the Jamaican education system showed that "while boys lag furthest behind in attendance and literacy, girls also perform below age- and grade-appropriate levels" (2005, vii). So while boys were performing below girls, the girls themselves were underperforming. In presenting the reasons for this overall unfavourable performance, the agency report pointed out that "alongside gender inequalities, the study shows an education system with wide variation and inequalities in terms of physical, social, and human resources, including staffing, quality of instruction and leadership. The net effect of these systemic inequalities is that significant numbers of both boys and girls perform at unacceptable academic standards, which puts them at a disadvantage for realizing their full potential."

An earlier study conducted in Jamaica (Evans 2001) revealed that boys tend to be more disruptive, do not pay attention, play a lot, fidget, move around, are absent from class and receive more corporal punishment than girls. In addition, teachers tend to treat boys differently from girls, and both boys and girls reported that boys were treated unfairly. The task to improve academic performance is multifaceted. And the present initiative at the school and national level is a good start.

Conclusion

I was able to be a successful leader based on the partnership that was forged with various stakeholders. It does not matter how good a leader someone is, he or she cannot do it alone. Hallinger and Heck (1996) contend that school leadership and its effects must stretch beyond the principalship and be diffused among the school community members. School leadership effectiveness is therefore highly dependent on the various stakeholders' abilities to cultivate effective schools. Truly effective school leadership should not be the responsibility of one individual; it should be a cooperative effort involving a number of individuals – from the state level to the district level to the classroom (Reese 2004).

References

Ackerman, R., and S. McKenzie. 2006. "Uncovering Teacher Leadership". *Educational Leadership* 63 (8): 66–70.
Bear, G.G. 2005. *Developing Self-Discipline and Preventing and Correcting Misbehavior.* With A. Cavalier and M. Manning. Boston: Allyn and Bacon.
Brookover, W.B., and L.W. Lezotte. 1979. "School Effectiveness and School Improvement". *International Journal of Leadership* 3 (4): 242–57.
Chrisman, V. 2005. "How Schools Sustain Success". *Educational Leadership* 62 (5): 16–20.
Evans, H. 2001. *Inside Jamaican Schools.* Kingston: University of the West Indies Press.
Ezenne, A. 2011. *Human Resource Management in Education: Developing Countries' Perspectives.* Charlotte, NC: Information Age Publishing, Inc.
Hallinger, P., and R.H. Heck. 1998. "Exploring the Principals' Contribution to School Effectiveness". *School Effectiveness and School Improvement* 9: 157–202.
Lambert, L. 2003. *Leadership Capacity for Lasting School Improvement.* VA: Association for Supervision and Curriculum Development.
Moran, S., M. Kornhaber and H. Gardner. 2006. "Orchestrating Multiple Intelligences". *Educational Leadership* 64 (1): 22–27.
Reese, S. 2004. "Effective School Leadership". *Techniques: Connecting Education and Careers* 79 (6): 18–21.
Sweeny, J. 1982. "Research Synthesis on Effective School Leadership". *Educational Leadership* 39 (5): 346–52.
Task Force on Educational Reform. 2004. *A Transformed Education System.* Kingston: Jamaica Information Service.
USAID (United States Agency for International Development). 2005. *A Gender Analysis of the Educational Achievement of Boys and Girls in the Jamaican Educational System.* Washington, DC: USAID. http://pdf.usaid.gov/pdf_docs/Pnade595.pdf.

CHAPTER 16

IMPROVING PERFORMANCE THROUGH RELATIONSHIP AND CULTURE

MARGARET CAMPBELL

THREE PRINCIPALS LED ST GEORGE'S COLLEGE during my six-year tenure as a teacher and senior teacher before I was appointed principal. By observing their differing styles, I identified the skills and characteristics which contributed to good school leadership and those which resulted in ineffective leadership. Those traits observed in the principals I served which contributed to ineffective leadership were poor communication and people skills, failure to communicate a vision and mission, a laissez-faire leadership style with a corresponding lack of monitoring and accountability, a dictatorial leadership style, and favouritism.

In 2006, the inconceivable happened. I was asked by a board member of a traditional all-boys secondary school to apply for the position as principal, and after a rigorous interview I was selected for the position. The fracas that followed, highlighted in the media, lasted for two months, as the country reacted negatively to the idea of a woman leading a boys' school. The fact that the outgoing principal was a respected alumnus and had done an excellent job of school improvement during his two years of leadership added fuel to the fire. Staff, parents, students, alumni and many in the society, openly resented my selection, focusing largely on gender and inexperience.

That first year was a challenge, the likes of which I had not experienced before and have not experienced since. I was careful not to make drastic changes that year unless they were urgent for school improvement. Instead, I spent a great deal of time observing, reflecting and planning. Before the start of school in September, I held meetings with smaller groupings of staff (ancillary, administrative, senior teachers and other teachers), to allow for more-personal interaction, as an antecedent to meeting with the staff as a whole. I also met with other stakeholders.

First Encounters

At the first meeting with parents for the academic year, a parent – a detractor intent on mischief-making – asked a question at the microphone requiring historic financial data, which he knew I could not reasonably address. As I questioned the bursar at the back of the room, the parent remarked to the audience, rudely using the vernacular, that I was ignoring him while he was asking his question. I maintained my pleasant demeanour, stiffened my spine and walked calmly to the microphone. I apologized to the audience and explained that I was obtaining the information from the bursar on their behalf. As I explained, the parent shouted something from the audience. I paused to address him, saying, "May I please have some respect", and the audience applauded. This was the first step to a positive relationship with parents.

Throughout the year, a handful of parents led by my antagonist, met on the campus in the mornings and remained talking in the parking lot well into the morning session. They were often rude and confrontational on many of the decisions that I made. I held my temper in check, always making sure to address them calmly and courteously but also firmly. I wrote a letter asking all parents to leave the campus by 7:45 a.m. when school started and offered a meeting space for those who needed it after that time. No one took up the offer of the meeting space, but the parents started leaving by 7:45 a.m. as requested. As principal, I have found that diplomatic solutions to problems with parents are usually more effective than declaring war. At the end of the day, however, parents must conform to the boundaries that are set for appropriate interaction with the school.

Academic staff meetings were largely monologues. Attempts to invite staff participation were met with stony silence, as teachers communicated their dissatisfaction through passive aggression. One of the teachers on staff, beloved by many, was reported for inappropriate conduct. Disciplinary action brought against him fuelled the staff's anti-principal campaign. Even staff who rejected his conduct, favoured their colleague in order to demonstrate their lack of favour for me. Those were dark days indeed and the horror stories of that year could fill many journal pages.

At the end of the year, the parent of a few paragraphs earlier, funded the preparation of a brochure lambasting the dean of students (new that year as well) and me. Students wrote the articles and created caricatures of the dean as a "country bumpkin" and me as the devil, complete with horns, tail and a pitchfork. The parent was observed distributing the offensive material on the campus. The document was libellous and mendacious, and on a personal note, quite hurtful. Two members of staff and a neighbouring principal sent me orchids of encouragement. Two supportive alumni, attorneys, offered to take the matter to court on my behalf. I rejected the offer, deciding to "take the high road" in the interest of diffusing fires and building relationships. The next staff meeting was alive with suggestions for the upcoming school year. I was puzzled. Staff members explained to me later that the staff felt justified in their ill-treatment of the principal but they were incensed by the idea of parents and students doing the same. There was an immediate improvement in staff relations.

The Alumni

The school has an active alumni association. The principal is an ex officio member of the executive board of the association. During my early years, I attended every meeting of the executive board to build relationships and encourage support of the school. The association was all male. The first meeting was amusing as some of the men, accustomed to their own company, swore as they spoke and then quickly apologized to me. After a few meetings, I took pity on the gathering and suggested that it would be better for me to give my report early in the meeting and take my leave, if they would allow. This worked very well.

In addition to the local alumni chapter, there were two active foreign chapters; one in the United States and one in Canada. I attended annual fundraising functions of both chapters to form relationships. At each function, I was asked to share for a few minutes about the school. I had a formula. I started by thanking the audience for contributing to the students' welfare through their presence and highlighted achievements especially in academics and sports. I continued by sharing a particularly touching human interest story about a student that subtly highlighted both how wonderful the student was and how much he deserved support. I ended by pleading for their generous contributions and pointed out that I would happily receive cheques at my table. The personal contact with the association's chapters was very important and influenced generous sustained donations to the school.

Over the years, maintaining contact with the alumni by attending and addressing functions, the distribution of electronic newsletters, maintaining a school website and so forth have been important in encouraging support from this stakeholder group. They like to be "kept in the loop". I am on the mailing list of several alumni groups. This allows me to monitor correspondences. I usually do so without interference, intervening occasionally to share positive happenings at the school or when misconceptions about the school arise and fires need to be doused before they spring into full flame. The three chapters used to operate independently. The school has proven to be a unifying force for them.

Community Engagement

My school is located on the outskirts of the inner city. Early in my first year, members of that community visited me seeking financial support. They insisted that the previous principals used to assist them. I pointed out that I did not have the personal resources to assist and could not use the school's funds in that way. I agreed to allow the members of the community's football team to use our field free of charge for training and selected one affordable item of their gear to seek funding to demonstrate my support of the community. Members of the community were awarded jobs on the campus for maintenance projects.

Once in those early days, a group of men from the community was asked to paint a building on the campus. They had done work for us in the past. They were joined by a new member who attempted to intimidate me into paying four times a reasonable rate for painting the building. When I refused, he became threatening. I stood my ground and assigned the job elsewhere. The other members of the group blamed him for causing them to lose the job. The next year the quoted price was reasonable.

When the school campus was invaded during the West Kingston incursion of 2008, and evidence pointed to the involvement of members of the surrounding community, I removed the privilege of using the field previously extended to the community's football team. I pointed out that if the community could not take care of the school then we would have to do it ourselves and that would start by making our property more insular. Some of the items stolen were returned. The community recommitted their support to the school and, after two months, was once again allowed access to the school's facilities with an improved and, from then on, a positive relationship.

In my experience, it is important for principals to be firm in demonstrating responsibility for the school. The board, alumni, parents, community and other stakeholders must understand from the leadership demonstrated that the principal is in authority. This does not have to be presented in a high-handed manner but with firmness, respect and humility, inviting appropriate and beneficial support.

Shaping a Positive School Culture

The guiding philosophies of my school are iterated in a vision statement, mission statement and in the school's motto, "For the greater glory of God". This philosophy of striving for excellence in order to give glory to God through service to humanity mirrors my personal philosophy, the driving force in my personal and professional life.

In order to motivate the school community to act on this philosophy, I define a theme annually which acts as a goal for the year. The theme is introduced at the first senior teachers' meeting for the year and then at all other meetings of staff and orientation sessions for students. The theme is also promoted to parents and alumni to engender community support and it is used for every school function for the academic year. Banners created for each theme are displayed throughout orientation week.

One year, I set a goal for the book-room coordinator: no parent or student should spend more than fifteen minutes collecting rental books. He rose to the challenge and we received commendations from many parents. One parent added her commendations but made the observation that the rooms where books were being distributed had cobwebs in the ceiling. She was right. In an effort to complete the distribution before the start of school, the rooms had not been thoroughly cleaned. If we would like to find cobwebs in the ceiling, they can always be found, but I encourage parents, as I share that story every year, that when they see the cobwebs, they bring along a cob webbing broom and help us to remove them. I ask annually for positive parental support of the school and an attitude of solving problems once they have been identified. Staff and students are encouraged in the same way. I encourage everyone to refrain from visiting my office once they have identified a problem, unless they have a few suggestions for solving it. In this way a problem-solving culture is being shaped in the school. So a culture has been established for the school. And as Lunenburg and Ornstein (2008, 69) note, the "organization's cumulative learning . . . [is] reflected in organizational structure, people, administrative processes, and external environment".

Senior Teachers and Middle Managers

Over the years, I have been very careful in the selection of senior teachers. These positions should not be seen as a reward for long service but should be offered to staff members identified as the most competent school leaders. Good senior teachers must first be good teachers in order to be an example for junior peers. They should also exhibit strong leadership qualities, be open to growth and be able to function as a part of a team led by the principal. In other words, it is folly to select someone who is incompetent even if she or he has been at the school for twenty years or someone who has demonstrated an inability or unwillingness to support the principal and administration. In one instance, in support of this philosophy, I selected a dedicated young teacher who at the time had a four-year tenure. He was the youngest in his department but stood out in his diligent performance as a teacher, demonstrating good leadership, intrinsic motivation and a spirit of volunteerism. After his selection, he was so focused on his role that he spared no time to focus on the resentment directed at him by his colleagues. He continues to excel as a highly efficient and effective school leader.

In another controversial selection, a new head was named for the physical education department, but the appointee had been approved for eight months' vacation leave and so an interim head had to be chosen. None of the other members of the small department could be considered for leadership. The mathematics teacher who was therefore asked to act had no experience as a head of department or teaching physical education and became the first female head of an all-male department. While I would not normally recommend this course of action because "on paper" she was completely unsuitable, this teacher was special. She demonstrated excellent leadership potential in her role as teacher. She did an outstanding job "holding the fort" in the face of tremendous opposition, until the new head of department returned from leave.

In my first year, I held weekly administrative team meetings with the vice principals. Later, I expanded the team to include the dean of students, director of guidance, campus minister and bursar, for greater distribution of leadership. The two vice principals each had their strengths but they did not work well together. At times their attitude towards each other was openly disrespectful. Rather than confronting them in an already tense situation, I demonstrated the respect I expected and the value I placed on their input. When one interrupted the other, I would ask that the speaker be allowed to finish. In a short time, the tone of our meetings became more positive. Friends we were not, but colleagues we became.

There were two senior teacher groups: form supervisors who met with the dean of students to address matters of discipline, and an academic council comprising heads of departments and the vice principals and led by the upper school vice principal. I combined the two groups and set about changing the culture so that senior teachers would see themselves as leaders; middle managers focused together on both academic and disciplinary concerns and all other aspects of school life.

Professional Development

As a leader in the field of education, the principal must also demonstrate the importance of learning by being a learner, participating in ongoing professional development and always growing (Lovely 2004). As principal, I have a firm commitment to the professional development of both teaching staff and support staff. Each year, areas of focus for teaching are identified and professional development is planned in support of that focus. In the past, external presenters were invited by the principal to do seminars and workshops. In the more recent past, I selected presenters from the academic staff of the school. For the past two years, however, a senior teacher has assumed responsibility for staff development at my request. Her job is made easier by the fact that staff members often volunteer to do presentations. Metacognition, brain-based learning and learning related to gender, teaching for critical thinking, personal health, collegiality and clinical supervision are some of the areas that have been addressed by staff members in development workshops. All staff-led workshops have met a high standard.

In order to maintain the momentum of teacher learning, I am constantly in research mode. I make it a point of duty to keep abreast of innovations in technology and to communicate my findings at every opportunity. In other words, I demonstrate that I am a learner to encourage others to do the same. I then encourage teachers to do their own research and share that research with their colleagues. It took some time to change the culture from one of individuality by "deprivatizing" teaching and fostering a culture of collegiality, which has been worth the effort.

Teacher Supervision and Evaluation

The effective supervision and evaluation of teachers is important to continuous school improvement (DiPoala and Hoy 2014). By fairly and honestly evaluating teachers for the purpose of benefiting from each other's strengths and providing remedies for identified weaknesses, improvements in teaching and therefore student performance can be realized. While the principal must accept responsibility for ensuring that systems of evaluation are in place, responsibility for the actual process must be delegated to senior teachers. At the start of the process, teachers identify goals and objectives for the academic year based on the outcomes of their previous evaluation and desired outcomes for the current period. During the period of evaluation, the supervisor is expected to visit classes. They need not stay for the entire session but are encouraged to perform three-minute walk-throughs. Feedback, verbal and in writing, should be provided to the teachers, highlighting positives of the lesson and areas requiring improvement. Teachers are then held accountable for addressing the weaknesses highlighted with the support of the head of department. Senior teachers are invited to openly share summaries of their observations with other senior teachers at monthly meetings. This allows other senior teachers to have input. Towards the end of the evaluation period, a formal evaluation is completed, spearheaded by the heads of departments, supported by input from form supervisors. Discussion of the evaluation is held with each teacher before both parties sign off on the form.

Senior teachers are evaluated in a similar way, using a form specially created to evaluate the teacher in his or her leadership role. Goals are set by the senior teachers based on feedback from their previous evaluation. At the end of the evaluation period, the teachers are asked to evaluate themselves using the form provided. They then participate in an interview with the administrative team of the school to review the evaluation. Strengths and weaknesses are discussed, and new goals are set to capitalize on strengths and address weaknesses in the next evaluation period. The process has been very effective in holding senior teachers accountable for performance in their roles.

Using Data to Make a Difference

Walter et al. (2014, 103) remind us that "principals and teachers have been given the enormous task of taking data . . . and turning this information into a systematic plan to improve instructional practice and student achievement". Therefore, both principals and teachers must be prepared to use assessment data to improve instruction. For St George's College, at the end of every reporting period, student performance data are analysed. Senior teachers are provided with summary data by teacher and by class for their analysis. Heads of departments are expected to focus on subjects and teachers, while supervisors are expected to focus on year groups and classes within year groups with the aim of identifying problem areas and creating strategies to address them. The analysis should be honest; for example, a head of department who indicates that the department is performing well must justify why teacher X has a class average performance of 52 per cent when all other classes in the group have averages over 70 per cent. The head of department must also describe problems identified and strategies that have been put into place by the teacher, head of department or the department to improve the students' performance.

In the case of CSEC data, grades are analysed as well as profiles in order to determine specific weaknesses in teaching and to modify curricula or teaching strategies. One year, in an attempt to improve mathematics performance, the curriculum was modified to utilize a recommended spiral approach to the teaching of the subject. Using this approach, a topic would be visited repeatedly throughout the year, with expanded scope in each instance. Mathematics performance fell. Research into the ways boys learn best revealed that they prefer to learn one topic at a time in great depth before moving to another rather than in the piecemeal approach we had taken. The scope and sequence of the curriculum was again modified to take greater advantage of this finding, and performance improved. As Boudett, City and Murnane (2013, 48) indicate, "educators and parents often want to trace a student's development" and their performance data are the primary source in this effort.

Student Discipline

Student leaders are very aware that the principal's office is one that hears and facilitates the implementation of good ideas, and they frequently make use of that knowledge. Many good innovations have come from them. When students approach me with a complaint, they are asked to suggest solutions and frequently asked to act on them; for example, when students complain about the canteen, they are encouraged to respectfully share their concern with the canteen manager and provide feedback on the result. The results have been very positive and I have not yet had to intervene.

I am unrelenting in my quest for appropriate student discipline. In my early years at the school, the standard of discipline was unsatisfactory. I wasted no time in addressing this as indiscipline compromises learning. One of our senior teacher positions is assigned as dean of students, with a significantly lighter schedule to allow time for him to be dedicated to the development of a *culture of discipline*, as opposed to the administration of punishment. In order to achieve this culture, required standards, defined in our code of conduct, were highlighted for a period with a planned and communicated date for enforcement. The requirement was then enforced consistently and rigorously, but not always rigidly, until it became the norm. For example, many students wore sneakers though the code of dress calls for dress shoes. For one term, we communicated our intention to enforce the rule the following term, frequently using multiple media. At the start of the next term, students who were still wearing sneakers were identified and their parents were called to bring replacement shoes or collect the student. However, where parents made a commitment to adhere to the rule by an agreed date, leniency was exercised. Over time, after consistently enforcing the rule, incidences of the infraction were significantly reduced.

While I expect discipline, I also anticipate indiscipline. Students, like all of us, make mistakes. Too many of them avoid taking responsibility when they do the wrong thing. Discipline will not improve in this type of environment. I therefore launched a campaign to improve the character of students by consistently communicating a four-step path to reconciliation. The junior students quote it along with me: "When I do the wrong thing: accept responsibility, apologize, accept the consequences, do whatever it takes to make it right." The students appear to be listening.

Managing students must be a school community affair which starts in the classroom. An engaging lesson is the first line of attack on poor discipline. Attentive students tend not to be disruptive. Teachers then must take full responsibility for discipline in their classrooms, referring only the most serious cases to higher authority. As teachers are considered for employment, they are asked to share the worst discipline they have encountered and how they responded. A situation of extreme student indiscipline is also posed and their response is examined to determine to what extent they see the locus of control for classroom behaviour as resting within themselves. Teachers are reminded often of their responsibility in this regard and training is provided in classroom management. Though I have very high expectations for proper discipline by all students, I also try to ensure that my expectations are reasonable and achievable.

References

Boudett, K.P., E.A. City and R.J. Murnane. 2013. *Data Wise: A Step-by-Step Guide to Using Assessment Results to Improve Teaching and Learning.* Cambridge, MA: Harvard Education Press.

DiPaola, M.F., and W.K. Hoy. 2014. *Improving Instruction through Supervision, Evaluation, and Professional Development.* Charlotte, NC: Information Age Publishing, Inc.

Lovely, S. 2004. *Staff the Principalship: Finding Coaching, and Mentoring School Leaders.* Alexandria, VA: Association for Supervision and Curriculum Development.

Lunenburg, F.C., and A.C. Ornstein. 2008. *Educational Administration.* Belmont, CA: Wadworth.

Walter, L.B., J. Shen, R. Leneway and J.M. Rainey. "Sustaining Data-Informed Decision Making". In *From Policy to Practice: Sustainable Innovation in School Leadership Preparation and Development*, edited by K.L. Suzan, 101–20. Charlotte, NC: Information Age Publishing, Inc.

CHAPTER 17

STUDENT SUCCESS
A Primary Concern

FAITH CLEMMINGS

I STARTED MY CAREER AS PRINCIPAL of Montego Bay High School in July 1997. Based on my experience as a classroom teacher, a form teacher, head of department and senior teacher, I assumed the role with a vision of incorporating into the programme of the school some things that I had hoped to see and of eliminating things I would have preferred not to see in the various schools I worked in over the years. I came with a determination to have a team working with me to create a school climate that emphasized and enhanced instruction and learning, a climate where each child, regardless of academic capability, can achieve his or her highest potential and leave school not only academically successful but also able to fit into society with grace, dignity and a sense of purpose.

Early Years as a Principal

The first few years were spent learning on the job, trying to make my own personal mark and getting my staff (academic, ancillary and administrative) to buy into the idea that we were a team and that every person's attitude and action had a direct effect in the successful functioning of this educational institution. From the outset, I tried to impress upon the students the importance of a sound education and the pivotal role they played in their own learning and development. It was challenging at times but, because of several good qualities already existing in the school, the foundation was there for me to build on. In the initial stages I also endeavoured to strengthen the parent-teacher association, the past students association and the general relationship with all the stakeholders. My purpose was to have each person working as an important and effective member of the Montego Bay High School family.

I believe that in every school the stakeholders are crucial to the success of the school. At my first meeting of the board of governors we frankly discussed the programmes of the school. The board freely expressed its expectations of me and I in turn expressed mine of them. Throughout my tenure, I had excellent support from the board of governors. There was constant dialogue between board and principal.

At the first meeting with the teachers (first with senior teachers and then with regular teachers), I shared my vision and my goals for the school. I reiterated my belief in the importance of teamwork. I reminded teachers that professional work and behaviour were expected from professionals. I made room for frank discussions, disagreements, suggestions, criticisms and goal-setting. Bear in mind that I was a teacher at this school before I became principal. The transition was smooth, mainly because of the cooperation from and the commitment of the teachers.

My next set of stakeholders was my precious students. My first address to them was quite easy. Having taught many of them, I had good relationships with them. However, in my role as principal, I had to set some guidelines. My main thrust to them was that they came to school for no other reason than to get a rounded education which would prepare them for further studies and for good social interaction and integration. I emphasized the importance of setting high standards of achievement at all levels.

In my first address to the administrative staff, I reminded them of the crucial role they played in the running of the school, as most times they were the first persons with whom the outside world came into contact. It was important that they be efficient and productive and that their interaction with parents, students, teachers and visitors reflect the pleasant tone of the school. I impressed upon them the importance of accuracy and promptness in their work for teachers, students and parents and that records must be treated with utmost care and confidentiality. I tried to impress upon the ancillary staff the importance of their role in keeping the school plant clean and attractive and helping in the guidance, protection and care of the students. The need for a high standard of performance in carrying out their responsibilities was emphasized, and they were made to know that the school's success depended heavily on them.

After outlining my vision for the school at my first parent-teacher association meeting, I was promised a school bus by a parent. This was delivered within weeks of the promise. The school was especially blessed during my tenure with past students' associations located in Montego Bay, Kingston, Miami, New York and Canada. Every effort was made to foster good relationships between these associations and the school.

The critical stakeholder was my employer, the Ministry of Education. From the outset, I reminded myself and my staff that we were answerable in everything to the ministry. I made sure that I knew the role of the officers with whom I had to interact. Fortunately for me and the school, although we had some moments of disagreement, the overall relationship between the ministry and the school during my tenure was very cordial and respectful.

My Leadership Style

Researchers suggest that teachers are inclined to be more satisfied when they perceive the principal as a trustworthy person who shares his or her experience and facilitates communication in the school context (Nguni, Sleegers and Denessen 2006). I tried to share my expectations and plans with my senior staff, get their feedback and then take it to the teachers. I had to understand, however, that the fact that the senior teachers might have unanimously agreed to a particular suggestion did not mean that the others would wholeheartedly agree. Sometimes, what seemed to have been an excellent idea among middle managers proved to be unrealistic or unworkable when examined from other angles by the teachers. In such a case, I had to graciously acknowledge the intuition and wisdom of a junior member and lead my seniors to accept it. Each teacher had to be made to feel that he or she played an integral and important role in the life of the school.

Another way of getting members of staff to work with me was to show interest in their personal life (without being inquisitive). A teacher who recently returned from maternity leave would be asked from time to time, "How is the baby doing?" Another who had lost a family member through death would be given a gentle rub on the shoulder with, "All the best for today." Teachers and other workers should not feel that they are simply "cogs in a wheel". Maxwell (2005, 108) states, "Don't ever underestimate the importance of building relational bridges between yourself and the people you lead."

A crucial aspect of my leadership style was a willingness to learn from everyone in the school community. Each person, I believed, had the ability to make a meaningful contribution to the school's welfare. I remembered having to repeatedly repair the support for the wooden platform in the auditorium. The last time I brought someone in to do some repairs, one of the ancillary members of staff suggested that I reinforce the platform; I thanked him and immediately put plans in place to install concrete support. In another example, we had a practice of awarding prizes to students who came first, second and third in their end-of-year examinations. I noticed, however, as I went through the students reports that there were students each year who got prizes for attaining first, second and third places but their averages were far from "prize worthy", while there were students who were tenth and fifteenth in position who had averages of eighty and above eighty and got no prizes. I shared my concern at a staff meeting. It was a junior member of staff who suggested that we could still keep the practice of awarding prizes to first, second and third because some students' 60 per cent may be their best. She further suggested that we introduce a "gold club award" for all students with averages of eighty and above. The suggestion was accepted and implemented and continues to this day.

Evaluation applies very critically to the students. Individual class teachers were expected to design ways of encouraging their respective classes to desire excellence both in their academic performance and behaviour. In my address to the students, the words, "This is Montego Bay High School and we do everything here to the best of our ability. We are the best!" would ring out. Department heads, in discussion with their teachers, would work out the monthly, weekly or fortnightly evaluation of students in addition to the end-of-term examinations administered schoolwide. The result of the analysis of these tests and examinations would be shared in the department and at senior teachers meetings. The principal, in turn, would invite parents to have dialogue with underperforming children. Follow up would then take place.

Evaluation or appraisal of staff is an integral aspect of the leadership function. Teachers' work plans had to be checked regularly and classes visited occasionally by both supervisors and the principal. Staff members were constantly reminded by their supervisors in their departments, and by me, of their duties and responsibilities. From time to time internal evaluations took place, and this was usually followed by evaluation in the suggested format by the Ministry of Education. Supervisors would meet with the teachers in their charge to discuss the findings and, if necessary, make referrals to me especially if there were disagreements in the conclusions reached by the supervisor. I would go through all the assessment reports to get feedback on the performance of staff members. If necessary, I would call in a teacher and have dialogue.

Discipline

Like every other school principal, I had my challenges. Occasionally, I would have to deal with a teacher who, even after much dialogue did not fall in line with some of the rules and guidelines of the institution. What made it even more difficult was when the teacher had excellent teaching skills and got good results but would not adhere to the rules. I found that after several attempts at firm but gentle persuasion and commending the good qualities, the teacher would fall in line.

Challenges also arose with the Ministry of Education sometimes with regard to funding for the refurbishing of key areas. All three laboratories, physics, chemistry and biology, badly needed refurbishing. In 2006, a massive fundraising drive and begging spree headed by the department head raised J$970,836 to improve the physics lab. On the heels of that, another drive was launched. We raised J$1,607,216.53 along with parents' contributions to the school's development fund to refurbish the biology lab.

Another challenge we encountered was having to teach a grade 9 achievement class that we got in October of the school year. Most of the students had not mastered the grade 8 material and so were ill-prepared for grade 9.

After much discussion with the teachers, we agreed to reduce the number of subjects they took, and under the innovative and skilful hands of the teacher of English they were given extra English classes and eventually achieved some measure of success.

Best Practices

Co-curricular Activities

At the school's annual prize-giving ceremony, prizes were awarded in many different categories. Prizes were given for outstanding character traits like honesty, helpfulness and resourcefulness, but most of the prizes and awards were for academic success. The CSEC results over the years have been outstanding. Each year we copped some of the top prizes at the CXC Award Ceremony put on by the Jamaica Association of Principals. In 2004, we had the island's top student, Donnalee Donaldson, in the CXC results. In 2006, we were the top school in the island and the top student in science, humanities and business (three of the four categories). Our results in English language, mathematics, science, Spanish and the business subjects have consistently been above the national average. We consistently had several students passing ten or more subjects, all with distinction.

The school would be amiss if it took all the credit for the high level of academic performance. We have had exemplary parents who ensured that their children did their work to the best of their ability and prepared themselves very well for their examinations. The proud community of parents, past students, Ministry of Education and well-wishers always called in to congratulate the school on its high standard of academic achievement. In addition to the measures taken to ensure academic success, much attention was given to how we used data from student performance at the classroom level and at the CSEC level to drive decisions regarding the deployment of teachers and the quality of supervision of teachers by heads of department. Comparisons were made of the quality of the passes in different subject areas in the CSEC examinations. The breakdown of the results in each subject was examined carefully. Strong areas were compared to weak areas, and instructions given for more effective teaching where necessary.

The Involvement of Past Students in the Life of the School

It was a blessing to have had many past students involved in different aspects of the school. At one time, over 60 per cent of the teachers were past students. The chairman of the school board was a past student. Among other board members were past students. During my tenure, two of the vice principals were past students. The programme of the school fostered the involvement of past students as we invited them to be guest speakers at our school functions and presenters on career day and at parenting seminars. In the surrounding hospitals, many of the doctors were past students, and they "looked out" for the present school family. Some branches of the alumni associations were more involved than others, but all expressed interest in the school and supported it in many ways, from financial support of building projects to helping with needy students, giving scholarships, and accepting invitations to speak with the students on health, legal and social issues at their club meetings. As these alumni shared some of their challenges and difficulties as students, they have been able to motivate and inspire the students.

The Involvement of the Parent-Teacher Association of the School

Burns (1993) accurately focuses on the need for families to work together in order to develop a support system for the development of their children. It is within this context that a partnership approach, involving the family and school, is taken to provide education in an atmosphere of trust and respect for all parties involved. As a result, each constituent including learner, parent, teacher and even school will benefit individually while at the same time enhancing the educational process. One of my very best experiences during my tenure was working with some dedicated, selfless, loyal and truly hardworking parents and teachers in the parent-teacher association. We spent hours late into the night, planning fundraising activities and working on the details of functions to be held and on many other things related to the life of the school.

In 2003, the school was empanelled by the Ministry of Education in the areas of leadership and management; teaching and learning; the learning environment, welfare social, cultural and personal development of the students and other areas. On a scale of one (weak) to five (excellent), the school was rated four. Areas were cited for improvement, and we made efforts to address them. Most important to me in my experience as a leader in my school was the way in which my Christian values determined how I dealt with situations or how I related to those with whom I came into contact. I saw myself as a servant-leader. The Christ-like spirit of a servant is a biblical distinction for Christian leadership. I could not operate outside of my Christian beliefs: my decisions, my interventions, my reprimands were undertaken professionally and firmly but were also accomplished with the utmost regard for the other person as my brother or my sister. Justice often had to be tempered with mercy. Total respect, compassion and sensitivity coloured my decisions. This in no way lessened the impact of my actions or pronouncements. Also as part of the school programme, Christian values were encouraged but not forced on anyone. Religious freedom was alive. In religious education classes, students were allowed to express themselves freely.

Conclusion

As I reflect, I cannot help but think of things that could have been done differently for greater effect or of a treatment that would have reaped greater rewards. I saw where my decision to learn from my mistakes and those of other principals helped me to grow in the post. There was one incident early in my tenure when I punished the entire school. I learned from it because if the same thing happened again, I would never repeat that approach. Standing back and away from the post, I am grateful for those who bought into my vision for the school at that time and who accepted willingly the "Family Affair" idea and worked with me. A strong belief and confidence made a big difference in how I handled setbacks, mistakes and even misgivings. The experience has made me a stronger, more determined person.

References

Burns, R.C. 1993. *Parents and Schools: From Visitors to Partners*. Washington, DC: National Education Association.

Maxwell, J.C. 2005. *The 360-Degree Leader: Developing Your Influence from Anywhere in the Organization*. CA: Nelson Business (Thomas Nelson Inc.).

Nguni, S., P. Sleegers and E. Denessen. 2006. "Transformational and Transactional Leadership Effects on Teachers' Job Satisfaction, Organizational Commitment, and Organizational Citizenship Behavior in Primary Schools: The Tanzanian Case". *School Effectiveness and School Improvement* 17 (2): 145–77.

CHAPTER 18

THE CAMPION EXPERIENCE
Cutting Diamonds

GRACE BASTON

I WAS ONLY THIRTY-SIX YEARS OLD when I first assumed the duties of principal of the Convent of Mercy Academy (Alpha Academy). My relative youth and inexperience could have been formidable obstacles to my taking over leadership from a woman who had served as the school's principal for almost fifty years, but there were several peculiar factors that made the transition remarkably smooth. First, I was a member of the religious congregation that had owned and led the school since its founding in 1894. The previous principal and I were both members of a religious community of women for whom the work of educating young women was a sacred mission (Sisters of Mercy).

The fact that I was an alumna of the school was also a significant factor. This meant that I knew, respected and loved its culture. My predecessor had been my own esteemed principal, a visionary woman, whose influence and impact will be celebrated forever by generations of graduates. Because we were members of the same community, we were friends as well as colleagues. This meant that I was not threatened by her presence and involvement in school matters after her retirement. I invited her to continue to participate in the life of the school as much as she could. I relied heavily on her counsel and insisted that she serve on the school board. She was a rich repository of institutional wisdom and experience on which I drew heavily and frequently. My predecessor understood her role as steward of the school and so was ready to let go of that stewardship at the appropriate time. She allowed me to take full control of the institution but generously responded to any request for assistance. I shall forever be grateful to her for her remarkable example of how one retires from active school leadership with grace.

In 2006, I assume the role of principal of Campion College. Edmund Campion, the patron saint of Campion College, was described by Sir William Cecil in the sixteenth century as "one of the diamonds of England" because of his brilliance. This is an epithet I often use when addressing the students of Campion College. I remind them constantly that they are some of Jamaica's finest diamonds. While this reminder is meant to be an affirmation of the giftedness and immense potential of each student, it is also a daunting and haunting challenge to myself as principal – the person charged with the responsibility for cutting these diamonds, because diamond cutting is that extremely difficult and complex process by which a diamond is transformed from a rough stone into a faceted gem. The reflections which follow are an attempt to document two specific forms of diamond cutting which take place at Campion College. One is the moral and spiritual formation of our students and the other is the assurance of the academic success and well-being of students from difficult socio-economic backgrounds.

Mission and Vision

The founders and owners of the school, the Society of Jesus (Jesuits) are explicit in the school's mission statement that Campion College is "a school committed to building the Kingdom of God – a world characterized by social justice, love and respect for the dignity of every person". Each graduate is to have the following profile: intellectually competent, loving, religious, open to growth and committed to doing justice. This mission is much broader than one narrowly focused on producing students with ten grade 1 passes on regional examinations. It calls for a rigorous programme of character formation, ensuring that we are not just turning out the brightest doctors, lawyers and business people who will be the future heads of North American corporations but, instead, that we are shaping men and women of integrity, rooted in faith and justice, who will be the leaders of our own national and regional transformation.

The Reality

The most common description of Campion College on the streets of Kingston is that it is a "rich, white, uptown school". I believe most people know that 95 per cent of the school's population is of African descent, and that just over 30 per cent of the students here are from primary schools. Children who attend privately managed schools (preparatory schools) are usually those from more-socioeconomically-advantaged backgrounds (OECD 2012). If we use the commonly accepted view that preparatory or primary school attendance is an indicator of a child's socio-economic status, then clearly not all Campion students are "rich" and they are certainly not all "white".

The fact that the average score of all students assigned to Campion College based on performance on the last Grade Six Achievement Test was 96.7 per cent is the clearest indicator of the academic potential of its students. The average Campion College student is intrinsically motivated to excel and is supported by parents who are fiercely committed to their children's success. Many authors emphasize the influence parental involvement has on a child's academic performance. The school's results on the examinations administered by the Caribbean Examinations Council are consistently among the best in the region. It has claimed the titles of top CSEC and CAPE school in Jamaica for the last nine years, and its students earn most of the coveted Jamaican scholarships after each exam cycle. This formula would be adequate if all that was required of Campion College by its leadership was high levels of student achievement, but the noble vision adumbrated in the introduction demands much more. Intellectual competence, as measured by standardized examinations, is only one facet of the profile of a Campion graduate. King and Furrow (2008, 704) suggest that "there exists a positive contribution of religion to adolescent well-being and that religion serves as both a protective influence and a catalyst for positive development". Therefore, each student, by the time of graduation is also to be religious, loving, open to growth and committed to doing justice. This vision calls the school to pay equally strict attention to the moral and spiritual formation of the youngsters in its care. All are to be exposed to a systematic and intentional process of values education.

Moral and Spiritual Formation

Students learn to be punctual because punctuality is modelled by their teachers; they learn to be respectful because they are treated with respect and witness respectful treatment of all within their school community; they learn compassionate service because they accompany their teachers who themselves perform works of charity. This is the philosophy that underpins values education and the moral formation of students at Campion College. It begins with the centrality of the teacher. The entire Campion staff is therefore exposed to the tenets of character education and its imperatives for the adults in a school community.

Each department has done substantial work, for example, on what it means to be intellectually competent in its subject. What should a Campion graduate know, be able to do and value after having studied history for five years here? Our belief is that the answer should be more than simply achieving a grade 1 pass at CSEC with a straight A profile. Surely this would be one very important indicator of competence, but our teachers are working hard to identify and then to develop the strategies to teach and assess the essential life values and attitudes relevant to their subject, without which a student should not rightly be called intellectually competent.

This is an ongoing conversation in our academic departments, which I believe will become even more crucial as teaching continues to move away from being a process of disseminating information. So much information is available to our students on their handheld iPhones that any teacher who is still dictating notes from a textbook is hopelessly redundant. Teachers will have to grapple with the question of what is worthy of being taught, and a good rule of thumb would be, "If you can Google it, don't teach it." Educators reflecting on the future of teaching and learning argue that the ethical dimensions of education are the ones that will come to the fore.

Approach to Discipline

Student Discipline

I have learned that regimentation and discipline are not synonymous. Where the former might be impressive – as in the precision and uniformity displayed by soldiers at a military tattoo, for instance – in a school setting, it can lead to the creation of student automatons – young people afraid to express their individuality and, worst of all, dependent on external structures to determine their actions, incapable of self-monitoring or of making moral decisions from internalized values. Discipline, on the other hand, although having many of the manifestations of regimentation which help in the maintenance of good order in the school environment, has as its ultimate goal, the forming of students into persons who are self-disciplined and truly free. My own approach to student discipline is to provide effective structures and systems that maintain order but at the same time leave ample room for student initiative, creativity and growth in personal responsibility. The ideal of a self-disciplined, self-reliant student will never be realized by mere regimentation. Student discipline has to involve multiple channels for student self-expression and leadership, as well as comprehensive programmes for intentional character formation.

Campion College, like many other schools, has a student handbook with detailed policies and guidelines governing all areas of student life. The posts of dean of discipline and assistant dean of discipline exist precisely for the promotion of discipline and good order. But their work is carried out in collaboration with the guidance department and the grade supervisors, the latter being the senior teachers charged with the "pastoral" care of the students at different grade levels. This collaboration ensures that discipline is not relegated to the punitive but takes into consideration care for the individual student.

Staff Discipline

The administration at Campion College has never asked teachers to be present at the start of the school day unless they have teaching assignments at that time. Teachers are also free to leave campus after their last class of the day. To many this seems a very lax arrangement, one inviting wholesale abuse by unprofessional teachers. Surprisingly, this has not been our experience at Campion. On the contrary, most teachers are at school at the start of the day and many stay long after their last class, grading papers, planning lessons or seeing students for individual help. This unusual freedom allowed to our teachers stems from the administration's insistence that teachers be treated as mature, adult professionals, who want to do their best at their job. Once again, the administration holds teachers accountable, while staying away from regimentation or any form of staff discipline that infantilizes the adults with whom we work.

Lesson plans have to be created and submitted, but apart from the use of a common template, there is no insistence on uniformity of planning style. Teachers are exhorted to dress professionally, but there is no "dress code" posted on the staff notice board. In recent years, the administration has had to deal with the complexity of leading an intergenerational staff with all the different expectations, worldviews, communication styles and cultures of a community of three generations of Jamaicans. The temptation to regiment is very strong, but the consensus is that the problem is better tackled through intentional community-building strategies and ongoing conversations about collegiality and common purpose. So staff-development exercises have included studying self-awareness tools like the Myers-Briggs Personality Profile and the Enneagram, exploring the differences between congeniality and collegiality in school culture, and events and gatherings aimed only at fostering camaraderie, trust and respect among staff.

The School Board

At the time of its founding, Campion College was owned and operated by the Roman Catholic congregation of priests known as the Society of Jesus, or the Jesuits. With their centuries old philosophy of education, known and respected throughout the world, they were very clear about the purpose of the new school started in 1960. Campion College was created to provide Catholic education to its students. This particular brand of Catholic education was Ignatian. Such education was not proselytizing, but the formation of men and women "for others". In later years, that mission was further distilled to create the profile of the graduate of an Ignatian school at the time of graduation or the "grad at grad" profile, which was loving, religious, open to growth, intellectually competent and committed to doing justice.

Like all boards, while it is busy with recommending appointments, leave or termination, ensuring that financial audits are timely and providing legal and other professional advice to the principal, its constant preoccupation is the extent to which the school is fulfilling its mission as a Roman Catholic, Ignatian institution. To this end, the board supports the efforts of the school administration in its character-formation initiatives, its efforts to ensure the welfare of students from challenging socio-economic backgrounds and in the promotion of the ideals of Ignatian education throughout the school community. A concrete example of this kind of support was the visit of a former board chairman to Jesuit schools overseas to study the formation of offices of development and alumni affairs in order to replicate that structure at Campion. This was the genesis of a successful capital campaign which saw the school raising over J$1 million to provide a library facility which would bridge the "digital divide" among its students.

The Role of the Co-curricular Programme and Chaplaincy Department

At Campion College, the whole purpose of the school's broad and rich co-curricular programme is values education, character formation and building community relations. Involvement in sports, the performing arts or any of the fifty–two clubs and societies is meant to teach discipline, dependability, teamwork, confidence, courage, perseverance, loyalty, and a host of other life skills, ideals and virtues.

One significant development in the school's co-curricular programme was the creation of the Campion College Home-Work Centre. This programme involves fifth- and sixth-form students providing tutoring and homework supervision for students from the neighbouring Chambers Lane community – an informal settlement with many of the characteristics of an inner-city community. A generous benefactor of the school, enthused about what this project could mean for the students of that community, donated an entire computer laboratory for the centre. The students from Chambers Lane have access to the Internet for their homework assignments, and their Campion tutors use special software to help those with reading challenges.

This project has contributed to the advancement of our mission in several ways. First, it sent a clear signal to the residents of Chambers Lane that Campion College was eager to enter into a respectful, mutually rewarding arrangement with them. That gesture alone has made a world of a difference in the quality of the relationship between the school and the community. The kind of partnership, in which both the school and the community contribute directly to the strengthening and development of each other, can provide a firm foundation for both educational renewal and community regeneration. Once relationships are established and continually cultivated, these relationships support school recruitment, after-school programming, student safety, parental involvement and student achievement (Chrzanowski, Rans and Thompson 2010).

Second, the project has provided an excellent learning resource for the students of Chambers Lane. The leaders of the community are always effusive in their commendations of this initiative. Third, and most significantly when looked at through the lens of the formation of our charges, the homework centre has provided an opportunity for our privileged students to come face to face with some of the grievous inequities that characterize Jamaica's education system. In their reflections on their service to the children, they often speak of the joy they get from sharing knowledge and forming relationships with their pupils, but they are also outraged by the gaps in the children's education.

Cura Personalis and the Thirty Per Cent

Cura personalis is best translated "care and concern for each individual person". Teaching and learning at Campion College is a dynamic, relational process in which creative methodologies, innovative techniques and resources are used to make every classroom a truly student-centred and interactive space. Twenty years ago, only 5 per cent of the students entering Campion College in First Form were from primary schools. Therefore, approximately 95 per cent of the student population was from upper-middle class and upper class Jamaica. In 2006, the then Jesuit chairman of the board sought permission to address a gathering of principals of primary schools, with the sole purpose of persuading them to send their students to Campion College. He explained that while the owners of the school celebrated Campion's evolution into the school of choice for Jamaica's brightest students, they did not want it to be an institution that catered only to the privileged social elite. Instead, the school wanted to attract the intellectual elite from all strata of Jamaican society, creating a more diverse and enriched population. The chairman assured the principals that Campion welcomed their students and valued their presence in the school community.

Today, over 30 per cent of Campion's population is drawn from primary schools, a movement owing to, in great part, the outstanding work being done in some of our primary schools but also, I believe, in some measure, a result of the chairman's earnest invitation. This shift in Campion's complexion delighted the owners of the school even as it perturbed certain others. Children coming to us from disadvantaged socio-economic backgrounds were to be provided with all the support they needed to ensure not only their academic success but their wholesome development, happiness and sense of well-being at Campion.

First, all members of staff had to be "conscienticized" about the peculiar problems that a child from a primary school background might experience at Campion. Initially, it was an awkward conversation because no one wanted to admit that evils like class prejudice or racism, even in latent forms, could ever be a part of our school culture. The school had an excellent system for managing discipline and so any reported incidence of bullying was thoroughly and speedily dealt with. We were all certain that no teacher would set out to intentionally alienate or make uncomfortable students from any background. And yet we knew so many past students "of humble circumstances" who spoke of their feelings of isolation during their time at Campion. What were those indirect, unintended signals that a student did not belong at Campion? At a Reflection Session on the theme "Students Falling through the Cracks", senior members of the leadership team engaged in extensive, honest self-evaluation around these difficult questions and their deliberations culminated in a strategy for the *cura personalis* of these special students.

The Role of the Guidance Department and the Office of Development and Alumni Affairs

The Office of Development and Alumni Affairs launched a campaign to procure scholarships for students who needed financial assistance to cover the cost of fees and other school-related expenses. The campaign was very successful and allowed the administration to invite any parent who was having difficulties meeting these obligations to apply for a scholarship. Further, the guidance department ascertained which students needed assistance with bus fare and lunch money and these were provided with bus cards and student cards.

The advent of the student card was most providential. While the most publicly celebrated benefit of this system of electronic payment by swipe-cards was the fact that schools would become cashless environments and therefore safer, at Campion College our enthusiasm about the student card (allows the school to remotely add money to a student's account) was because it allowed the school to assist students with lunch money without the embarrassment that characterized such programmes in the past. At one time, students "on welfare" were issued lunch tickets which they presented at the canteen. Another system involved keeping a special register of such students in the canteen, so that the servers would be able to recognize them. Both of these arrangements were unsatisfactory because they exposed the students being assisted in ways that deterred many in genuine need from coming forward. Preserving the dignity of students receiving assistance with lunch money is important in any school, but in an environment like Campion College, it is vital.

The guidance department overcame a similar obstacle with the establishment of the Breakfast Club. The provision of a simple breakfast for students who leave home without this important meal is a feature of welfare programmes in many schools. It was important at Campion that we not call it a programme but a club and that, from the outset, all students were invited to take advantage of its services. So today, some students go to the Breakfast Club because they leave home very early and do not have a chance to have a proper breakfast; some, because their parents cannot afford to provide breakfast at home; some, because they are excited about what is being served that morning; and others, because they simply prefer to have breakfast with their friends at school. It was an ingenious way to remove the stigma which is usually attached to this essential programme.

The Digital Divide

As part of its strategic development plan, Campion is committed to the optimum integration of appropriate technology in its administrative functions and its curriculum delivery. This is in keeping with the recommendations of the report (OECD 2010) which gives a number of reasons that technology is important to an educational system. Those pertinent to our effort include (1) technology can perform several key functions in the change process, including opening up new opportunities that improve teaching and learning – particularly with the affordance of customization of learning to individual learner needs, which is highly supported by the learning sciences; (2)the skills for an adult life include technological literacy, and people who do not acquire and master these competencies may suffer from a new form of the digital divide, which will impact their capacity to effectively operate and thrive in the new knowledge economy; and (3) technology is an integral part of accessing the higher-order competencies, often referred to as twenty-first-century skills, that are also necessary to be productive in today's society. Many of the school's management functions are already automated, parents receive school reports as e-documents, teachers are increasingly making use of e-learning sites, and students are required to have access to technology for their individual research and collaborative work. Here again, 70 per cent of our students have all the technology they need available to them at home, but the remaining 30 per cent could be left behind as the school moves in the direction of becoming an e-school.

Campion College is committed to bridging the "digital divide" that separates the students whose parents can provide enhanced learning environments for them at home from those whose parents simply cannot. The major capital project these past two years has been the construction of a modern library media centre precisely to address this gap. The new library will have small, technology-rich rooms which any group of students can reserve for working collaboratively on projects. It will provide high-speed Internet access throughout the building and a wide range of digital learning resources for all students.

The Principal: Leader, Educator, Administrator

After fifteen years as a high school principal, I still suffer from the "impostor syndrome" that afflicts so many women in positions of leadership. Feelings of inadequacy have always lurked in my consciousness, but over the years I have made peace with them. I try to integrate them into my personality as a form of humility and work hard to make sure that they do not debilitate me. When I confessed my feelings of inadequacy as an administrator to a board chairman once, his reply was that my job was "to inspire". My concern at the time was that I knew so little about timetabling, curriculum review, plant maintenance, fundraising, financial management and all the rest of the nitty gritty of high school management. What did my knowledge of philosophy, my passion for social justice and my formation as a Sister of Mercy have to contribute to moving the mission of Campion College forward? I have thought often about his response and have come to see the wisdom in it.

There were people to do all the nitty-gritty things I worried about, but someone needed to inspire them – to paint for them the broader picture of meaning and mission. That alone convinces me to give of my best in a context of low salaries and less than desirable working conditions. Students needed the same inspiration – to think of their education as not just a tool for their own development but for the transformation of their society, their region, their world. I have learned much about those aspects of high school administration that were so foreign to me when I first started out, but those are not the skills I draw on every day as a leader. At most, I use those skills to supervise the people carrying out those administrative tasks. The skills I use are those that come from my convictions, my ideals, my vision, my very person.

Were I to be asked to offer advice to a new principal, these would be my humble suggestions:

- Make time for self-care, especially for activities that renew and energize you.
- Cultivate the skill of active listening. It is the *sine qua non* of leadership.
- Believe that there is an abundance of talent and potential in your staff waiting to be tapped and act on that belief.
- Pay attention to the 90 per cent of your staff who get excited about a new development in education and learn to listen respectfully to the negative 10 per cent without allowing them to dampen your enthusiasm.
- Never call a meeting for the sole purpose of sharing what could have been communicated by a memo.
- Randomly invite staff members to have tea or coffee with you some mornings.

- Beware of fads in educational theory and practice, but remain open to change.
- Do not take ingratitude from parents, students or teachers personally.
- Actively seek student feedback about everything, but remember that they are children and the school is not a democracy.
- Students are idealistic and like "causes"; capitalize on their generosity and pull them out of themselves in acts of service to the sick, elderly and poor.
- Get to know your parent body and make good use of their skills and other resources.
- Parents can be wildly irrational in matters concerning their children – listen to them politely and then speak your truth.
- Relate respectfully to the Ministry of Education but with the support of your chairman. Do not be afraid to challenge what seems unreasonable or counterproductive coming out of that entity.

References

Chrzanowski, D., S. Rans and R. Thompson. 2010. *Building Mutually Beneficial Relationships between Schools and Communities: The Role of a Connector.* Evanston, IL: Asset Based Community Development Institute. http://www.abcdinstitute.org/docs/Building%20Mutually%20Beneficial%20School-Community%20Relationships.pdf.

King, E. P., and Furrow, J. L. 2004. "Religion as a Resource for Positive Youth Development: Religion, Social Capital, and Moral Outcomes". *Developmental Psychology.* 40(5). 703-13. http://dx.doi.org/10.1787/9789264175006-en.

OECD (Organisation for Economic Co-operation and Development). 2010. *Are the New Millennium Learners Making the Grade? Technology use and Educational Performance in PISA.* Paris: OECD Publishing. http://eskills4jobs.ec.europa.eu/c/document_library/get_file?p_l_id=10713&folderId=10545&name=DLFE-2306.pdf.

———. 2012. *Public and Private Schools: How Management and Funding Relate to Their Socio-economic Profile.* Paris: OECD Publishing.

CHAPTER 19

ISSUES OF IMPORTANCE
Analysis, Reflection and Action

DISRAELI M. HUTTON AND BEVERLY JOHNSON

IN ORDER TO MAXIMIZE THE LESSONS learned from the experiences documented by the effective and successful principals, we examined a number of areas which were germane to their performance. These areas ranged from the ones that represent challenges to their efforts to improve student outcomes to those which facilitated their effective performance. The Jamaican public school system, for example, has developed based on a kind of stratification whereby the children of the poor tend to end up in what is perceived as the non-performing schools, some of which are aided by a shift system which too often fail to advance learning. A brief examination of the historical development of the school system provides an explanation of this phenomenon.

One of the issues which must be addressed with more creativity and determination is violence and indiscipline in schools, which is rooted in and is a reflection of the wider society. The question is, What approaches can be employed to address this problem after so many years of attention and intervention efforts?

Also, with a shift in the gender balance, over 70 per cent of our current principals are females. How does this impact the education system? In addition, those principals who shared their stories seem to display a particular type of personal leadership. Is there then a relationship between this particular leadership trait and their success as school leaders? Finally, active community participation is a major factor in the success of schools. In fact, building support by engaging businesses, alumni, parents, churches and others from the community in general is a strategy that can positively impact the overall running of a school.

The issues that seem to arise from the presentation of the authors include those related to systems structure, such as the nature of the Jamaican education system, the impact of the shift system, and the overall physical and resource requirements for improving performance. The other area is related to challenges and interest, such as indiscipline and violence and the particularities of leadership, respectively. This section will propose solutions which should lead to even greater performance by school leaders. In the end, it is about how these issues are addressed that will make or break a principal's resolve and, more importantly, impact the effective running of a school.

Analysis and elucidation of these issues are necessary, not only to bring a sense of completeness of the book, but also to inform those who seek to learn from the experiences related by principals. Arising from this overview are eight areas representing issues for analysis and elaboration and recommendations for action. Both internal and external stakeholders will have an opportunity to treat the information as a source for reflection and basic guidelines to improve school performance. The areas selected are as follows: (1) Jamaican school system overview, (2) planning option – backward planning, (3) shift system and its impact, (4) mentorship for performance, (5) geographical and economic challenges, (6) violence and indiscipline in schools, (7) gender leadership, and (8) personal beliefs and community support.

Jamaican School System Overview

In the 2013 sectoral debate, the then minister of education, Ronald Thwaites, provided a composite picture of Jamaica's education system. He pointed out:

> Nearly seven hundred thousand (700,000) children and young people are in schools; 69,000 in tertiary institutions, 44,330 registered in our 13 publicly funded tertiary institutions (2011-12 data). [There are] almost one thousand and twenty five (1,025) public schools, six hundred (600) private ones, [and]

three thousand (3,000) basic and infant [schools]. Of the forty five thousand (45,000) employees in the public education sector, twenty seven thousand (27,000) of them are teachers.

Jamaican public schools can be placed in three categories: primary, all-age, and combined primary and junior high; traditional high schools; and upgraded high schools, or secondary schools. Primary, all-age, and primary and junior high are a mix that offer education to students aged six to fourteen years. Note that the junior high segment of the primary and junior schools, which goes up to the age of fourteen years, was designed to serve as a bridge between the primary schools and secondary schools. Traditional high schools are those schools which usually cater for the best-performing students at the secondary level in the Jamaican school system. Some of these schools have been in existence for over two hundred years.

Upgraded high schools or secondary schools, originally known as junior secondary schools, were established in the 1960s to accommodate the students who did not gain entrance to a traditional high school. They were subsequently upgraded and classified as secondary schools, but most of them continue to perform below the traditional secondary schools. According to Miller (1999), the mix of schools at the lower level is a reflection of the historical development of the school system in Jamaica. In the initial stages, all-age schools were the dominant ones, and they provided basic education for children up to grade 9 or age fifteen. The primary schools were later created to serve children ages six to twelve. These schools placed a greater emphasis on the formal preparation of children from an earlier age, despite the presence of basic schools, which are mainly community or privately owned. Overall, at the primary level, academic performance remains weak for many of the primary schools, but there are some schools at which student performance is outstanding (Hutton 2016a). For decades the traditional high schools have been the backbone of the Jamaican education system, and a number of these schools are over two hundred years old (Hutton 2016b). Black (1983) points out that some of the oldest schools in Jamaica were founded in the eighteenth century during the height of slavery. Three of these schools which continue to make a contribution to the Jamaican education system are Manning's High in Westmoreland, Rusea's High in Hanover and Wolmer's High in Kingston.

In 2011, of the 999 public schools, there were 109 upgraded secondary; 52 traditional; and 838 primary, all-age, and primary and junior high schools. High schools not only attract the best-performing students but also receive additional funding (through their strong alumni networks, investments and income-generating projects). In many instances, they receive more than three times in excess of the annual allocation provided by the central ministry (Hutton 2014a). What was also noticeable is that the academic performance of the church-owned schools was superior to many of those owned by the state. With greater effort on the part of the central ministry, coupled with the work of high-performing and effective principals, the performance landscape of upgraded high schools is changing rapidly. This was not necessarily the case fifteen years ago, when these schools admitted students who did not meet the academic requirements to go to traditional high schools. In fact, some of the upgraded schools are now outperforming the traditional high schools. This shift is making it much easier for parents to send their children to these upgraded schools with the confidence that they will receive a quality education.

Many of our schools, regardless of the level, continue to face problems with overcrowding, high absenteeism, inadequate furniture and dilapidated plant among other factors. The spectre of indiscipline and violence is a primary concern. And this problem cannot be resolved easily when the country itself is trapped in a spiral of violence.

Planning Option: Backward Planning

Even though the principals ably outlined the areas of focus they pursued in order to realize the successes they shared, the question is, Could more have been accomplished if they applied more efficient planning techniques and approaches? Certainly, one would expect more could be achieved with greater efficiency as a result of better planning. One approach which has been used successfully in education is backward planning. Wiese (2015, 13) indicates that while backward planning has been used for "large-scale, complex systems as a way to accurately predict the future, an increasing amount of attention is being focused on the implementation of backward planning in smaller contexts such as educational, business and project management". Wiese, Buehler and Griffin (2016, 148) outline the steps of backward planning as "starting with the target goal or completion time in mind, and working back toward the present by identifying the steps needed to attain the goal in reverse-chronological order".

Like any other organization, schools do plan and likewise face the problem of underestimating the time required to complete the projects they implement. Optimistic bias is therefore a real problem which stems from factors that are external to the project being implemented, "such as competing activities, interruptions, delays, and procrastination" (Wiese, Buehler and Griffin 2016, 147). Backward planning or design can be used in an undetermined type of setting. For instance, in the classroom setting, the three stages required for backward planning include identifying desired outcomes, determining acceptable evidence, and planning learning experiences and instruction (Wiggins and McTighe 1998). For the first stage, the goal is to determine what the learner should know, understand and be able to do. At this stage, the standards for performance must be established (McTighe and Wiggins 2004). At the second stage, it is important that the data be collected and analysed in order to determine whether learning meets the standards set at the first stage. The evidence must be based on a range of sources of assessment and different types of measures (Hamilton et al. 2009). For the third stage, focus is on the selection of content and experience to be taught and the techniques and methodology which will be most appropriate for imparting the skills, knowledge and understanding. Ball Foundation (2016) identifies four stages for backward planning appropriate for a workplace setting and which, in our view, can be appropriated by school leaders:

1. Define your goal. This means that the organization has to decide on the goal to be accomplished.
2. Identify the steps and sequence needed to achieve your goals. Determine what is required, when, and the resources necessary to implement the tasks identified. The more precise the information gathered, the better the chances for a timely implementation process.
3. Create a deadline-driven timeline. Identify completion date, milestone, and related steps to be completed, *in reverse order.*
4. Seek support. Seek input from others who will be impacted by the final

outcome. Any input from others who should be in the know will be of worth.

Backward planning provides the tool to plan and execute projects and programme with greater assurance of success. The extent to which every effort is made to remove optimistic bias will bring the project into a more realistic and predictable framework and thereby increase the chances for success.

The Shift System and Its Impact

The shift system was first introduced to the Jamaican education system in 1972 (on a trial basis), and Jones Town Primary and Tarrant Secondary were the first two schools to start this experiment. With severe overcrowding facing both primary and junior secondary schools, the government had to find a cost-effective means of providing school space and deal with other related issues. The shift system, common in many developing countries, has reaped some level of success. In addition to reducing overcrowding, the shift system assisted countries such as Jamaica in moving closer to achieving universal primary and secondary education. With the increase in the number of school spaces, access was also increased, which was a primary limitation of many education systems in developing countries.

But even with the shift system in place, a space study conducted by Hutton (2005) showed that overcrowding remained a significant problem. For secondary schools it was projected that by the academic year 2009/2010 the net space needs would be 89,539 if no changes were made to class size, the duration of secondary schooling, and the present capacity of the schools. And at the primary level, the net space requirement projected for that period was 26,419. The true figure would be 55,448 spaces but there were 29,029 dead or unused spaces which were identified, especially in rural schools. The impact of the shift system was pointed out by the Task Force on Educational Reform (2005, 51):

> In Jamaica the number of instructional hours per school day as stipulated by the Regulations should be no less than 4 at the Primary, All Age and Secondary schools on a shift system, and 5 hours for whole-day schools. By comparison, the average number of instructional hours for the United States for example, is

6 hours per day. The hours of instruction refer to the hours that a teacher and students are present together imparting and receiving educational instruction respectively.

For the removal of the shift system to be a reality, Hutton (2008) revealed that 24,000 spaces would have to be provided at the primary level and, in the case of secondary schools, 42,000 additional spaces had to be found. Johnson (2004), who examined the impact of the shift system in three primary schools in the parish of Portland, Jamaica, said that the benefits of the shift system included alleviating overcrowding, increasing student enrolment, improving the utilization of plant and facilities, increasing teacher employment, and providing an avenue of employment for new teachers and facilitated promotion. On the other hand, the weaknesses of the shift system included facilitating truancy and poor attendance, reducing coverage of the curriculum, limiting teaching and restricting individualized consultancy time for students.

The shift system has indeed made some contributions to the strengthening of the education system. In a period when the government of the day was unable to build schools to keep up with the increase in the population of children of school age, bearing in mind that universal education was a goal for primary and secondary education, the shift system played a significant role. Initially, it was intended that the shift system would be used as an interim solution to the problem of overcrowding. However, over forty years since its introduction, it continues to exist in some schools. Nevertheless, the government has pledged to remove the system by providing additional space by constructing new schools. Some schools have taken the initiative to raise funds to construct additional classrooms in order to have a single shift or school. The then minister of education, Ronald Thwaites announced at a press conference in September 2015 that "during this academic year, approximately 30 schools will be removed from the shift system. It is also anticipated that the remaining 48 schools still on shift will be removed by 2017" (Cunningham 2015, 1).

The shift system was used to address some important deficiencies in the education system, but over time its own limitations were revealed. Most critical among them is that valuable teaching time is reduced. A related problem continues to be the inability to manage students arriving for the afternoon shift which tends to lead to disruption in some schools. Based on world standards, students need to have more organized learning time at schools. Some of the traditional secondary schools which did not go on shift or did not spend much time as shift schools have a distinct advantage. Most evident is that as far as available learning time is concerned, they have a full-day schedule with over six hours of contact time for the students.

Mentorship for Performance

For the most part, mentoring in Jamaica, for many years, has been limited to children in a mentor-mentee relationship, usually managed by social services. Mentoring as it relates to the neophyte teacher has just begun to be treated as an area of importance in the field of education. In fact, only three principals mentioned that mentoring was used in their schools, and in one case it was the senior students being trained to mentor the younger ones. What is known is that for some schools, the new teachers are likely to be placed in a disadvantageous situation by being assigned to teach and take on administrative responsibilities without adequate support and preparation. While some of these teachers are able to survive through sheer determination, others wilt under the pressure of disruptive students, who are always willing to test the teacher's mettle. Worst of all, is the fact that some new teachers are given the academically challenged students because they are seen as university or college trained and are assumed to have the skills to manage. Searby and Brondyk (2016, 3) reveal that "mentoring occurs in multiple contexts and levels . . . [and] in P-12 schools, mentoring is often used to induct, develop and retain teachers and administrators"; so in a context where mentoring is so diverse, how is it defined? Zachary (2005, 3) said that "mentoring can be best described as a reciprocal and collaborative learning relationship between two (or more) individuals who share mutual responsibility and accountability for helping a mentee work toward achievement of clear and mutually defined learning goals". The New York City Department of Education (2016, 1) describes the mentor as one who "promote[s] the growth and development of the beginning teacher to improve student learning. . . . When new teachers are hired, they are given a full program and are expected to impact student learning immediately without the benefit of any period of apprenticeship." But Searby and Brondyk (2016) expand the scope of the target group to include

(1) pre-service teachers who are provided with mentoring support in their placement, (2) new teachers employed to schools who are assigned mentors to support the induction period, (3) teachers in the system who are provided with mentoring support as necessary and, finally, (4) senior leaders including principals and vice principals who are also provided with mentoring support based on the needs to be addressed.

At the School of Education at the University of the West Indies, one goal of the teacher preparation programme is to equip "potential teacher mentors with the knowledge, skills and disposition needed to perform successfully as teacher mentors in their school setting" (McCallum 2013, 111). The New York City Department of Education (2016, 1) elaborates on some of the basic requirements to become a mentor: "5 years of teaching in the New York City public schools. Mentors should also demonstrate mastery of pedagogical and subject matter skills; evidence of excellent interpersonal skills; and a commitment to participate in professional development."

The Jamaican education system has started to take note of mentoring in the school system, but the programme is really in its infancy. The central ministry, teacher preparation institutions and the principals, through their professional organization, should seek to formalize the mentorship programme in the school system. Hutton (2014b) recommends that one feature of the proposed master's programme for the preparation of school leadership and management should be a mentorship component. Because mentoring can assist at all levels of the organization and stages of preparation, a comprehensive programme should be developed to target students, teachers and administrators and it should involve pre-service, in-service and ongoing mentoring intervention.

Geographical and Economic Challenges

All the chapters focused on challenges brought about by geographical and economic situations in Jamaica. Research has indicated that the geographical location of a school affects its effectiveness (Gordon and Qiang 2000). Of the seventeen schools highlighted, five are located in rural areas, while twelve are located in urban or suburban areas. Schools from rural areas have smaller populations but older and less conducive infrastructure. These challenges

Issues of Importance: Analysis, Reflection and Action   237

pose greater economic challenges for the principals as they have to seek financial assistance for the daily operation of the schools and solicit funds to build or improve the general infrastructure. Moreover, such assignments are more challenging in that those schools have parents who are either subsistence farmers or unemployed. In contrast, most of the schools located in urban areas have better infrastructure and more-affluent parents except for three schools located in the inner city. Such schools have scarce resources and violence is pervasive. Undeniably, the challenges were compounded by the limited resources provided by the government.

Vision-2030 Jamaica (2009) identified a number of factors which are impeding the development of the education system and schools in particular. In many ways these factors are related to financial constraints that the country continues to experience. Some of these are poor academic performance (although there is evidence of improvement in a number of areas), overcrowded or sometimes underpopulated schools, poor student attendance, dilapidated plant, and lack of equipment for effective teaching and learning among others (Vision-2030 Jamaica, 2009). Despite these challenges, however, the principals were able to achieve levels of performance and success that need to be duplicated exponentially if the education system on a whole is to achieve its performance goals and objectives.

Differences in location and resources did not deter the effective principals from realizing success regarding student achievement and the general effectiveness of the schools. What was it they did that made the difference? Fifteen of the seventeen principals interviewed cited the forging of partnerships with stakeholders as a major contributor to their effectiveness. These stakeholders were able to assist them with the financial, human and material resources necessary to improve the infrastructure and learning environment. Stakeholder groups included parents, community members, alumni associations, past students, businesses, overseas and local foundations and funding agencies. Many of the schools also had income-generating projects to augment the grants received from the Ministry of Education. Most importantly, many principals cited the need for good financial management and accountability. Craig (2007, 28) agrees and suggests, "Special funding is not necessarily a prerequisite for the most critical improvements in education." Further, he remarked, "Even the poorest countries can, without special financing embark on educational improvements through adequate planning, the abandonment of ineffective operations, and the realignment of resources to achieve desired goals."

Violence and Indiscipline in Schools

The issue of violence and indiscipline, which includes disruptive and aggressive behaviour, has become a serious challenge to the education system and, specifically, teaching and learning. But other activities which fall within the realm of criminality, such as extortion and the operation of gangs, have also increased in schools, especially those located in the urban and suburban parts of the country. The Draft Safe School Policy (2016, 9) indicates that in 2013 "there were 298 reported incidents including 4 murders, 168 fights; 64 cases of theft; 25 cases of wounding; and 8 incidences of sexual offences". These are alarming statistics and, even though the central ministry has made an effort to arrest the situation, there is little sign of any reduction in most of these types of cases. A number of initiatives have been implemented by the Ministry of Education and other agencies and entities to address indiscipline in schools. These include (1) guidance and counselling services, (2) parent support system through the National Parenting Support Commission and (3) the safe schools programme, which provides school resource officers. The appointment of deans of discipline to take a planned approach to address the problem of indiscipline in school has been a major initiative of government.

The initiatives of the schools which would complement the national efforts have been highlighted by some of the principals who have contributed to this text. Fourteen spoke to indiscipline in schools, while two specifically addressed violence in society and its impact on schools. As they brought these issues to the fore, the principals offered some insights on how they were addressed. One principal suggested that he took a multifaceted approach in maintaining discipline. That meant engaging and reminding members of staff of their professional roles and setting high standards as well as emphasizing good parent-teacher relationships, student-teacher relationships and relationships among staff. Parental involvement, open communication and leadership capacity building were also strategies embraced. Another principal who was faced with acts of indiscipline, such as skin bleaching, short skirts, tight pants, truancy and unpunctuality, took a zero-tolerance approach and with the assistance of parent engagement was able to transform the school. He actually visited the students' homes on Saturdays, took the parent-teacher association meetings to the community and took on a "fatherly role" with the students.

Principals discussed initiatives such as student and staff handbooks, creating and fostering a positive school climate and professionalism from staff. Most importantly, they set high standards for all, and parents were actively engaged. Indiscipline of students and teachers normally accompany underachievement, consequently, three principals suggested that they ensured that the adults in the schools modelled the kinds of behaviour they desired. One principal made transportation arrangements to address punctuality issues. He also monitored the students' behaviour on the routes to ensure compliance. One female principal also testified to taking a zero-tolerance approach to indiscipline. Revising school rules, applying sanctions and rewards, installing and empowering student leaders, and engaging the parents and the police were among some of the initiatives utilized.

The solution to the problem of violence and indiscipline will be no easy task as this phenomenon is a direct reflection of the wider society. Learning from the international community, a schoolwide approach and progressive disciplining approach have demonstrated some success. But it seems that greater cooperation and collaboration which involves all stakeholders is necessary to address the problem of indiscipline in schools. In fact, accountability on the part of everyone is essential. And at the personal level, the deliberate validating and valuing of students are also critical to engendering this disciplined environment where, as one of the principals pointed out, "Teachers must see themselves as bearers of good news and recognize [that] the success of the students lies with them." Other initiatives and approaches which occur at the classroom and personal level in addressing the incidence of indiscipline include training of staff in classroom management, consistency and rigour, fairness, building student leadership capacities, having accountability structures and systems in place, and most importantly, spiritual and moral development.

Gender Leadership in Schools

Females form the majority at almost all levels in the school system. For example, in the public schools, where primary, all-age, primary and junior high represent the pre-secondary level and the secondary level (which comprises upgrades and traditional high schools), 76.5 per cent of the principals are females and 23 per cent are males (Hutton 2013). This general pattern holds for education officers, teachers in training in colleges and universities, and even those who are in training in the Aspiring Principals Programme. The pattern is broken only at the level of the school board, where 72 per cent of the chairpersons are males and 28 per cent are females (Hutton 2016b).

A review of the literature reveals that there are three views articulated in comparing the effectiveness of school leaders by gender: (1) females leaders are more effective than males leaders, (2) male leaders are more effective than female leaders, and (3) there is no difference in the leadership performance of male and female leaders (Bass and Bass 2008). However, increasingly, research on gender leadership suggests that male principals lead differently from their female counterparts (Johnson 2012; Mertz and McNeely 1998; Rosenblatt and Somech 1998). While the leadership stories in the book did not specifically address gender differences, one principal did suggest that after fifteen years as principal, she still suffered from an "impostor syndrome" that she believes affects many women in positions of leadership. There were also three female principals who stated that they had to rigorously defend many decisions they made. This could be attributed to the notion that many people believe that female leaders are not as effective as male leaders (Appelbaum, Audet and Miller 2003). In highlighting the strengths of female leaders, Paustian-Underdahl, Walker and Woehr (2014, 1130) opine that "based on these social roles, women are typically described and expected to be more communal, relations-oriented, and nurturing than men, whereas men are believed and expected to be more agentic, assertive, and independent than women".

For the Jamaican school system, a closer examination of the emergence of female leaders, especially in the school system, is necessary. Further research is necessary on the impact of the rapid replacement of male principals with female principals. In schools, it is well known, for example, that male students, especially boys, respond to female principals differently than their male counterparts. This fact could have implications for how boys learn and equally their behaviour in schools. So every effort must be made to resist the practice of employing males in preference of females and vice versa.

The evidence supporting the effectiveness of leadership based on gender difference is inconclusive. One could conclude that the debate about the advantage and disadvantage of male and female leadership will continue for some time to come. The best that can be accomplished at this time is to seek to benefit from the strengths of both male and female principals.

Personal Beliefs and Community Support

The principals under discussion were themselves teachers with seemingly strong and successful teacher-training backgrounds. Most of them had at least a first degree in one of the disciplines such as languages, sciences, psychology or mathematics. And the majority of those with a master's degree earned it in educational administration or one of the traditional disciplines. Generally, a number of the principals attributed their success to their spirituality. Of course Jamaica is known to be a "God-fearing" country so it should not be surprising that some of the principals embrace religion. A few also highlighted the fact that their personal qualities or innate tendencies also played an important role in the accomplishments they achieved. In fact, in some cases both their faith-based embrace coupled with their personal qualities made the difference in their performance. One principal stated, "It was my passion for the job coupled with my faith in God and my positive attitude that allowed me to go on." Speaking on the role of personal qualities, another principal mentioned, "When you are convinced that what you are implementing is for the good of the organization, you have to be determined and courageous in the face of resistance." This male principal who worked at a technical school, again, pinpointing the role of his disposition reasoned, "My passion was to transform this newly upgraded technical school . . . into an institution of academic excellence." In instances when they are confronted with challenges for which they did not have an immediate answer, the name of God was evoked, "I am now in the second sojourn at the secondary level and I pray God to continue to guide my steps."

The other factor which made a difference in their success was the extent principals elicited support from their internal and external constituents. A number of them highlighted the fact that building a good relationship was central to their effectiveness. A principal from one of the upgraded high schools said, "We offer parental training, invite experts to address relevant and pertinent issues, engage in school improvement projects such as painting and road patching and student mentorship." Another principal said, "The parents are included in every aspect of school development. The community members are allowed to use our football field in the afternoons for structured training, supervised by a member of the Board of Management." It is of interest that the relationship was also symbiotic in this case. In other words, the giving was not only from community to school but also from school to community.

The relationship between school and community is not always a healthy one. In some cases people from the communities relieve the schools of valuable items including equipment such as computers, multimedia systems, televisions, fridges and stoves. For one principal, this behaviour and attitude was addressed by "forging partnerships [that is] getting the surrounding community to respect, appreciate and protect the school instead of preying on it. Informal talks proved most successful". In another case, the response of the community was very different, even though both of these examples are from inner-city communities: "I find the parents from . . . the inner-city communities very supportive and cooperative, contrary to popular opinions that parents of low socio-economic status rarely support PTA meetings."

It is important that principals take deliberate steps to build a wholesome relationship between school and community. This is especially true for rural communities, where life "revolves" around the school. The need to make the relationship a mutual one signals an even higher level of school-community relationship. The benefits are numerous and include (1) securing the school and property, (2) addressing the problem of student discipline, (3) focusing on the academic performance of students and (4) assisting the parents themselves to advance their academic goals.

Effective school leadership demands of principals the capacity to identify strengths and pair them with particular needs within the institution. The function of the principal is to get the best out of the staff for the development of the school. It calls on their ability to provide effective leadership, within a transparent administration, led by proactive planning and accountability (Shepherd 2015) and proper management of resources. As the principals in this book charted their journey, they offered some solutions to some of the critical challenges that face all school leaders, especially school leaders in the Caribbean and other developing countries. It is therefore important to look critically at how they address these challenges.

References

Applebaum, S.H., L. Audet and J.C. Miller. 2003. "Gender and Leadership? A Journey through the Landscape of Leadership". *Leadership and Organizational Development Journal* 24 (1): 43–51.

Ball Foundation. 2016. "Backwards Planning: A Great Strategy for Those Who Find It Hard to Get Started". http://careervision.org/backwards-planning-great-strategy-find-hard-get-started/.

Bass, B.M., and R. Bass. 2008. *The Bass Handbook of Leadership: Theory, Research, and Managerial Applications*. New York: Simon and Schuster.

Black, C. 1983. *The History of Jamaica*. Harlow, UK: Longman Group.

Craig, D.R. 2006/2007. "Constraints on Educational Development: A Guyanese Case Study". *Journal of Education and Development in the Caribbean* 9 (1 and 2): 1–30.

Cunningham, A. 2015. "Several Schools to Be Removed from Shift System". *Gleaner*, 5 September. http://jamaica-gleaner.com/article/lead-stories/20150905/several-schools-be-removed-shift-system.

Draft Safe School Policy. 2009. *Learning and Working in a Secure and Safe Environment*. Kingston: Ministry of Education.

Gordon, A, and W. Qiang. 2000. "Education in Rural Areas of China and South Africa: Comparative Perspectives on Policy and Educational Management". UNESCO. http://unesdoc.unesco.org/images/0012/001218/121853E0.pdf.

Hamilton, L., R. Halverson, S.S. Jackson, E. Mandinach, J.A. Supovitz and J.C. Wayman. 2009. "Using Student Achievement Data to Support Instructional Decision Making". http://repository.upenn.edu/cgi/viewcontent.cgi?article=1298&context=gse_pubs.

Hutton, D.M. 2005. Presentation to the Policy Committee of the Ministry of Education and Youth of the Findings of the Space Rationalization Study and Recommendations for Ameliorating the Physical State of the School Facilities. Education Transformation Team, Kingston, Jamaica.

———. 2008. "Lessons from the Transformation of the Jamaican Education System".

In *Reconceptualising the Agenda for Education in the Caribbean: Proceedings of the 2007 Biennial Cross-Campus Conference in Education, 23–26 April, 2007, School of Education, the University of the West Indies, St Augustine, Trinidad and Tobago*, edited by L. Quamina-Aiyejina, 383–94. St Augustine, Trinidad: School of Education, University of the West Indies.

———. 2013. "Interpreting the Demographic Variables Related to High-Performing Principals in the Public Education System In Jamaica". *International Studies in Educational Administration* 41 (1): 57–73.

———. 2014a. "Cost Sharing and the Financing of Public Education: Applying a Comprehensive Model". *Journal of the Commonwealth Council for Educational Administration and Management* 42 (3): 3–18.

———. 2014b. "Preparing the Principals to Drive the Goals of Education for All: A Conceptual Case Developmental Model". *Research in Comparative and International Education* 9 (1): 92–110.

———. 2016a. "Critical Factors Explaining the Leadership Performance of High-Performing Principals". *International Journal of Leadership in Education Theory and Practice* (March): 1–21. http://www.tandfonline.com/doi/pdf/10.1080/13603124.2016.1142118.

———. 2016b. "The Rating of High-Performing Principals' Performance on Their Leadership Dimensions by Senior Administrators, Middle Managers and Classroom Teachers". *Research in Comparative and International Education* 9 (1): 1–14. http://rci.sagepub.com/content/early/2016/02/26/1745499916632423.full.pdf?ijkey=oDLWlvK7Bc7u2Hy&keytype=finite.

Johnson, B. 2012. "The Relationships between the Principals' Roles in Instructional Supervision and School Effectiveness in Selected Primary Schools in Jamaica". PhD dissertation, University of the West Indies, Mona, Jamaica.

Johnson, V.E. 2004. "A Comparison of Teachers' and Students' Opinions about the Effects of the Shift System in Three Portland Primary Schools". Master's thesis. University of the West Indies, Mona, Jamaica.

McCallum, D. 2013. "Teachers as Leaders: Building the Middle Leadership Base in Jamaican Schools". In *School Leadership in the Caribbean: Perceptions, Practices and Paradigms*, edited by P. Miller, 105–24. Oxford: Symposium Books.

McTighe, J., and G. Wiggins. 2004. *Understanding by Design: Professional Development Workbook*. Alexandria, VA: Association for Supervision and Curriculum Development.

Mertz, N.T., and S.R. McNeely. 1998. "Women on the Job: A Study of Female High School Principals". *Educational Administration Quarterly* 34 (2): 196–222.

Miller, E. 1999. "Educational Reform in Independent Jamaica". http://www.educoas.org/portal/bdigital/contenido/interamer/bkiacd/interamer/Interamerhtml/Millerhtml/mil_mil.htm.

New York City Department of Education. 2016. "Mentoring Guide for Principals". http://schools.nyc.gov/NR/rdonlyres/249FFD6F-4018-41E9-B957-FCC9E98BF786/0/PrincipalsMentoringGuideEdited813.pdf.
Paustian-Underdahl, S.C., L.S. Walker and D.J. Woehr. 2014. "Gender and Perceptions of Leadership Effectiveness: A Meta-Analysis of Contextual Moderators". *Journal of Applied Psychology* 99 (6): 1129–45.
Rosenblat, Z., and A. Somech. 1998. "The Work Behaviour of Israeli Elementary School Principals: Expectations versus Reality". *Educational Administrative Quarterly* 34 (4): 505–32.
Searby, L.J., and S.K. Brondyk. 2016. "Introduction: The Complexities of Identifying Mentoring Best Practices". In *Best Practices in Mentoring for Teacher and Leadership Development*, edited by L.J. Searby and S.K. Brondyk. Charlotte, NC: Information Age.
Shepherd, D., ed. 2015. "What Is the Role of Education Today?" *Next Generation* 2 (1): 24.
Task Force on Educational Reform. 2005. *A Transformed Education System: Report*. Rev. ed. Kingston: Jamaica Information Service.
Thwaites, R. 2013. "Ministry of Education (A Call to Action): Sectoral Debate 2013–2014". Ministry of Education, Kingston, Jamaica. http://www.japarliament.gov.jm/attachments/956_Sectoral-Presentation-2013.pdf.
Vision 2030 Jamaica. 2009. *Education Sector Plan*. http://planipolis.iiep.unesco.org/upload/Jamaica/Jamaica_Vision_2030_Education_sector_plan.pdf.
Wiese, J. 2015. "Backward Planning: Examining Consequences of Planning Direction for Time Prediction". PhD diss. Wilfrid Laurier University, Canada.
Wiese, J., R. Buehler and D. Griffin. 2016. "Backward Planning: Effects of Planning Direction on Predictions of Task Completion Time". *Judgment and ing* 11 (2): 147–67.
Wiggins, G., and J. McTighe. 1998. "What Is Backward Design?" https://www.fitnyc.edu/files/pdfs/Backward_design.pdf.
Zachary, L. 2005. *Creating a Mentoring Culture: The Organization's Guide*. San Francisco: Jossey-Bass.

CHAPTER 20

STRENGTHENING STRUCTURES AND SYSTEMS FOR SUCCESSFUL SCHOOL LEADERSHIP

DISRAELI M. HUTTON

FOR PRINCIPALS TO HAVE THE NECESSARY impact on student performance, they must be both successful and effective leaders. Hutton (2016, 168) states that "successful leadership is about implementing the basic structures and systems which provide the platform on which effective leadership performance is achieved whereas effective leadership is more about the direct actions that are taken to impact students' achievement and overall performance". This chapter focuses mainly on those factors which are the essential structures and systems necessary for building successful leadership. These can be placed into three categories. First are systems to support student learning and training and education for teachers and principals. Student support systems are provided primarily by school leaders, while training for principals is provided currently by the National College for Educational Leadership and allied services. The training of teachers is provided by universities, teacher-training institutions and professional development programmes initiated by schools and the central ministry. Second are the systems to facilitate the decentralization of the education process, which will be realized through regional authorities, schools boards and the practices of school leaders. Third are the structures to facilitate the implementation of crucial education processes, which include critical school evaluation and performance (National Educational Inspectorate); teacher quality (Jamaica Teaching Council); and school facilities (central ministry). The activities which are important to leadership success are therefore related to the work of the central ministry, the decentralized entities, the schools and those who lead them. It would seem that the effort to establish the basic framework for successful leadership cannot be accomplished by all concerned operating independently, but instead working collaboratively, with the ultimate goal being improved student performance.

Student Performance and Support System

The primary role of the school is to effect student learning. This essential function should never be overshadowed by the commitment of school to a plethora of activities which may or may not advance the cause of the learner. In the Jamaican context, the concept of *in loco parentis* (standing in the place of the parent) remains an important role of schools, especially for some learners who are coming from a disadvantaged economic and social background. While there is a greater awareness that the parent must be "standing in his or her own place" and thus playing the role of effective and responsible parent, the Jamaican situation demands that the school should continue to take on at least some of the parental roles.

Student performance has shown some positive results over the past ten years in Jamaica. The Task Force on Educational Reform (2005) has provided the framework for the implementation of significant change and transformation, and the two political parties (that formed governments over the period) have taken on the task of transforming the education system. Certainly, progress has been made over the past ten years. For example, the task force report indicates that for the Grade 1 Readiness Inventory which was administered in academic year 2002/2003, only 37 per cent of the children achieved mastery in all components of the inventory. The four components include visual motor coordination, which is coordinating of eyes and hands; visual, which is seeing effectively; audio, which is hearing effectively; and number-letter recognition, which is being able to identify both numbers and letters. In terms of the performance of the students assessed, based on the mastery of numbers and letters, 63 per cent of males demonstrated mastery while 73 per cent of females demonstrated mastery. This means that only 68.6

per cent of the cohort demonstrated mastery on this component. (Note that the Grade 1 Readiness Inventory was administered during the first term for those children entering primary school, but this has been discontinued for a number of years.) The performance of students on the Grade One Individual Learning Profile varied according to school type in 2012. The percentage of students attaining mastery in all five subjects was 26.9 per cent for primary schools; 17.1 per cent for all-age schools; 20.9 per cent for primary and junior high schools; and 64 per cent for kindergarten/preparatory schools.

In 2003, the results of the Grade Four Literacy Test showed that a total of 57.4 per cent demonstrated mastery, which represents 45.5 per cent of the boys who took the test and 70.4 per cent of the girls (Task Force on Educational Reform 2005). In 2014, the data on literacy in public schools showed that girls continued to outperform boys with 55.8 per cent of girls achieving mastery, while 44.2 per cent of the boys achieved mastery. Overall, 75 per cent of the students achieved mastery on the literacy test (Planning Institute of Jamaica 2015). This is more than a 19 percentage-point improvement over the past twelve years and suggests that much effort would have been made by schools and the central ministry to improve performance in this vital area, which is necessary for further learning.

Regarding student performance in public secondary schools in 2003, 32.6 per cent were successful in CSEC, gaining a grade of 1, 2 or 3. This represents 35.6 per cent of males and 30.7 per cent of females. For English language, 48.8 per cent were successful, earning a grade of 1, 2 or 3; this represents 53.9 5 per cent of girls and 40.1 per cent boys. In 2014, 38.6 per cent of the students were successful in five or more subjects, earning a grade of 1, 2 or 3. Sixty-six per cent of those who sat English language passed with grades of 1, 2 or 3 and 55.5 per cent of those who sat mathematics passed with grades of 1, 2 or 3 (PIOJ 2015). So while there has been improvement in performances by students, the performance in mathematics continues to lag behind the performance in English language. With 2015 being the target date for achieving many of the academic goals set out in the report of the Task Force on Educational Reform (2005), it is obvious that the education system will fall short on the accomplishment of many of these goals.

There is evidence of efforts to improve student performance. For example, the study of high-performing principals in Jamaica showed that one of the factors which received attention was the effort by these principals to enhance students' support systems. Hutton (2011, 8) asserts that "the high-performing principals envision their most important role as one of providing the platform and support system to facilitate the development and achievement of the students through programmatic activities which target their personal needs and aspirations". Evident also, is the fact that student support extends beyond the provision of the basics such as breakfast, bus fare and transportation. Hutton (2013a, 83) indicates that school leaders sought to help students to develop self-confidence by guiding them "to believe that they can make a difference in their own lives, but they will have to demonstrate personal commitment and conviction in order to achieve success". In practice, "The principals also support students' performance through a wide variety of interventions, ranging from physical facilities, new and enhanced academic programmes, new technology including computers, and software to enhance learning including those for literacy" (Hutton 2011, 8). In concurring, Williams and Fox (2013, 41) make reference to supportive learning environments in the Jamaican education system which ensure that "students are encourage[d] to think and ask questions, [where] learning sessions are inclusive, [and students are given] ... sufficient time on task and both instruction and assessment are related to the diversity of students and culture of the school".

Leadership Preparation and Performance

Assessment of Leadership Performance

One of the recommendations of the Task Force on Educational Reform (2005, 36) is the need for all principals to engage in "continuous training in school management and leadership in a variety of accredited institutions". This recommendation is in accordance with the recognition that the role of principals in transforming teaching and learning is central. But there were other voices which called for the training and strengthening of the principalship in schools. For example, Anderson (2004) reports on a study conducted by Dennis Minott on school performance in CSEC, a regional examination, which indicates that the poor performance of the students is directly related to poor leadership provided by principals.

In a consultative workshop conducted at the start of the 2006/2007 academic year by the School of Education and the Ministry of Education on the performance of school administrators, including principals, ten areas of concern were identified. These areas can be placed into four categories (Hutton 2014):

1. Motivation and relationship: that is, demonstrating ability to relate to stakeholders, inspiring and motivating stakeholders, and demonstrating an appreciation of aesthetics.
2. Student discipline and safety: that is, managing student discipline and appreciating the safety and security needs of the school and the ability to address these needs.
3. Visioning: that is, strategizing the vision of the school, planning for the achievement of a vision, and formulating and communicating a vision that is grounded in reality.
4. Using data: that is, analysing and interpreting data related to student performance, and recognizing, interpreting and responding to trends.

These deficiencies, although identified some time ago, still exist today. For example, in the area of school discipline, the problem remains a major concern for the education system, which is seen as one of the obstacles to effective teaching and learning. Further, in a study of high-performing principals by Hutton (2011), nine categories of effective performance are classified according to three dimensions: personal competencies, students' performance and relationship management. These categories and dimensions represent some of the areas pertinent to the performance of the Jamaican school principal, and these need to be incorporated into activities principals undertake to enhance student outcomes.

The findings of the National Education Inspectorate, through its assessment conducted between 2010 and 2014, endorse the need for better preparation and selection of principals and other school leaders. The data showed that although leadership and management were satisfactory, being within the 50 per cent range, the fact is that 43 per cent of leadership and management were rated as unsatisfactory. It should be noted that the forerunner to the new National College for Educational Leadership programme were the Mount St Vincent programme in Canada, which provided training for primary school principals and the University of the West Indies programme, which provided training for secondary school principals between 2006 and 2011. These interventions represent concerted efforts on the part of the central ministry to provide systematic training of principals. Although limited, both programmes would have had an impact, but they were short lived. Nevertheless, feedback provided by graduates of the Secondary School Principals Programme delivered by the School of Education, University of West Indies, indicated significant levels of satisfaction by participants and, in fact, a number of them were promoted to the headship of schools (Hutton 2013b). It should also be noted that the Mico University College offers a bachelor's degree in school management and leadership and this programme continues to attract principals and senior teachers.

Leadership Preparation: National College for Educational Leadership

The National College for Educational Leadership was established in 2011 based on the leadership deficiencies presented above and consistent with the recommendation of the Task Force on Educational Reform (2005). The entity is aggressively delivering its charge, with over 330 principals having been trained between November 2012 and September 2013 (Dunkley-Willis 2014). The training package is designed on a modular basis and aims to correct leadership and management deficiencies displayed by existing principals. The National College for Educational Leadership completed the training of the first cohort of aspiring principals in 2014. The programme consists of four modules presented over 120 hours, which includes transformational leadership, instructional leadership, community leadership and organizational leadership. A practicum is also included for trainees to implement and apply what they learn during the presentation of the modules.

The basic plan of the college is to train aspiring principals who will be equipped to perform in schools across the country. This approach must be seen in light of the fact that all principals will be required to complete the aspiring programme before they can be approved in a position. The prospects for the programme seem positive, but its effectiveness must be judged with the passage of time. Only then can meaningful assessment of the quality and impact of the programme be determined.

Continuous improvement in the delivery of the Aspiring Principals Programme will be necessary in order to maintain quality and respond to the leadership needs of the school system in Jamaica. So it is a reasonable policy to require that all principals complete a basic professional certification programme in order to assume the post of principal. Those who are already in the post of principal will be required to complete a similar programme within a given period of time. However, the process cannot be based on a one-off certification. Performance must be continuously evaluated. Licensure should therefore be a requirement for all principals to maintain their position as school leader. This should be renewed within a three-year period and based on the criteria established for performance in the first instance.

Qualities of an Effective Principal

The qualities of effective leadership in the Jamaican school system have been discussed in the study on high-performing principals (Hutton 2011a). These were principals who emphasized strong personal qualities which included factors such as passion, empathy and enthusiasm. In addition, they advanced a philosophy which is shared with staff and students and school community. As Hutton (2011b, 57) explains, "In an almost unified natural response, the principals shared a strong philosophy regarding the role of education and schooling in the development of the learner. They believe in the supremacy of the learner in the process of schooling and strongly feel that all programmatic activities conducted by the schools should be geared toward addressing the learner's needs and interests." High-performing principals exhibit a strong commitment to the work they do and seek to engage those problems which are most challenging. As Hutton (2011b, 58) points out, "They constantly reflect on the problems that schools must address . . . advance solutions which are shared with teachers and other constituents (and) they are motivated to action by their own successes." Davies (2009) concurs with the role of personal abilities and qualities of principals in making a difference in school performance. In assessing her encounter with one of the school principals in the public education system, Davies concludes, "Were it not for his own intense commitment to school and student improvement, his creative thinking and decisive action to change established internal school organizational processes to increase teaching effectiveness, nothing might have changed in the school" (333). But the principals' ability to perform is constrained by external factors. Miller and Hutton (2014, 84) declare, "School leaders enact leadership within a broad regulatory framework, influenced and impacted by social, economic, global and other factors. Nevertheless, their interpretation of the regulatory framework and of other events and factors in the environment is a personal and intense activity that therefore situates the very practice of leadership within each individual." So the recruitment and training of principals must be informed by what has been learned from our local research, even though limited. What is evident is that those who are recruited to become principals and effective or high-performing principals must be able to apply these personal qualities in order to be effective.

The pool of principals who were identified as high-performing represented only 12.5 per cent of the principals in the public school system (Hutton 2013b). How many of the remaining number of principals have the personal qualities to engage the external and internal challenges faced by the school system? Can training and monitoring help to improve the performance of those who remain weak and ineffective? Or is it necessary to implement polices to replace those who are unable to make a difference in the performance of the school to which they are assigned? These are the issues that the central ministry, principals and their organizations, and stakeholders have to address. Since the study reported by Hutton (2011), many of those who were identified as high-performing have left or are leaving the system, mainly as a result of retirement. There are clear signs that through the effort of the National College for Education Leadership and a more deliberate approach to recruiting principals and the effort of training institutions such as the University of the West Indies, principals are better prepared to function effectively. The real question is, to what extent will these positive changes make a significant and profound difference in student performance?

Structures and Systems for Education Transformation

The strengthening of the structures and systems to transform the education system was signalled with the publication of the Task Force on Educational Reform's final report in 2005. Further elaboration of the recommendations for the decentralization of the education system ushered in the formation of the Regional Education Authority, the National Education Inspectorate, the Curriculum and Assessment Agency and the Jamaica Teaching Council. The National Education Fund was launched in 2010. The establishment of these agencies was facilitated by the Education System Transformation Programme of the Ministry of Education which was funded by the Government of Jamaica along with international agencies such as the World Bank and the International Development Bank. Much of the work was accomplished between 2005 and 2009.

Decentralization of the Education System

The decentralization of the education system, which originated with the transformation of the education system, must be viewed within the context of the modernization of the Jamaican public sector. The Government of Jamaica, in its drive to improve the performance of the public sector, established the Public Sector Reform Unit in 2003 which includes four ministries of government, as well as the Ministry of Education. The mission of the Public Sector Reform Unit was to "drive forward the implementation of the agenda for modernizing government, improving the quality, coherence and responsiveness of public services and for promoting a strong and professionally well-managed public sector, capable of enabling and facilitating the achievement of the national goals" (Public Sector Reform Unit 2002, 12). As Hutton (2008) points out, the overall aim of the education transformation process and, specifically, the democratization of education, was to improve students' outcomes and accountability. Thus, within this framework, the "transformation of the education system must be treated as part of the national effort on reform, which will provide the broad contextual basis for the authentic change to benefit all aspects of the Jamaican society" (96).

Unlike a number of other Caribbean countries, the Jamaican school system had some level of governance established at the lower level; for example, as outlined in the 1965 Education Act, school boards have been a permanent part of the Jamaican landscape. And since the 1980s, regional entities have had some responsiblity for recruitment of teachers and performance evaluations. The Task Force of Educational Reform (2005, 36) made a number of recommendations which included the strengthening of "governance and management at the school level". These interventions would include the upgrading of the regional entities to become regional authorities which would have been established within a legal framework. While regional authority would bring governance of school from the traditional centralized approach through which decisions are taken by the central ministry, the experience of Jamaica under such a system is not encouraging. For example, even though the Ministry of Health established the Regional Health Authority in 2003 as an autonomous entity to operate within a designated legal framework, the ministry remained reluctant in handing over important decision-making roles and providing the financial and human resources for the authority to function effectively. The local government (which represents the second level of government in Jamaica) has been pursuing a path of decentralization since 1993. The expectation was that a legal framework would have been created to provide the necessary autonomy for local government to function fairly independent of the central government. Twenty years later, the political directorate is unable to facilitate the reform to make local government an independent entity. As Hutton (2009, 305) concluded, "Decentralization has a greater chance of realizing its objectives when the capacities and capability are in place for the lower bodies to assume responsibility for the new roles."

Regional Education Authority

The primary role of the Regional Education Authority was to provide the structure for the decentralization of the education system. At present schools are allocated to six regional entities. By combining two of the existing school regions, there would be five instead of six regional authorities. Regional Education Authorities would be established within a legal framework in order to provide the autonomy to function with some level of independence in making decisions and managing resources without the involvement of the Ministry of Education. The role of the Regional Education Authority would include the provision of more efficient education services by making education policy more relevant to stakeholders; enhancing the responsiveness of the education system to the clients; allowing for increased participation of stakeholders in decision making; and performing some of the functions that are usually carried by the central ministry.

The establishment of the Regional Education Authority has still not been realized after a number of efforts made to agree on an appropriate design for operation. At present, school boards provide the framework for the governance process at the level of the schools. But, as pointed out in the 2014 National Education Inspectorate report, the boards are not as effective as required in the primary schools in general and rural primary schools in particular. This structure needs to be examined in light of the ineffectiveness identified. The inspectorate's 2014 report indicated that in the schools with ineffective leadership, a few boards had not been constituted: "Consequently, these schools did not benefit from the strategic oversight that is afforded by this mechanism. Many boards in this group did not operate at the strategic level and so systems of accountability tended to be weak" (20) and have limited knowledge of what to do to improve school performance. For the schools identified as having effective leadership and management in place, the board "systems of governance were highly developed. . . . Most board members were visible and integrally involved in the school's planning processes" (19).

The establishment of the existing regional entities which was proposed by the Task Force on Educational Reform to be upgraded to regional authorities is one level of the decentralization process. The strengthening of school boards and especially those for small schools is also a vital step in the decentralization process. There are a number of proposals including the provision of boards for clusters of schools. However, these initiatives must be tested to determine their effectiveness. What is certain is that schools will be placed at a great disadvantage if boards are weak or, in some cases, non-existent.

National Education Inspectorate

The establishment of the National Education Inspectorate represents one of the interventions to strengthen the performance of schools and the systems which are necessary for more successful and effective principals. The importance of this action stems in part from the agency's role in advising the Ministry of Education and the cabinet and parliament of Jamaica. Over the period 2011 to 2014, the National Education Inspectorate has inspected some 803 schools, representing 84 per cent of the 954 schools identified. The assessment of school performance over the three-year period shows similar weak performance in the area of leadership and management. In fact, only 57 per cent of the schools were rated as effective and above in the area of leadership and management (Thwaites 2014). Also, of the 129 schools which were assessed in 2014, primary schools were assessed to be less satisfactory in their academic performance when compared with secondary schools. This finding seems to be consistent with Hutton's on high-performing principals which shows that only 8.35 per cent of primary, all-age, and primary and junior high schools are identified as high performing by regional directors and senior education officers in Jamaica (Hutton 2013b, 62). In fact, only 125, or 12.5 per cent, of the principals were identified as high performing. As Hutton opines, "If effective student performance is aligned with quality principalship, immediate action [has] to be taken to improve the pool of principals in both primary and upgraded secondary schools."

Based on the accumulated results of the assessment of four areas related to school performance – leadership and management, teaching support for learning, curriculum and enhancement programmes, and students' progress for the 803 schools – the National Education Inspectorate report shows an overall effectiveness of schools to be 45 per cent and ineffectiveness 55 per cent. The Jamaican schools must improve performance in all four areas in order to significantly impact student outcomes.

For the 2015 report, which provides the overall assessment for all 953 schools, 47 per cent and above are assessed as satisfactory and 53 per cent as unsatisfactory and below. In the areas of student progress, 47 per cent are assessed as satisfactory and above and 53 per cent are assessed as unsatisfactory and below. For the areas of leadership and management, the results of the assessment show that 59 per cent and above of the schools are assessed as satisfactory and above and 41 per cent are assessed as unsatisfactory and below. This suggests that improvement is being made in the performance of schools, especially when compared with the performance at the commencement of the transformation process in 2005. However, this is far below the target set for 2015 by the task force's report, especially in the area of student academic performance. It should be noted that one of the roles of the National Education Inspectorate is to provide continuous monitoring of the schools to ensure that performance reaches a minimum standard that is sustained.

Jamaica Teaching Council

The responsibility of the Jamaica Teaching Council includes "maintaining and enhancing professional standards, regulating, registering and licensing teaching professionals. It will provide strategic direction and advice on training, teacher supply and distribution, quality assure teacher education and review and oversee conditions of service for teachers" (Government of Jamaica 2008, 3). The council has established standards for both teachers and principals, and the code of regulations which outlines the responsibilities and conduct of teachers and principals is being revised. The process has been somewhat contentious, with the teachers' union objecting to a number of clauses that teachers feel are not in their interest or that of the teaching profession.

The standards for teachers address three categories of teachers' work in schools: teaching delivery skills, building relationships, and personal development and deportment. Both training and support systems must be provided to ensure that teachers are able to display the required behaviour in each area. For principals, fifteen areas of standards fall into three categories: teaching and learning, personal and professional development, and systems management. For the standards to be relevant they need to be internationally benchmarked by the Ministry of Education; but as importantly, local needs must be paramount in determining the critical set of standards. How they are generated is the important factor. Wide consultation of both primary and secondary stakeholders is essential to identifying and responding to the need for effective leadership.

Implementation of performance standards for both teachers and principals is just the first step. Measuring and monitoring the performance of principals and teachers according to these standards are the only way to bring confidence in the work of the Jamaica Teaching Council. This approach would also assist the council to satisfy the basic requirements for stakeholder involvement while at the same time adhering to local and international standards. But the need for greater accountability for the stewardship of principals and teachers requires fundamental changes in recruitment, workplace behaviour and evaluation practices. The situation wherein principals can do the minimum (or less) and retain his or her position until retirement is untenable; for example, the system must be strengthened to ensure that jobs are retained as a result of performance and not personal relationship or length of service. Much of the practice regarding running an organization is learned from the business sector. For example, chief executive officers are employed on contract for a specific period of time and they retain their jobs or contracts based on performance. This is one approach that should be adopted by the education system despite the fact that the teachers' organization continues to resist this approach. Even though an evaluation system is in place for both teachers and principals, the results of the evaluation are not being used on a consistent basis to improve their performance. The logical outcome of the evaluation process is to employ professional development strategies to address areas of weaknesses identified in teacher and principal performance.

School Plant and Facilities

Hutton (2011, 13), in his study of high-performing principals observes that they "posited the view that, in addition to facilitating learning, the physical environment and the quality of the facilities are true representations of the conscience of the school and the pride the school community has in itself and stakeholders". In fact, in almost all cases in which high-performing principals were interviewed, the plant and facilities were at a high standard. In a number of cases where additional facilities were required, the principals, along with their teams, would seek to acquire needed facilities using funds they raised through their own efforts. This is not necessarily the case with some schools for which leaders were willing to wait an inordinately long period of time for the central ministry to provide the facilities they needed. In some cases it could take years before a response would come.

Based on some of the recommendations arising from the report of the Task Force on Educational Reform (2005), many initiatives are being undertaken including the improvement of school plants. The state of the capacity of the schools was highlighted by the report – namely, (1) the need for greater capacity to facilitate the leading needs at the secondary level; (2) the poor quality of the facilities at the early childhood level; and (3) the overcrowding at the primary level resulting from the emphasis on universal access which resulted in massive overcrowding. The poor condition of school plants was reported by KPMG (1998) including major problems with maintenance and repair of facilities, inadequate toilet facilities, poor security, lack of adequate furniture and sparcity of science laboratories and libraries.

A study of space needs conducted by the Education Transformation Team (2005) showed that, based on existing parameters for class size, the school system required over 115,958 additional spaces to address overcrowding and the abandonment of the shift system. The actual available space then was 472,030, and it should be noted that there was no guarantee that the spaces met the basic standards for student occupancy. The situation would be far worse if the new parameters of space per child would be applied. The study shows that 428,941 additional spaces were required. The actual available space would have been reduced to 266,308 spaces, based on the new parameters which would take approximately two existing spaces to make a new space. This information was based on a five-year projection taking into consideration factors such as student population, location of new and projected housing settlements, and areas of economic growth. The period considered was 2004–2005 to 2009–2010. Over the past ten years, fifteen new schools have been built, providing space for three thousand additional students. Fifteen schools have been removed from the shift system. It was argued that the shift system reduced the number of hours available for academic and other developmental work necessary to enhance student performance; thus, it has been recommended that the shift system be phased out.

Conclusion

Strengthening systems and structures is necessary to support the work of principals and central leadership in the school system. Increasing the pressure on primary stakeholders such as principals and teachers is essential for greater accountability. The decentralization of the education processes and system will help to strengthen governance, especially at the lower levels of the education system. Everything has to be done to ensure that factors directly related to school performance are functioning at optimum level. The elevation and retention of effective and successful principals in all schools, the employment of teachers who can consistently make a difference in students' performance, and the building of strong community support for the schools are vital to the overall performance of students. While the factors addressed in this chapter are not necessarily all the most critical ones related to the structures and systems required for successful school leadership, they are the ones impacting the Jamaican education system at this time. It is the responsibility of principals and other school leaders to be in tune with the structural and system changes being implemented and to seek to benefit from the opportunities provided and, indeed, continue to influence the process as critical stakeholders in the effort to improve student performance.

References

Anderson, G. 2004. "Grades Plunged: Many Schools Performing Well Below Expectation". *Daily Gleaner*, 16 May, A1, A3–A4.

Davies, R. 2009. "School Leadership, Teacher Qualifications and Student Achievement in the Lower Primary Grades: Is There a Connection? Case Study of a Jamaican School Principal's Student Improvement Initiative". *Caribbean Journal of Education* 31 (2): 308–39.

Dunkley-Willis, A. 2014. "Plans to Start Mandatory Training for Principals in 'Tablets in Schools' Programme". *Jamaica Observer*, 12 January. http://www.jamaicaobserver.com/magazines/career/Plans-to-start-mandatory-training-for-principals-in--tablets-in-schools--programme_15760800.

Education Transformation Team. 2005. *Space Audit and Rationalization Study: Report on Secondary and Primary School Space Needs and Proposed Interventions*. Kingston: Ministry of Education.

Government of Jamaica. Cabinet Office. 2008. *Modernisation of the Ministry of Education*. Kingston: Government of Jamaica. http://www.cabinet.gov.jm/current_initiatives/ministry_education.

Hutton, D.M. 2008. "A Conceptual Framework for Guiding the Transformation of the Jamaican Public Education System". *Journal of the University College of the Cayman Islands* 2: 93–113.

———. 2009. "Decentralization of the Public Education System in Jamaica: Learning from the Experiences from Local Government and the Public Health Sector". *Caribbean Journal of Education* 31 (2): 281–307.

———. 2011a. "Revealing the Essential Characteristics, Qualities and Behaviours of the High-Performing Principal: Experiences of the Jamaican School System". *International Journal of Educational Leadership Preparation* 5 (3): 1–15. http://www.ncpeapublications.org/volume-5-number-3.html.

———. 2011b. "Profile of High-Performing Principals: Some Revelations of the Jamaican School System". *Journal of the University College of the Cayman Island* 5: 48–74.

———. 2013a. "Training Programme for Secondary School Principals: Evaluating Its Effectiveness and Impact". *International Journal of Educational Leadership Preparation* 8 (1): 31–48. http://www.ncpeapublications.org/attachments/article/536/Hutton.pdf.

———. 2013b. "Interpreting the Demographic Variables Related to High-Performing Principals in the Public Education in Jamaica". *Journal of the Commonwealth Council for Educational Administration and Management* 41 (1): 57–73.

———. 2014. "Preparing the Principal to Drive the Goals of Education for All: A Conceptual Case Developmental Model". *Research in Comparative and International Education* 9 (1): 93–112.

———. 2016. "Caribbean Perspectives: Practising Successful and Effective School Leadership". In *Successful School Leadership: International Perspectives*, edited by P. Pashiardis and O. Johansson, 165–77. London: Bloomsbury Academic.

Miller, P., and D.M. Hutton. 2014. "Leading from 'Within': Towards a Comparative View of How School Leaders' Personal Values and Beliefs Influence How They Lead in England and Jamaica". In *Building Cultural Community through Global Educational Leadership*, 70–90, edited by S. Harris and J. Mixon. Beaumont, TX: NCPEA.

PIOJ (Planning Institute of Jamaica). 2015. *Economic and Social Survey Jamaica 2014*. Kingston: Planning Institute of Jamaica.

Public Sector Reform Unit. 2002. "Government at Your Service: Public Sector Modernization Vision and Strategy 2002–2012". Ministry Paper no. 56 (September).

Task Force on Educational Reform. 2005. *A Transformed Education System: Report*. Rev. ed. Kingston: Jamaica Information Service

Thwaites, R. 2014. "Briefing on Findings of National Education Inspectorate (NEI) Report, 20 August 2014". Ministry of Education, Kingston, Jamaica.

Williams, C.W., and K. Fox. 2013. *School Effectiveness in Jamaica: What Do Successful Schools Look Like?* Kingston: Inter-American Development Bank.

INDEX

absenteeism, 130, 231
acceptance, 10, 126
accountability, 39, 56, 74, 121, 147, 149, 156, 175, 187, 194, 235, 237, 243, 256, 258; accountability matrix, 72, 87; accountability structures, 77, 239
administrators, 15, 18, 36, 42, 56, 159, 167, 183, 184, 188, 190, 22, 235
alumni. *See* past students
appraisal, 31, 50, 56, 99, 183, 210
assessment, 5, 6, 49, 55, 159, 202, 249–51, 256, 259
assumptions, 153, 168
attitude, 27, 29, 84, 154, 155, 241, 242
authority, 19, 198, 255

behaviour: acceptable, 108, 111; authentic, 2; leadership, 3, 41, 83; modification, 147, 186, 239, 242; principal, 38; student, 33, 42, 51, 59, 60, 126, 132; teacher, 11, 60, 97, 207, 252; unacceptable, 13, 108, 160
behavioural profiles, 17
benchmarks, 57, 258
best practices, 211
building relationships, 83, 196, 258

challenges, 21, 36, 58, 81, 115, 147, 183, 210, 229, 253
change, 168
characteristics: of effective leader, 11, 252–53; of effective school, 11–13, 73, 150; personal, 34; teacher, 60, 155

collaboration, 53, 58, 74, 99, 133, 142, 188, 191, 239
commitment, 27
communication, 16, 17, 34, 53, 58, 60, 74, 194, 208, 220, 238
community, 13, 20, 26, 36, 37, 40, 42, 44, 51, 73, 74, 132, 144, 186, 197–98, 229, 241
competitive, 137
competition, 71, 93, 110, 112, 137, 143, 176
computers, 26, 40, 81, 173, 177, 242, 249
computer room/lab, 93, 97, 135, 157, 221
conceptual skills, 17–18
conflict, 178–79,
conflict resolution, 96, 161
consistency, 157
continuity, 31
control, 13, 51, 140, 146, 190, 204
cooperation, 74, 126, 207, 239
coordination, 144, 247,
criteria, 109, 176, 252
criticism, 43, 207
culture, 115, 130, 167, 171, 172, 181, 182, 188, 194, 198, 199
curriculum, 136

data, 5–6, 32, 33, 61, 66, 68, 71–72, 77, 202
decentralization, 19, 246, 254–56
decision-making, 18, 74, 111, 255

263

delegation, 60, 156, 169
democratic leadership, 57
digital divide, 221, 224–25
direction, 19, 43, 44, 95, 116, 167, 225, 258
discipline: addressing/maintaining, 59–60, 97, 107–8, 126; indiscipline, 228, 229, 231, 238, 242, 250; student, 42, 60, 70, 119, 132, 146–47, 203–4, 218–19; staff, 219–20. See also punishment
diversity, 70, 192, 249

education officers, 29, 40, 188, 240, 257
effectiveness: leadership, 2–3, 19, 26, 133, 240–42, 252; school, 11, 12, 19, 26, 31, 34, 38, 60, 82, 154, 256–57; teaching, 6, 10, 253
efficiency, 14, 83, 231
empathy, 4, 18, 95, 252
employment interview, 16, 136, 140, 185,
empowerment, 19, 41, 99, 123, 175, 189; in staff, 117, 144, 190; in students, 123, 126, 183, 239
equity, 2, 56, 94, 141, 149
ethics, 41, 156, 218
evaluation, 7, 11, 14, 49, 53, 61, 98, 209, 246, 258–59
expectations, 11, 39, 74, 154, 156, 186

facilities, 16, 92, 104, 109, 110, 113, 137, 234, 241, 249, 259–60
fair play, 41, 66, 68, 126, 168
family, 7, 51, 111, 138, 153, 160–61, 165, 178
feedback, 39, 50, 66, 81, 98, 140, 202, 203, 227, 231
flexibility, 14, 137, 159–60

gender, 33, 155, 192, 194, 201, 228
gender diversity, 70–72, 192
gender-focused teaching, 33, 122
gender leadership, 240–41
goals, 2, 9–11, 15, 45, 61, 85, 94, 95, 106, 137, 140, 154, 178, 183, 186, 207 232, 238, 241, 254

health, 41, 44, 85, 92, 110, 134, 164, 201
hierarchy, 108
hiring, 16, 99
home/school partnership, 12, 13
honesty, 4, 29, 57, 97, 154, 211
human resources, 84, 102, 192, 255
humour, 155

improvement, 1, 16, 20, 31, 32, 37, 49, 72, 75, 85, 98, 119, 121, 125, 130, 141, 190, 201, 228, 248, 252
input, 12, 21, 99, 108, 184, 189, 223
instructional leadership, 11, 39, 61, 75, 106, 142
integration, 224
integrity, 4, 29, 34, 94, 97, 154, 216
Internet, 81, 97, 187, 221, 225
intuition, 98, 208

Jamaica Teaching Council, 84, 258
justice, 52, 94, 149, 213, 216, 217, 220, 226

knowledge, 17, 27, 28, 48, 61, 99, 100, 110, 111, 131, 171, 222, 225, 226, 232, 256

leadership: authentic, 2; behaviour, 2, 3; building, 27, 60, 184; concerns, 10, 14, 39, 61, 75; definitions, 14, 106, 107; educational, 164, 170,

174; effective/successful, 3, 19, 20, 21, 29, 41, 61, 128, 129, 149, 185, 243, 246, 256, 258; gender, 240–41; ineffective, 18, 194, 256; instructional, 106, 142; moral, 41–42; perspectives, 10; preparation, 249, 251; professional, 12, 13; and management, 14, 15–16, 19, 106; school, 130, 192, 193, 216, 242; shared, 16, 165, 180; skills, 17; supervisory, 75; teacher, 190; team, 166; traits, 3, 4, 229; transformational, 3, 106, 115
learning, 6, 12, 27, 38, 42, 56, 75, 81, 105, 124, 131, 139, 141, 145, 149, 184, 186, 189, 190, 201, 225, 235, 249
listening, 226
literacy, 7, 26, 43, 66, 67, 81, 82, 118, 136, 192, 225, 248

maintenance, 188, 197, 226, 260
management: conflict, 179; defined, 14–16, 73, 106; financial, 59, 237; functions, 14, 17, 20; human resources, 104; responsibilities, 14, 20; roles, 17, 20; school, 19, 44, 127, 249; skills, 17, 20
meetings, 81, 105, 195, 196, 210
mentorship, 81, 100, 142, 158, 159
mission, 11, 40, 79, 85, 95, 104, 106, 194, 198, 216
mistakes, 180, 204, 213
monitoring, 16, 42, 47, 49, 96, 97, 99, 106, 159, 194, 219, 253, 257
morale, 41–43, 105, 144, 154, 158, 177,
motivation, 117, 158, 144; of staff, 45, 50, 56; of stakeholders, 72, 250; of students, 48, 162

National Education Inspectorate, 3, 35, 39, 84, 246, 256

needs, 56, 83, 99, 105, 109, 113, 118, 129, 131, 133, 137, 140, 187, 225, 240, 250, 252
non-performance, 32

open-door policy, 70, 174, 178
organizing, 15, 17, 106
orientation, 4, 159, 198
outcomes, 1, 5–6, 20, 27, 56, 60, 72, 81, 108, 154, 164, 169, 250, 254, 257

parents, 92, 126, 212, 242; and parental involvement, 13, 26, 32, 42, 52, 60, 66, 72, 83, 98, 132, 173, 184, 210, 211, 217, 239
partnerships, 12, 58, 73, 104, 112, 132, 134, 148, 184, 188, 189, 192, 212, 237
passion, 27, 175, 180, 226
past students, 26, 40, 73, 83, 94, 98, 113, 139, 189, 196–97, 207, 208, 229, 237
performance: academic, 21, 48, 68, 103, 159, 184, 192, 209, 230; of principal, 127, 240, 241; of school, 45, 129, 252, 257, 260; of students, 6, 32, 39, 48, 49, 53, 65, 66, 71, 76, 84, 102, 105, 118, 142, 160, 161, 230, 247; of teachers, 175, 183, 202
personal qualities, 3–5, 27, 52, 77, 127, 241, 252, 253
philosophy, 2–3, 164, 198, 199, 218, 226, 252
placement, 40, 48, 81, 98
planning, 13, 17, 38, 106, 238; backward, 231–33; curriculum, 140; lesson, 97, 171, 219; proactive, 243; strategic, 116; succession, 86
policies, 143, 172, 182
positive behaviour, 159
power, 4, 28, 174, 175

principal: behaviour of, 2–4, 38, 145, 201, 242, 249; functions, 14, 16, 17, 68, 225, 231, 242; strategies, 30, 33; skills, 145
problem-solving, 18, 136, 199
proficiency, 43
punctuality, 15, 58, 82, 85, 119, 157, 218
punishment, 51, 70, 97, 108, 132, 186, 197, 204

recruitment, 16, 33, 105, 131, 142, 149, 182, 253, 254, 258
regional authority, 40, 255
regulations, 29, 59, 75, 162, 233
rehabilitation, 26
relationships: interpersonal, 30; with stakeholders, 37, 43, 83, 88, 94, 119, 194
reliability, 6
responsibility, 2, 1, 16, 19, 29, 37, 74, 117, 123, 132, 139, 174, 189, 204
research, 11 33, 57, 70, 92, 160, 184, 203, 208, 236, 240
rewards, 82, 126, 132, 141, 147, 158
risk, 14, 45, 69, 154
roles, 9, 16, 29, 40, 43, 61, 106, 113, 145, 172, 190
rules, 77, 97, 107, 132

safety, 156, 222, 250
school: achievement, 94; board, 40, 56, 127, 145, 188, 220–21; characteristics, 13, 73; culture, 198; effectiveness, 26, 34, 100, 104, 115, 154, 156, 159–61, 188; plant, 133, 259–60; single sex, 33, 122
security, 44, 82, 158, 250
screening, 173
selection, 199, 232, 250
self-esteem, 2, 13, 154, 159

shift system, 233–35
software, 221, 249
staff: appraisal, 30, 50, 168, 210; deployment, 53; development, 2, 38, 48, 56, 94, 104, 124, 170; welfare, 51
stakeholders, 1, 16, 27, 37, 58, 73, 83, 111, 116, 145, 188
standards, 59, 99, 106, 232, 258
strategies, 37, 40, 72, 104, 124, 132, 179
students: discipline, 42, 51, 59, 107–8, 119, 126, 132, 146, 186, 203, 218; learning, 131, 141, 145, 149, 209; nutrition/welfare, 51, 123, 183; performance, 5–6, 10, 21, 32, 39, 48, 55, 67, 71, 84, 118, 142, 247–49
supervision, 31, 43, 75, 98, 141, 183, 201
success, 43, 57, 75, 129
support, 158, 165

tardiness, 10, 119
targets, 5–6, 9, 52, 71, 83, 104, 130, 156, 175, 186, 232, 236, 248, 257
teachers: behaviour, 11, 30, 60; discipline, 219; effectiveness, 6, 10; evaluation, 31, 39, 43, 50, 168, 254; leaders, 190; preparation, 5, 105, 182, 191, 236; professional development, 30, 37, 72, 93, 117, 124, 144, 170 ; supervision, 76, 141; working with, 50, 56, 73, 96, 98
technical skills, 182, 187
technology, 16, 96, 134, 155, 173, 201, 224–25
termination, 220
tests, 32, 33, 66, 124, 192
theft, 28, 133, 238. *See also* security
time management, 36
time-table, 92, 121
training, 3, 5, 12, 19, 28, 105, 119, 124, 128

transformation, 2, 9, 45, 49, 104, 111, 247, 253, 254
transformational leadership, 3, 41, 99, 106
transition, 27, 37, 60, 85, 111, 187
trends, 74, 250

values, 2, 14, 41, 45, 49, 95, 106, 153, 156, 158, 160, 218

vending, 148, 185
violence, 96, 107, 224, 238
vision, 39, 40, 79, 83, 85, 99, 104, 128, 147–48, 166, 177, 216, 237, 250

women, 3, 225, 240
workforce, 185, 190, 191, 232
workshops, 170, 201, 250

CONTRIBUTORS

DISRAELI M. HUTTON is a senior lecturer, School of Education, University of the West Indies, Mona, Jamaica. Dr Hutton is a graduate of the Mico Teachers' College and the College of Arts, Science and Technology in Jamaica. He holds an undergraduate degree in technology education from Buffalo State College; a master's degree in supervisory management and training and development; and a PhD in educational administration and supervision in higher education, both from Bowling Green State University. His work experience spans both the private and the public sectors, and he has taught in the public school and tertiary education systems for many years His areas of specialization are educational leadership and management, educational supervision, and technical vocational education training. Dr Hutton has published a number of articles and book chapters on school leadership, the financing of education, and technical and vocational education and training.

BEVERLEY JOHNSON is a lecturer, the Mico University College, Kingston, Jamaica, and adjunct lecturer, School of Education, University of the West Indies, Mona, Jamaica. Dr Johnson is a graduate of the Mico Teachers' College and of the University of the West Indies, Mona. She started her teaching career at the Half Way Tree Primary School, where she rose to the posts of senior teacher and acting vice principal, and went on teach at the Duhaney Park Primary School prior to assuming the principalship at Jericho Primary School. Dr Johnson serves as deacon and church and circuit secretary at the Jericho Circuit of Baptist Churches, lay preacher, writer at the Caribbean Christian Publication, secretary of Jamaica Baptist Union Education Committee, chairman of Children's Ministry of the

Jamaica Baptist Union Christian Education Committee, as well as serving on three school boards.

O'NEIL B. ANKLE is principal of Jonathan Grant High School, Spanish Town, Jamaica. His primary education began at New Providence Primary School, and his secondary education at Kingston College. He obtained the diploma in teaching from G.C. Foster College and a bachelor's degree from New York Institute of Technology in 1988. He did post-graduate studies at Nova South Eastern University, gaining a master of science in teaching and learning in 2002. He served as principal at Green Park Primary and Junior High School in Sandy Bay, Clarendon, from 2003 to 2011.

GRACE BASTON is principal of Campion College, Kingston, Jamaica. She attended the Alpha Preparatory School, after which she completed her secondary education at the Convent of Mercy Academy, Alpha. She began her tertiary education by pursuing a bachelor's in theology at the University of the West Indies, Mona, and continued in that field by doing theological studies at Collegio Missionario in Italy. Between 1991 and 1992, she pursued a diploma, after which she went to Columbia University, New York, where she did an master's in philosophy and education. Between 1985 and 1990, she taught Spanish, English and religion at Alpha Academy. In 1990, she was promoted to vice principal and served in this capacity for four years, becoming principal in 1994. She has been the principal of Campion College since 2006.

MARGARET CAMPBELL is principal of St George's College, Kingston, Jamaica. She began her formative education at the Lady of the Angel Preparatory School and her high school education at the Immaculate Conception High School. She completed her bachelor's degree in computing at the University of the West Indies, Mona (1985–1989), and an MBA at the Nova Southeastern University (1992–1994). She also did a postgraduate diploma in mathematics education at the School of Education, the University of the West Indies, Mona. She taught at the Ardenne High School from 1998 to 2002 and lectured in mathematics education at the School of Education, the University of the West Indies, Mona, from 2004 to 2006, when she went assumed the post of principal at St George's College.

DENNIS M. CLARKE, now retired, was principal of Dinthill Technical High School, Linstead, Jamaica. He is a past student of Woodside All Age, where he received his formative education. His quest for knowledge and academic prowess led him to acquire a junior teachers' certificate from Caenwood Junior College in 1971, a teachers' certificate from Mico Teachers' College (1972–1974), a diploma from the College of Arts, Science and Technology (1979–1981), a bachelor of education from the University of the West Indies, Mona (1982–1984), and a master of education from the University of the West Indies, Mona (1989–1991). He taught at a number of schools in the education system. He was education officer with the Ministry of Education, Jamaica, and principal lecturer (industrial arts) at the Mico Teachers' College. He served as principal at Thomas Technical High School (1992–1999) and at Dinthill Technical High School (1999–2012). In 2015 he was awarded the Order of Distinction from the Government of Jamaica for distinguished service to education and agriculture.

FAITH CLEMMINGS, now retired, was principal of Montego Bay High School, Montego Bay, Jamaica. She started her early education and the Lowe River Primary School her secondary school education at Westwood High School for Girls. Her tertiary education began at the Shortwood Teachers' College (1968–1970), where she completed the certificate programme in language. She pursued Spanish, French and linguistics at the University of the West Indies, Mona (1976–1979). She also completed a master's in linguistics at the University of the West Indies, Mona, in 1986. Her teaching career covers Clarendon College, Westwood High School, Titchfield High School, Immaculate Conception High School and Montego Bay High School. She became principal at Montego Bay High School in 1997 and continued in that post until her retirement in 2009.

Contributors

GARTH GAYLE is principal of Charlie Smith High School, Kingston, Jamaica. He obtained his formative education at Kingston College. His education continued at the G.C. Foster College of Physical Education and Sports, where he received a diploma in teaching as well as a bachelor of physical education (1982–1986) and master of science in education from the Southern Illinois University. His teaching career started in 1982 at Kingston College, as a teacher of physical education. His career continued at St George's College as teacher/sports master from 1987 to 1991; Excelsior Community College as sports director/senior lecturer (1991–2005). He also served as principal at the Angels Primary School between 2006 and 2014.

ERROL V. JOHNSON, now retired, was principal of St Mary High School, Highgate, Jamaica. He received his formative education at the Preston Primary School in St Mary and completed his high school education at St Mary High School. Between 1976 and 1979 he pursued the bachelor of science in chemistry at the University of Rajasthan, India, where he graduated with honours. He completed his diploma in education at the University of the West Indies, Mona (1982–1993). He received his master's in psychology from the University of the West Indies, Mona, in 2004. Colonel Johnson did all his teaching at St Mary High School. He became acting vice principal in 1984 and was subsequently appointed vice principal in 1985 then principal in 1993, until his retirement in 2013.

CARLENE McCALLA-FRANCIS is principal of Kensington Primary School, Portmore, St Catherine, Jamaica. She had her early entry in the teaching fraternity when she worked as a pre-trained teacher at the Grateful Hill Primary School in St Catherine, 1978–1981. Her formal training began at the St Joseph's Teachers' College (1981–1984) where she majored in primary education. She then obtained a bachelor's degree in primary education from the University of the West Indies, Mona, in 1996 and completed the master's in 2003. Prior to her becoming principal, she worked as a classroom teacher at the Maxfield Park Primary (1984–1994) before joining the staff at the Kensington Primary School in 1996 as a classroom teacher.

ESTHER McGOWAN is principal of Morant Bay Primary School, Morant Bay, St Thomas, Jamaica. She attended Cairn Curran and Caledonia All Age schools in rural Westmoreland, where her formative education was cemented. Her high school education took place at Manning, also in Westmoreland. Her tertiary education began at Shortwood Teachers' College in 1980 and she graduated with her certificate in primary education in 1983. She completed the undergraduate and master's degrees in educational administration at the School of Education, the University of the West Indies, Mona. Over her eleven years as principal, Morant Bay Primary has become one of the most respectable schools in the parish of St Thomas.

MONICA McINTYRE, now retired, was principal of Ocho Rios High School, Ocho Rios, St Ann, Jamaica. Her formative education began at the Cocoon Primary School and was completed at Lucea Primary School. Since high school education was not required at that time, she began tertiary education at the Caenwood Junior Teachers' College followed by studies at the Bethlehem Teachers' College. She also completed a master of science in administration at the University of the West Indies, Mona. Her career as a teacher began at the primary level where she taught grades 1 to 6 at the Peggy Barry, Sandy Bay and Jericho Primary Schools, and and she went on to become principal of Merlene Ottey and Ocho Rios High Schools.

CYNTHIA PEART, now retired, was principal of Papine High School, Kingston, Jamaica. Her primary education was at Windward Road Primary School, followed by secondary education at Kingston Technical High School. She went on to pursue tertiary education at the University of the West Indies, where she did a certificate in education and a master of science in education. Her initial teaching experience was at the St Elizabeth Technical High School, where she was a science teacher from 1974 to 1976. She continued her teaching at Papine High School where she served first as a science teacher then as principal between 1976 and 2011.

PAULEEN PAMELA REID is principal of Holland High School, Martha Brae, Jamaica. She started her formal training as a student at the Brandon Hill All Age School in Clarendon and completed her secondary training at Vere Technical High School. Her tertiary training was at Shortwood Teachers' College (1976–1978), where she completed the teaching certificate. She later pursued a bachelor of arts in English language and social science (1982–1985) at the University of the West Indies, Mona. She completed a master's in educational leadership at Central Connecticut State University. She taught at a number of schools, including Calabar High School, St Mary High School, Ocho Rios High School, Frome Technical and William Knibb High School, before becoming principal of the newly opened Holland High School in Trelawny in 2004.

BRADLEY ROBINSON is principal of John Mills Infant Primary and Junior High, Kingston, Jamaica. He is a past student of Titchfield High School. He has a diploma in teacher education (secondary) from the Mico College (1999–2002); bachelor of arts in guidance and counseling from the International University of the Caribbean (2002–2006), and is currently pursuing a master's in educational administration at the University of the West Indies. His teaching career involved a number of schools including Mount Pleasant All Age School, Ardenne Preparatory, Holy Trinity High School and John Mills Primary and Junior High. He served as principal of Woodford Primary from 2009 to 2014.

ESTHER TYSON, now retired, was principal of Ardenne High School, Kingston, Jamaica. Her formative education was completed at Chapelton Primary School in Clarendon and her secondary education was at Ardenne High School. She earned a bachelor of arts in English, a post-graduate diploma in education and a master's in language education from the University of the West Indies, Mona.

She has been involved in education since the 1970s. She taught first at Ardennne High School, then Manchester High School and later at St Andrew High School for Girls, where she served as vice principal. She then moved on to Ardenne High School, where she served as principal from 2000 until her retirement in 2011.

EVERTON WALTERS is principal of Edwin Allen High School, Frankfield, Jamaica. He began his formal education at Mount Moriah Primary School. His secondary education began at Alston High School and ended at Edwin Allen High School. He went on to the Church Teachers' College and the University of West Indies, Mona, where he completed his tertiary studies. He also studied at Connecticut State University in the United States and Mount Saint Vincent University in Canada. He taught at Alston High School for thirteen years. In 1996, he became the principal of Aneon Town All Age and served in that capacity for eleven years.

JOAN WINT, now retired, was principal of Denbigh High School, May Pen, Jamaica. She attended New Works Elementary School in Westmoreland, where she gained her formative education. Her secondary education was at Clarendon College, where she completed sixth form, and her tertiary education started at Shortwood Teachers' College, where she completed her certificate programme in language with geography and history (1969–1971). She completed her undergraduate degree in language and literature with social science from 1981 to 1984 at the School of Education, the University of the West Indies, Mona. She spent the major portion of her career as an educator at Denbigh High School, starting 1972 as a classroom teacher and senior teacher before being appointed principal in 1985. She retired in 2009.

www.ingramcontent.com/pod-product-compliance
Lightning Source LLC
Chambersburg PA
CBHW021137230426
43667CB00005B/155